THE HEART ATTACKED

'Our national history and current events teach us that Italy is a country in which it is practically impossible to keep a secret, but where it is equally impossible for a mystery to be resolved.'

Carla Mosca, 'Antigone', May/June 1986

THE HEART ATTACKED

**Terrorism and Conflict
in the Italian State**

by Alison Jamieson

**Foreword by
Richard Clutterbuck**

Marion Boyars
London · New York

First published in Great Britain and the United States
in 1989 by Marion Boyars Publishers
24 Lacy Road London SW15 1NL
26 East 33rd Street New York NY 10016

Distributed in Australia by
Wild and Woolley Pty Ltd, Glebe N.S.W.

Distributed in the United States by
Rizzoli International Publications, New York

British Library Cataloguing in Publication Data
Jamieson, Alison
    The heart attacked: terrorism and conflict
    in the Italian state.
    1. Moro, Aldo   2. Brigate rosse
    3. Kidnapping — Italy — Rome 4. Political
    crime and offenses — Italy — Rome
    I. Title
    364.1'54'0924   HV6604.I82M6

Library of Congress Cataloging-in-Publication Data
Jamieson, Alison.
    The heart attacked.
    Includes index.
    1. Terrorism — Italy.   2. Moro, Aldo, 1916–1978 —
Kidnapping, 1978.   3. Brigate rosse.   4. Terrorists —
Italy — Attitudes.   I Title.
    HV6433.I8J36   1988   303.6'25'0945   87–23864
ISBN 0–7145–2871–4 original paperback

Typeset in 11/12½ Times by Ann Buchan (Typesetters), Middlesex
Printed and bound in Great Britain at
The Camelot Press Ltd, Southampton

CONTENTS

FOREWORD

Why did they do it? Most of the Red Brigadists were intelligent and young, some of them genuinely dedicated to ideals of brotherhood and justice; they had acquired at university the political skills of analysis, communication and persuasion, skills which should have enabled them to contribute more than most to influencing peaceful progress in society. Why did they throw these skills aside and turn instead to the gun, killing people in cold blood, often preceding the killing with the prolonged and excruciating mental torture of kidnap — perhaps the most loathsome and inhuman of all man's inhumanities to man?

How did a few dozen such people, a hard core aided by a few hundred part-timers, dominate the political life of Italy for 10 years, killing and kidnapping politicians, judges and industrialists, disrupting the process of law? And how, in the end, did the fragile, chaotic and corrupt system of Italian democracy, already bombarded by criminal gangs and constant economic crises, survive this onslaught and emerge with its rule of law strengthened by the ordeal?

The kidnapping and murder of Aldo Moro — the attack on the heart of the state — was the high point of the Red Brigades' campaign but was, in the end, their undoing. One aim was to smash the 'historic compromise', the strategy of political co-operation between the Communists and the other parties, of which Moro was prime architect. This aim was partially achieved in that the agony of party leaders in deciding whether and how to negotiate his release and their bitterness at having failed to prevent his death undid much of Moro's work — the 'government of national unity' voted in on the day of his kidnap outlasted Moro by a mere six months.

The crisis and humiliation did, however, jerk the Government into legislation to provide the powers for the police and intelligence services to deal with terrorism effectively.

The Italian government was supported by a majority of politicians, press and public in its decision not to release any terrorists convicted or on trial to save Moro's life. Experience shows that such terrorists in practice go on to take more lives (as did the German terrorists released to save the life of a leading politician in West Berlin, Peter Lorenz, in 1975). It would have been better, however, if the government had made this clear in advance. Political kidnaps to coerce governments are less likely to occur at all when they have announced unequivocally that they will not make concessions to terrorists. The governments of France, Germany, Italy, UK, Canada, USA and Japan made a joint declaration to this effect at their Venice summit in June 1987. It has been reported that all the members of Mrs Thatcher's cabinet in Britain have signed statements requesting that no concessions be made if they are taken hostage. Terry Waite, the Archbishop of Canterbury's envoy, did the same before setting off in January 1987 to meet the kidnappers of other hostages in Lebanon. So did Dr Hanns-Martin Schleyer before he was kidnapped in Cologne in 1977 by German terrorists demanding the release of comrades who were convicted murderers. Chancellor Helmut Schmidt, while announcing that he would make no concessions, showed great subtlety in playing for time. First, he tacitly raised no objection to Schleyer's family attempting to negotiate his release for a ransom (though the negotiations proved abortive as the family could not also release the hostages). Second, Schmidt arranged for Ministers and senior officials to be seen visiting certain Arab capitals, the kind of places to which terrorists might be released; he knew that the journalists would conjecture that, despite his denials, he was considering the possibility of doing so. The result was that Schleyer was kept alive for six weeks, during which German security forces twice located the apartments where he was being held and only missed rescuing him by a day in each case.

Andreotti's government in 1978, whilst maintaining its declared intention of not giving way to terrorism, could have followed Schmidt's example by showing some guile and flexibility in creating a climate for negotiations. The art of such behaviour lies in ensuring that the adversary always believes that he has more to gain by going on talking. Once he feels that there is nothing more to be gained he will probably salvage what he can by killing the hostage — if only to add to the terror and bargaining power when he takes another hostage.

Success in saving the hostage's life will depend also on how well the negotiator can bring himself to look through the kidnappers' eyes; and on whether the hostage has psychologically prepared himself for the ordeal. Schleyer clearly had, while Moro had not.

There has not been, and is never likely to be, a more perceptive and unbiased analysis of the Moro crisis than this one. Alison Jamieson has no axes to grind; she talked freely to all sides — to families of the victims, judges, prosecutors, politicians and convicted terrorists in and out of prison; because of her objectivity, compassion and determination to understand, she inspired trust, sincerity and candour in their responses. Thereby she has communicated her understanding to me, as she will to others who read this book. After grappling with terrorism for many of my 35 years as a soldier and writing about it for another 15, I have never read anything from which I learned so much about why such terrorists do what they do.

The repercussions of Aldo Moro's murder broke the main body of the Red Brigades, due both to popular revulsion and to the disillusion and discord in their ranks which bred the *pentiti* (repentant terrorists) whose information led to hundreds of arrests. The campaign was brilliantly conceived and handled by General Dalla Chiesa, who was later murdered by the Mafia because of his parallel success against them. Nevertheless, as Alison Jamieson points out, the conflict is far from over. A number of fanatical BR survivors are still killing people in Italy, illustrating — as Adriana Faranda told her in her interview — how easy it is to shoot people down on the streets or in their homes in a free society (the only deterrent being a high prospect of getting caught). There is some evidence of their collaboration with the equally battered but resilient terrorists in France and Germany in an anti-NATO and anti-imperialist context; also with Middle Eastern terrorists cooperating with them. The lessons of this book will remain vitally important to anyone who wants to see terrorism defeated without sacrificing the freedoms it aims to destroy; and there are no lessons better than the lessons of experience which this book provides.

Ms Jamieson's genius in talking to people generates the heartbeat which makes the book what it is. Her interview with Adriana Faranda, who has so far served nine years of a 30 year sentence for her part in the murder of Moro and his five bodyguards, is both moving and immensely revealing. Faranda undoubtedly feels remorse for these and other crimes and for the anguish she caused the families of the victims; yet her reasons for doing them remain freshly in her mind and she has vividly expressed them. Her answers to the author's penetrating questions help to explain why Aldo Moro's daughter has forgiven her (as the Pope forgave the man who tried to kill him) and regularly visits her in prison. It helps us to understand, not only the terrorists, but also the remarkable qualities of Italian culture, religion and humanity which have endured through so many centuries of political disruption, personal cruelty and war.

Along with its vivid interpretation of Italian terrorism in the 1970's and 80's, this book gives us encouragement for the future too. The terrorists emerging from its pages were not ten feet tall. They were appallingly cruel, like cats holding a mouse in terror before they kill it, and they sometimes revelled in the power and exhilaration of using a gun; but their reactions after doing so were akin to those of '*quattro gatti*' or 'a bunch of kids' as Faranda herself says, astonished by their own temerity and wondering what would happen next. They were often incredibly naive and amateurish. Faced by a realistic and efficient intelligence organization, laws offering seductive temptations to waverers anxious to get off the hook, and an imaginative and courageous opponent in General Dalla Chiesa, they crumbled very quickly. This book will, I hope, convince the critics of *pentitismo* that, if it had been blocked on ethical grounds, many hundreds more people would now be dead, including many more of the terrorists themselves. Intelligence about terrorists saves lives and humane methods of acquiring it cannot be wrong. Understanding the terrorists is the first step along the road to acquiring intelligence, as it is for successful hostage negotiations, and that is why this is such a valuable as well as such a fascinating book.

Richard Clutterbuck
Exeter

INTRODUCTION

16th March 1978, 9 am. A handful of Italian revolutionaries kidnap Christian Democratic party President Aldo Moro, plucking him from the midst of his five-man bodyguard squad, all of whom die in a hail of gunfire. During the following 54 days, as Italy's investigative forces comb the country looking for Moro, the Red Brigades not only succeed in keeping his prison a secret but circulate freely throughout the country, delivering 24 letters from Moro to his family and colleagues within Rome, and distributing nine printed communications of their own in Rome, Genoa, Milan and Turin. They also claim responsibility for two murders, six woundings and six attacks on property during the period. Attempts to establish some basis for negotiation are petering out when a telephone call to a friend of Moro's discloses where his body can be found — dumped in the boot of a Renault 4 in central Rome. The arrogance of this final gesture — Moro's body was recovered in Via Caetani exactly half way between Christian Democratic and Communist party head-quarters — marked the peak of left-wing terrorism in Italy. Mario Moretti, mastermind of the project, summed up:

> The connection between symbolic gesture and military risk is a close one. For us, that symbol was worth the risk, we had to indicate clearly whom we considered responsible for the tragedy. But it was a calculated risk. Guerrilla warfare

is at a disadvantage under normal conditions of war, in the usual alignment of one force against another, but wins when it succeeds in concentrating its strength in a specific time and in a specific place. In Rome at that moment there were tens of thousands of police and carabinieri dispersed throughout the metropolitan area, but in Via Caetani, for those few minutes, we were superior.[1]

1st March 1985, 10 am.   The morning session of the Appeal trial for the Rome column of the Red Brigades is about to begin in the courtroom of the Foro Italico, a former gymnasium specially converted for criminal trials where maximum security is required. Six marksmen patrol the roof and four more stand in look-out towers at each corner, observing every detail of traffic movement around the perimeter of the building. A dozen armoured vans stand outside, engines running, while overhead two helicopters hover, aerial escorts for the vehicles which have just brought the terrorists from Rebibbia prison to the courtroom. All forces are on the alert should an escape attempt occur. It might seem unlikely — but only yesterday a Red Brigades prisoner hit a guard over the head with his handcuffs and tried to make a break for freedom. He gave up after a volley of warning shots was fired into the air.

The main entrance to the court is through a zig-zag series of fences and barriers, so anyone trying to leave in a hurry would have to negotiate these obstacles before clearing the guarded perimeter. Close circuit television screens scrutinize all those entering — after the checks on identity, briefcases and clothing have been completed.

Inside, the 53 prisoners, of whom 32 received life sentences in the Court of Assizes or first grade trial, are ranged in six 'cages', carefully assigned according to their chosen degree of co-operation or not with the authorities. The judge and jury file in, taking their seats behind a podium with the inscription, 'The law is equal for all'. Everyone stands respectfully except those in the cages, who pointedly ignore what is going on around them, and continue to chat, smoke, read newspapers and comics; even to kiss, cuddle and caress. Once, a child was conceived in such conditions, the couple's companions shielding them from the gaze of officialdom.

The cages are surrounded by carabinieri whose positions are rotated every hour — to prevent collusion with the terrorists or to prevent boredom and inattentiveness? They certainly seem bored, but then none looks more than twenty years of age, they were just boys when Moro was kidnapped.

The hearing gets underway. The usual impassioned speeches by defence lawyers explaining the minor role played by one client, the change of heart of another. Some of them become highly emotional, shouting, 'Your sentence is an act of war!', or, trying another tack, 'The political battle cannot be the object of this trial!' One paints a tragic picture of his client who has written the date of her entry to prison on the wall of her cell and below it, 'Date of exit — never!' He is not asking for mercy, he protests, merely justice.

At midday, as the morning session draws to a close, the public gallery fills up with friends and relatives of the prisoners. Babies and young children wave. Old women, shabbily dressed and with scuffed shoes, look uncomfortable. Ordinary, poor, sad people caught up in events beyond their understanding and control. From the cages the prisoners blow kisses and wave back cheerfully. They are wearing brightly coloured pullovers, neatly pressed shirts and blue jeans. Their hair is clean and shiny. They are my age, they look like my friends. But these are people who have wounded and killed in cold blood, people who loathed the world they lived in so much that they were prepared to risk life and liberty in order to change it. What produced such hatred, how could they shoot and kill? But not all those women in the public gallery are trying to catch the eye of a loved one. Some must be here for another reason, perhaps to see justice done on behalf of the policeman son or the husband who served in a political protection squad — victims whose names have been almost forgotten beside those of the more illustrious figures who perished with them. What must they be feeling about the prisoners in the cages? What do they expect from this trial?

And these confident-sounding prosecution magistrates who lay the charges so carefully before us, who for years have fought terrorism in the certain knowledge that the more efficiently they do their job the more likely they are to fall victim to terrorist bullets themselves — what do they think and feel? What is it like to deal with terrorism as part of an everyday job?

We all talk easily and casually about terrorism and in many respects we feel on familiar ground. We all think we know what groups like the Red Brigades stand for, what they hope to do and how they hope to do it. But what do we really understand about them, how they live and why they believe what they do?

Adriana Faranda is a sensitive, intelligent and attractive woman of 38, the mother of a 17 year old daughter. Between 1976 and 1979 she was a full time clandestine member of the Red Brigades. Nowadays she rejects the use of violence as a means to a political end, and talks candidly about her past actions and ideology. Her professed anguish for the heartache and suffering she has caused is convincing in its sincerity, yet the Rome column of the Red Brigades of which she was a founder member was responsible for seventeen murders, eleven attempted murders, four woundings, four kidnaps and four robberies. She and her companion of thirteen years, Valerio Morucci, freely admit their roles in the planning and execution of Aldo Moro's kidnap and of the murder of his bodyguards, although both claim to have opposed Moro's killing from the start. But even after Moro's death they remained within the Red Brigades for a further six months, participating in other acts of violence until February 1979, their final break with the organization. What were the beliefs that were so strong, so passionate that Adriana Faranda could risk her life and abandon a child she loved to commit these acts of violence? How could she say, as she did in that Rome courtroom, 'We believed it was necessary to kill today in order to live tomorrow'? Just why and how has she changed?

With a criminal record of such appalling proportions,

Faranda and Morucci could hardly have expected demonstrations of forgiveness, yet this has been offered publicly by one
of those who has suffered most from their actions — Aldo
Moro's daughter, Maria Fida. Displaying an astonishing
spirit of Christian charity, she went in person to Rebibbia
prison in Rome to hear their confessions of repentance and to
forgive them. In her words, 'For Christians, forgiveness is a
necessity rather than a duty,' her meeting with Faranda and
Morucci had symbolized 'a meeting of two sufferings fused
into one.'

And Carole Tarantelli, two short months after her
husband's murder by the Red Brigades in 1985, made her own
pilgrimage to Rebibbia, not to forgive her husband's
assassins, but to talk to ex-terrorists in an attempt to
understand them and to encourage a process of political
maturing towards a gradual re-integration into the society
they once tried to destroy. But how can women like Maria
Fida Moro and Carole Tarantelli allay their suffering by
gestures of reconciliation? Can they forgive?

I have tried to strip away the veil of generalizations and
misunderstandings which surround the phenomenon of
terrorism, and the Italian experience in particular. Having
spent hours discussing their experiences with those who have
been directly involved I have been able to look at it from the
inside, without, I hope, falling victim to the emotional or
political prejudices to which a native Italian might be prone.
In the course of my researches I have often been asked what
prompted me to write this book. I wrote it to find the answers
to the questions in this Introduction — in other words, to try
to understand.

Reference

1   'L'Espresso', 2/12/84

1
ITALIAN TERRORISM — A PERSPECTIVE

Throughout its 40-year history the Italian Republic has been battered by violence from many directions and from shore to shore: in the south it has had to cope with the internecine warfare of the Mafia and the Camorra, in its northern region of Trentino-Alto Adige with nationalist violence, while both left and right-wing terrorism have ranged from Reggio Calabria to Turin. Moreover, in recent years a combination of Italy's economic and military policies, its political alliances and its strategic position in the Mediterranean have left it vulnerable to the spread of Middle Eastern conflicts on to its soil.

In the 19 years from 1969–1987, 14,591 terrorist attacks were committed in Italy; 1,182 people were injured and 419 died. 1979 was the year in which attacks peaked at 2,513, but 1980 saw the worst death toll — 125. 193 deaths, or almost half the total, have been attributed to the neo-fascist right; 145 to the far left and 63 to the actions of Middle Eastern terrorist groups.

TABLE 1: TERRORISM IN ITALY 1969–1987

	Terrorist attacks	Deaths caused by terrorism
1969	398	19
1970	376	7
1971	539	2
1972	595	5
1973	426	40
1974	573	26
1975	702	10
1976	1353	10
1977	1926	13
1978	2379	35
1979	2513	24
1980	1502	125
1981	634	25
1982	347	23
1983	156	10
1984	85	20
1985	63	20
1986	24	2
1987	8	3
TOTAL	14,591	419

SOURCE: Ministry of the Interior.

Notes on statistics

i)   From 1969–1987 there were 148 deaths from left wing

terrorism and 193 from right wing terrorism. This latter figure is considerably weighted by the 85 deaths in the Bologna station attack of 1980.

ii)   In purely numerical terms, of the 359 attacks which caused death or injury, 74% are attributed to the far left, 7.6% to the far right and 7% to non-Italian terrorist groups. The rest are non-attributable.

iii)   Between 1969 and 1980 there were 697 'signs' or group headings under which terrorist attacks were claimed. Of these 484 were of the left, 119 of the right. The origins of 92 have not been ascertained. (Source — *Rapporto sul Terrorismo*, Ed. Mauro Galleni, Rizzoli, Milan, June 1981).

Of the two extremes, the terrorism practised by the far right is more terrifying to the man in the street. One reason for this is the indiscriminate use of explosives in public places, tactically timed to cause maximum injury and panic. This is known as *stragismo*, or slaughter tactics, and forms part of the so-called 'stragegy of tension' which characterized the years 1969–1974. In contrast, the far left in Italy never targets indiscriminately and generally only uses explosives against property.

The major *stragi* attributed to the far right are the attacks of Piazza Fontana, Milan, in December 1969 (17 dead, 88 wounded); Piazza della Loggia, Brescia, May 1974 (8 dead, 94 wounded); the 'Italicus' train, August 1974 (12 dead, 105 injured); Bologna station, August 1980 (85 dead, 177 injured); and the 'Rapido 904' train, December 1984, (15 dead, 267 injured). This last explosion occurred on the same stretch of railway tunnel between Bologna and Florence as that of the 'Italicus' ten years earlier. However, in none of these attacks has legal culpability been finally established. Hence another reason for the greater fear of right-wing terrorism; its perpetrators are shadowy, elusive creatures whose ideology is obscure and of whose aims little is known save that they hope to undermine national stability through the erosion of public confidence in the forces of law and order. Were this erosion to take place, the supporters of a military or dictatorial regime would manipulate the fear and unrest caused by continuing terrorist attacks to seize power on a 'protection of civil order' mandate, just as Mussolini's carefully planned rise to power came about through a wave of discord and strikes which he and his fascist squads alone seemed able to crush and control.

One theory as to why less is known about right-wing subversion is that such information might shed an unfortunate light on the activities of those in high places. Indeed it has been proved that members of the Italian security services have given cover to those engaged in right wing atrocities. After the initial claims that the Piazza Fontana bomb was the work of left-wing extremists were discredited, a number of neo-fascists were arrested, including security services agent Guido Giannettini. Considerable evidence, backed up by the confessions of 'penitent' neo-fascists, pointed to their guilt, and in 1979 they were sentenced to life imprisonment by a Catanzaro court. However, in 1985, several trials and sixteen years after the event, the Appeal Court of Bari overturned this verdict and completely absolved not only an anarchist called Valpreda (against whom the security services had apparently fabricated evidence) but also the fifteen neo-fascist defendants. That years of investigations had led nowhere flew in the face of logic: the establishment of innocence for all seemed to negate the very fact of the tragedy. Ironically, the verdict was announced almost five years to the day from the explosion at Bologna station.

In recent years Italian authorities have met with considerably more success in dealing with the other extreme of political violence. Left-wing terrorism in Italy took its doctrinal inspiration from a basis of Marxist/Leninist ideology and its active momentum from the revolts of students and workers in the late 1960's. The largest and most notorious urban guerrilla group to engage in the armed struggle, has been the

Red Brigades, or *Brigate Rosse* (BR). The left-wing equivalent of 'the strategy of tension' were the years 1978–80, dubbed the 'years of lead' when hardly a day went by without news of an armed robbery, assassination or kidnap.

Despite the consummate show of strength realized through the Moro kidnap, the Red Brigades were unable to bring their political ambitions to fruition: the recognition of guerilla warfare in Italy, of themselves as political subjects and the mobilization of mass support for their revolutionary projects. Not only could they not enlist the backing of the working classes whom they claimed to represent, but they also alienated their erstwhile allies on the extra-parliamentary left, directly contributing to the reinforcement of the democratic structure they had hoped to destroy. Although revolutionary terrorism became more widespread and intensified after the Moro kidnap, the dissent which arose within the revolutionary movement over Moro's fate initiated its fragmentation and defeat. And by the early 80's, thanks to the virtual disappearance of consensus over the use of violence within the groups traditionally receptive to political militancy, to more efficient police and intelligence work and to the greater understanding of terrorist structures provided by the evidence of imprisoned militants who decided to collaborate with the authorities, most of the proponents of the armed struggle were behind bars.

Since the end of 1984, however, there has been a resurgence of left-wing terrorism, albeit on a reduced scale. In the same week of December 1984 an attempted jewel robbery in Bologna and an attack on a Metro Security Express van in Rome, both involving loss of life, were carried out by a new generation of Red Brigades; the amassing of funds is one of the pre-requisites for any large-scale terrorist operation. Various documents were discovered during raids in 1984, including a BR hit list of 1,400 potential victims. The name of Professor Ezio Tarantelli, political science lecturer at the University of Rome and economic adviser to the trade union organization CISL was amongst them. However, the Italian authorities felt it beyond their capabilities to extend protection to all those under threat and some, including Tarantelli, were left in ignorance of their appearance on the list. Some foreknowledge of his vulnerability might have helped Tarantelli to escape the ten BR bullets fired at him at point blank range in the courtyard of Rome university on 27th March 1985.

In 1986 the Red Brigades attacked twice in the month of February, killing a former mayor of Florence as he drove to work in the city, and wounding an economic adviser to Prime Minister Craxi in Rome. In February 1987 two police officers providing an armed escort to a post office cash-carrying van in Rome were murdered and a third was seriously wounded. In March a senior official in the Ministry of Defence was assassinated — once again in Rome.

In April 1988 a Christian Democrat Senator was shot dead in his apartment in the sleepy provincial town of Forli, near Bologna.

Tactics and targets may vary over the years, but the desire both to exploit and to create social and political grievances, driving a wedge through the loose coalitions of convenience which keep Italian governments afloat, remains a hallmark of the BR, for whom all parliamentary parties are a sham, existing only as repositories of vested interests. The Italian Communist party (PCI) which should champion the proletarian cause, is held in particular derision, having in the BR view abdicated its responsibilities in a greed for power encouraged by the Christian Democratic party during almost 40 years of majority rule.

And Italy is not alone in facing a renewed terrorist challenge. Throughout the 1980s co-ordinated attacks have been carried out on military bases or on personnel in nearly every European member state of NATO. The specific targeting of people and places under the US umbrella represents a strike at what the Red Brigades termed 'the Imperialist State of Multinationals' (SIM) — the domination and exploitation of the working classes by economic means (US owned multinational companies) and military pressure (NATO). Moreover, the explicit aim of attacking the 'imperialist' enemy embodied by NATO and the increasing regularity of terrorist actions perpetrated by Middle Eastern groups on European soil suggest that terrorist forces with diverse aims may be pooling resources. Were international co-operation to be maintained or stepped up, the semi-defeated European groups could be very quickly revived.

The Aldo Moro affair represented an attempt by the Red Brigades to 'bring the attack to the heart of the state.' In the end they failed because the 'heart' and the 'state' were myths they themselves had created and did not correspond to the real world whose complexities they had failed to understand. On that occasion the attack failed. But others have taken place and new ones are threatened. Former Red Brigadist Valerio Morucci no longer believes you can transform society into something purer and better with the use of violence, and talks of this belief as a 'meaningless dream'. But there are still many today who harbour such dreams.

2
ALDO MORO AND
THE POLITICAL SCENE

'Moro was kidnapped to put the Christian Democratic party on trial' — says Valerio Morucci, Rome column leader and Aldo Moro kidnapper. The easy logic which equates a politician with his party sounds superficial and naive; yet to understand its significance is to understand the collective history of the party which has dominated post-war Italy and the individual story of a man whose life was dedicated to its survival.

Aldo Moro was born in the region of Apulia, south eastern Italy, on 23rd September 1916. His father was an elementary school headmaster, his mother also a teacher. Both were devout Christians and attended church daily, an example their son was to emulate. In 1920 the Moro family moved to Taranto, where Aldo began his schooling, quickly proving a conscientious and intellectually outstanding pupil. Another move followed in 1934, this time to the provincial capital and university city of Bari, whose historical and cultural origins owe much to centuries of Greek occupation.

It is frequently claimed that the east-facing position of Bari, its climate and its past have endowed its inhabitants with a cynical form of pessimism and a detached superiority which distinguishes them from their more sociable compatriots. These qualities were present in Aldo Moro, although in his case they were softened by two other elements which were an unending source of strength and consolation to him throughout his life — his religious belief and his profound emotional attachment to his family. Amidst the bitterness and despair of his Red Brigades prison they were his only consolation, giving him the courage to face his own death and at the same time to bring comfort to his wife Noretta through his letters: 'Be strong, my dearest, in this absurd and incomprehensible trial. These are the ways of the Lord.'[1]

The years of Aldo Moro's youth were dominated by the rise of fascism. While his contemporaries went off to fight in Mussolini's Abyssinian war, Moro pursued his law studies at Bari university. In 1937 he became President of the Federation of Catholic Students (FUCI) for Bari, and was elected national President in 1939. He was also a member of the Federation of Fascist Students (GUF), but as membership was compulsory, it cannot be inferred that he nursed particular sympathies for the fascist cause. Moro took his studies seriously and indulged in few frivolous pastimes, his main leisure activities being chess and going for long walks. In the stultifying political climate of fascism, the only legal outlets for serious debate and discussion were to be found in organizations such as FUCI and *Azione Cattolica* (Catholic Action) which acted as an internal critic of religious policy and doctrine, and was frequently controversial. For some years the ecclesiastical adviser to FUCI in Bari had been Monsignor Giovanni Battista Montini, but he had been obliged to resign his post in 1933 when his insistence that the church and associated organizations should demonstrate greater social involvement was proved to be incompatible with the dictates of fascism. Montini's belief in the socio-political role of the church would be tested to the limit some forty-five years later, when as Pope Paul VI he was requested by Aldo Moro to mediate with his terrorist captors.

Aldo Moro graduated in jurisprudence in 1938, and for the next two years divided his time between his law studies and

FUCI. In 1941 he obtained a lectureship in the Philosophy of
Law at Bari university, and began to turn his attention to the
specific problems of the student in his university environment. With some perspicacity for 1942, he observed that
'one should not be surprised at the young student who looks
at the university and unfortunately finds it infinitely smaller
than his own life.' University education should be 'a teaching
adapted to life, a quest for values . . . an integrated part and
proof of a cultural search in which the mind can satisfy its
deepest needs'.[2] Adriana Faranda, Red Brigades member
and Moro kidnapper, would later admit to remarkably similar
preoccupations about her university environment, where the
sense of restriction, of being unable to stretch one's wings,
was just one of the inspirations behind the student revolution
of 1968.

Military service caused Moro to abandon FUCI and the
university for a brief period, but by 1944, when most of Italy
had forsaken fascism in favour of co-operation with the
Allies, he was able to resume teaching and engage in private
legal work. As the prospect of an Allied victory drew closer, a
Committee of National Liberation was established, composed of all the banned political parties, to prepare for
constitutional legitimacy and the return to democracy. For
many young people such as Aldo Moro who had only known a
fascist dictatorship, the longed-for political freedom also
brought in its wake acute difficulties of choice. It was, says a
contemporary, an 'awkward entry' to make. For a while,
Moro flirted with the idea of joining the Socialists who were
intellectually attractive, but instinctively he was drawn back
to the right by his religious beliefs. Moro's participation in
university politics through FUCI and membership of Catholic
Action inclined him to continue his involvement through the
Christian Democratic party. The DC, founded in 1919 by the
Sicilian priest Don Sturzo, aimed broadly to promote modern
ideas of democracy and equality within the traditional moral
and religious framework of Roman Catholicism. Moro began
to attend meetings of the DC as early as 1944, although he did

not join immediately. Having made his choice, Moro obtained the active support for his DC candidature from Archbishop Mimmi of Bari, and went forward to contest the 1946 elections to the Constituent Assembly, whose task was to draft the new constitution. Together with a referendum on the retention or abolition of the monarchy, these elections would realize the dream of democratic participation for a whole generation, and open the door to a liberated, post-war Italy. Aldo Moro was duly elected for the constituency of Bari-Foggia, and took his seat in the new Constituent Assembly in Rome.

The phrase 'to do things the Italian way' is a metaphor for compromising, getting by, or simply arranging things as well as possible. The Italian Republic was founded on this basis in 1946. On the left, the Socialists (P.S.I.) and Communists (P.C.I.) were strongly in favour of voting away a monarchy which had shown itself to be anachronistic, weak and ineffective. The Christian Democrats were divided on the issue of the monarchy, although a slender majority favoured its retention. The referendum gave the Republicans (P.R.I.) a majority of 2 million (of 32 million votes cast). The amnesty of the following year which set free an estimated 40,000 fascist offenders from prison inevitably led to speculation that a deal had been struck between anti-monarchists and fascists keen to save their own skins. Even the constitution had to take into account the eternal Italian dichotomy, epitomized, according to Italo Pietra, within the very character of Aldo Moro — 'It is based on the formula of cohabitation, on the necessity of understanding the other side's point of view, on a Catholic/ Marxist compromise.'[3] A frequent comment at the time was that the constitution seemed to be written 'half in Latin, half in Russian'. However the encouragement towards political polarity was the first trap that the new democracy fell into: right and left wings of Italian politics have lived since the war in perpetual fear of elimination by the other — both electoral and, at times, physical. Many Christian Democrats who took their seats in the Constituent Assembly after the war had cut

TABLE 2: GOVERNMENTS UNDER THE REPUBLICAN CONSTITUTION OF 1948

| | | | | No. of days | |
President	Parties	Formed	Resigned	Duration	Crisis period (no gov't)
DeGasperi	DC PLI PSLI PRI	31/5/47	5/5/48	347	11
DeGasperi	DC PLI PSLI PRI	23/5/48	12/1/50	599	15
DeGasperi	DC PSLI PRI	27/1/50	16/7/51	535	10
DeGasperi	DC PRI	26/7/51	6/6/53	704	17
DeGasperi	DC	16/7/53	28/7/53	12	20
Pella	DC	17/8/53	5/1/54	141	13
Fanfani	DC	18/1/54	30/1/54	12	11
Scelba	DC PSDI PLI	10/2/54	22/6/55	497	14
Segni	DC PSDI PLI	6/7/55	6/5/57	679	13
Zoli	DC	19/5/57	19/6/58	396	12
Fanfani	DC PSDI	1/7/58	26/1/59	209	20
Segni	DC	15/2/59	24/2/60	374	30
Tambroni	DC	25/3/60	19/7/60	116	7
Fanfani	DC	26/7/60	2/2/62	556	19
Fanfani	DC PSDI PRI	21/2/62	16/5/63	449	36
Leone	DC	21/6/63	5/11/63	137	29
Moro	DC PSI PSDI PRI	4/12/63	26/6/64	205	26
Moro	DC PSI PSDI PRI	22/7/64	21/1/66	548	33
Moro	DC PSI PSDI PRI	23/2/66	5/6/68	833	19
Leone	DC	24/6/68	19/11/68	148	23
Rumor	DC PSU PR	12/12/68	5/7/69	205	31
Rumor	DC	5/8/69	2/7/70	186	48
Rumor	DC PSI PSDI PRI	27/3/70	6/7/70	101	31
Colombo	DC PSI SPDI PRI	6/8/70	15/1/72	527	33
Andreotti	DC	17/2/72	26/2/72	9	121
Andreotti	DC PSDI PLI	26/6/72	12/6/73	351	25
Rumor	DC PSI PSDI PRI	7/7/73	2/3/74	238	12
Rumor	DC PSI PSDI	14/3/74	3/10/74	203	51
Moro	DC PRI	23/11/74	7/1/76	410	36
Moro	DC	12/2/76	30/4/76	78	90
Andreotti	DC	29/7/76	16/1/78	536	54
Andreotti	DC	11/3/78	31/1/79	326	48
Andreotti	DC PRI PSDI	20/3/79	31/3/79	11	126
Cossiga	DC PSDI PLI	4/8/79	19/3/80	228	16

President	Parties	Formed	Resigned	Duration	Crisis period (no gov't)
					No. of days
Cossiga	DC PSI PRI	4/4/80	27/9/80	176	21
Forlani	DC PSI PSDI PRI	18/10/80	26/5/82	220	33
Spadolini	DC PSI PSDI PRI PLI	28/6/81	7/8/82	405	16
Spadolini	DC PSI PSDI PRI PLI	23/8/82	13/11/82	82	18
Fanfani	DC PSI PSDI PLI	1/12/82	29/4/83	149	97
Craxi	DC PSI PSDI PRI PLI	4/8/83	27/6/86	1057	36
Craxi	DC PSI PSDI PRI PLI	1/8/86	3/3/87	214	45
Fanfani	DC/Independents	17/4/87	28/4/87	11	91
Goria	DC/PSI/PSDI/PRI/PLI	28/7/87	12/3/88	227	33
De Mita	DC/PSI/PSDI/PRI/PLI	14/4/88			

SOURCE: *Il Tempo* (Rome).

their seats in the Constituent Assembly after the war had cut
their political teeth in the Catholic groups which had been
tolerated under fascism. The solid, nationwide structures
already in existence provided the platform from which the
DC could consolidate and expand its influence, 'building a
bridgehead to state power through the church.'[4]
approval in the face of the lay opposition. Italy's new-found
allies, as well as many native Italians, recognized the tenacity
and the potential force of a strong, proud and united
Communist party, and took steps to control it. Massive
American aid was provided to boost the Italian economy, for
which the price paid was adherence to sternly anti-communist
foreign and economic policies. The agricultural landowners,
the third major political force in the country after church and
industry, looked to the DC to save them from socialism and
expropriation. If the raw materials of DC power consisted of
catholicism and anti-communism, the finished product
emerged in the form of infiltration and control of the public

sector maintained by a spoils and favours system. Italy's economic problems in the 1930's had led to the near collapse of industry and of its creditors, the banking institutions. The rescue operation had placed effective control of industry in the hands of the State, and had endowed the ruling élite with great powers of patronage. This ruling élite came to be identified with the Christian Democratic Party.

The DC's power was further enhanced by the fragmented nature of the political opposition: the Communist Party (PCI) was strong in the North but lacked a sound national infrastructure; the Socialist Party, weakened in 1921 by the Communist breakaway, was thrown into more disarray by crucial differences in foreign policy. Elections held in 1948 gave the DC an unequivocal mandate — they obtained a landslide victory on 18th April, taking 48% of the votes cast, the PCI as the next largest party taking a mere 18.9%. The task that the Christian Democratic politicians immediately set themselves was to reconcile as far as possible the needs and demands of a geographically, socially and economically disparate nation. Their leader from 1948 until 1953 was Alcide De Gasperi, who took on the formidable job of dragging a basically peasant Italy into the modern industrial world.

In the 1950's Italy's transformation began in earnest and, despite many political and social tensions, the economy grew rapidly, facilitated by the discovery of natural gas and oil. The country gave an outward impression of affluence that was not reflected in the working conditions of those whose labour had created it.

Aldo Moro began to work his way up through the DC Party hierarchy, earning himself a reputation as a sound, methodical thinker and a cautious believer in the virtues of gradual progress rather than dramatic innovation. His first significant post came when he was asked to join Antonio Segni's government in 1955 as Minister of Justice. From 1953 the powers of the DC had been circumscribed by a steady falling off of political support; no longer enjoying an absolute majority in Parliament, the party was compelled to govern

with the backing of other parties, including the neo-
fascist Italian Social Movement party (MSI). In 1956 the
Italian Communist party suffered a damaging blow to its
morale and credibility when Soviet Premier Krushchev
revealed the atrocities perpetrated by his predecessor, Stalin.
Anti-communism became fiercer and the self-justifying
propaganda of the right wing gained more sympathy.

The brief tenure of office of Prime Minister Amintore
Fanfani in 1958 seemed to offer the Socialists, who were
moving towards the right, realistic prospects for sharing
power. Fanfani's government did not last however, and in
1959 he was forced to resign both as Party Secretary and as
Prime Minister. His replacement as Secretary was Aldo
Moro, who by now had gained a further two years experience
as Minister of Education. With his intellectual astuteness and
his recognized ability to reconcile and compromise, Moro
seemed the fitting choice to smooth over the cracks in a
troubled party. But the right of the DC was determined to
give no ground to the left, and when Antonio Segni became
Prime Minister again in 1959 he declared a 'no deal' principle
with the Socialists. After a long period of crisis Fernando
Tambroni finally achieved a working majority in April 1960
with the aid of the 24 MSI deputies in the Chamber. The
MSI's decision to hold its party conference in July in Genoa, a
Communist party stronghold, was a sign of its new
confidence. In protest, three general strikes were held in
Genoa, and demonstrations took place all over the country.
Police reaction was fierce: 5 were killed in Reggio Emilia, 4 in
Sicily and hundreds were injured. Public opinion, including
that of the DC itself, forced Tambroni's resignation and the
MSI conference did not take place. The circumstances of
Tambroni's departure gave his successor Amintore Fanfani
and Party Secretary Aldo Moro the opportunity to edge the
DC leftwards towards co-operation with the Socialists. Two
other things favoured this move: Pope John XXIII, who had
taken office in 1958, was deeply concerned about a potential
alliance between Catholic and non-Catholic forces, but
Moro's personal religious sincerity and his powers of

persuasion were ultimately to convince him that membership of a lay political party precluded neither membership nor support of the Catholic Church. Pope John subsequently expounded this reconciliation in the encyclical *Pacem in Terris*, in which he accepted the principle of a dialogue between Marxists and Christians. The other influence which had hitherto acted as a break on centre-left collaboration in Italy was transatlantic paranoia over communist infiltration and subversion. With President Kennedy in the White House this was publicly toned down and Italy ostensibly allowed greater freedom to run her own affairs.

Fanfani broke new ground in 1962 with his 'opening to the left', a coalition composed of the DC and the Social Democrats. Aldo Moro was beginning to talk of 'parallel convergences' to refer to the conciliation between political forces of right and left, and at last Italy seemed to be emerging from the dark ages. 1963 saw Moro as Prime Minister for the first time, uniting the centre-left in a four-party coalition of DC, Republicans, Socialists (P.S.I.) and Social Democrats (P.S.D.I.).

Despite, or perhaps because of, this spirit of reconciliation, dissatisfaction and mutual fear on the political extremes led to autonomous action by those with vested interests to protect. One man convinced of the necessity to act was the head of the Italian carabinieri, (the military branch of the police force), General Giovanni De Lorenzo. Confident that government by the centre-left could only be of brief duration, he prepared a plan to ensure the smooth transition back to right-wing control. Without consulting either the Prime Minister or the Interior Minister, but apparently with the collaboration (later he was to say on the orders) of President of the Republic Segni, De Lorenzo's plan proposed the arrest of important left-wing figures such as politicians, trade unionists and media figures, and their subsequent detention in Sardinia for an unspecified period of time. He also envisaged the occupation of key centres such as police stations, telephone exchanges, newspaper and post offices. Naturally the effect of such a move would have been the arbitrary abrogation of the constitutional order and, effectively, would have set in motion a military *coup d'état*. De Lorenzo had used the resources of 'Sifar', the military security service, to compile reports and files on whomsoever he chose in public life, and also to forge links with the CIA, whose involvement in the plot, as part of the aim to reduce the communist influence in Italy, was subsequently revealed. The full facts of the De Lorenzo conspiracy and his 'Solo plan' did not emerge until a government enquiry was published, very tardily, in 1971. Even then, allegations that a *coup d'état* was in preparation were considered unfounded, and the commission of enquiry merely concluded that De Lorenzo had exceeded the limits of his authority. De Lorenzo resigned and was later elected as member of Parliament for the Monarchist party (which merged with the MSI). No judicial action was taken against him, nor against the President who had allegedly encouraged him, for Antonio Segni had died.

In 1968 widespread student revolt spread across Italy and caused predictable confusion and dissent within the centre-left coalition headed by Aldo Moro, and in May Moro was forced to resign and go to the polls. The results were favourable both to the DC, who obtained nearly 40% of votes cast, and to the Communists, who made gains at the expense of the Socialists. In general, the parliamentary left had taken the side of the students in their demands for reform, and had publicly stated that retaliation had been over harsh. Yet because of their participation in the governing majority, the Socialists had been unable to distance themselves from the State's treatment of the student revolutionaries, leaving the PCI to provide the only serious and effective opposition to government policy. Aggrieved at having made such scant progress electorally and in terms of policy influence during six years of power-sharing, the Socialists looked for a scapegoat and found one in the man who had led three governments of the centre-left — Aldo Moro. Moro yielded the premiership to Giovanni Leone and began a fourteen-month period of exile from office.

The sense of failure is frequently a prelude to radical rethinking and, in the case of a far-sighted politician such as Aldo Moro, caused a revision of his concept of social democracy in an attempt to discover a new basis for the resolution of contrasting political ideologies. The process of both political and self analysis which ensued, described by a colleague as a '*riforma di mentalità*', a '*momento di verifica*', was probably the most significant intellectual and spiritual reassessment of his entire career. The ideas conceived during this period in the wilderness remained at the heart of his political philosophy until his death.

The only way to extend national consensus, according to Moro's rationale, was to find the common ground between left and right and to act on it by 'making the parallels converge'. The inspiration for the 1946 Constitution was based on religious and political freedom, equality of opportunity and tolerance of individual choice. These ideals were to be harnessed to political practicability. Moro did believe that a 'qualitative leap' was required to cross the boundary between principle and pragmatism, but crucially, this leap was not to imply a debasement of principle. Always the Christian before the politician, Moro saw God's action in sending His son to live amongst mankind as the supreme example of the qualitative leap.

Aldo Moro's political philosophy gradually evolved from the experience of centre-left government in the 1960's to open out even wider parameters towards the 'historic compromise' or conciliation with the Communist party during the 1970's. Moro realized the impossibility of effective government without the co-operation of the second largest political party; PCI Secretary Enrico Berlinguer knew the strength of his party but also feared a reaction against it — the coup d'état in Chile proved to him that 51% of a democratic vote was inadequate protection against super-power opposition. For Moro and Berlinguer the 'historic compromise' was a pact of protection and an assurance of progress, held together by a respect for agreed differences. Moro's leftwards shift marked his breakaway from the mainstream of Christian Democrat thinking, and served to deepen his isolation. The vulnerability of his position was indicated on the official Italian visit to the new Ford administration in Washington in September 1974 by President Leone and Foreign Minister Moro. By then Richard Nixon had at last been hounded out of the White House in the wake of the Watergate scandal, but to Moro's chagrin, one of the few survivors of the Nixon era was Secretary of State Henry Kissinger. Moro had little in common with his US counterpart either personally or politically, due at least in part to a personality clash between the reserved, committed Catholic and the extrovert, aggressive Jew. Whilst the US was providing military assistance to the Israelis in the Middle East conflict, Italy's foreign policy had moved steadily under Moro's guidance towards a pro-Arab position. And in domestic affairs, Moro's declared policies of political rapprochement with the left alarmed Kissinger in their implications for NATO security. Moro had affirmed in a speech of July 1974 that Italy's political salvation could lie in 'nothing other than a force of national solidarity' and he had insisted on recognizing in the Communist party a 'valid and important interlocutor' to whom it was necessary to give 'due attention and dialogue'.[5]

After Moro's death, his widow asserted that Moro's US visit in September 1974 had been marred by ill-feeling between the two delegations. Signora Moro went further, stating that her husband had actually received specific threats not to continue with his pro-left policies, and recalls with clarity her husband's account of the warning, confirmed by other family members and close friends:
'You must give up your policy of bringing all the political elements of your country into direct collaboration. If you don't you'll pay dearly for it'.[6]

In 1976, Aldo Moro allowed himself to be elected President of the Christian Democratic party. This was conceived largely as an honorary post, a recognition of distinguished service to the party without specific responsibilities, although in Aldo Moro's case his customary dedication to the political and social problems of the day continued undiminished. The regularity of violent demonstrations and street battles throughout 1977 caused him great distress, not only from the point of view of national stability, but also for the obvious discontent of the thousands of young people who seemed directionless and desperate. In the course of his university teaching he tried to talk to and understand the causes of the widespread malaise, and, according to a family friend, helped to 'save' more than one student from taking up the path of armed confrontation. Moro was proud of his close and even affectionate relationship with his pupils; indeed, at the height of anti-student feeling in March 1968 he had been one of the few politicians to praise the honesty and the intellectual contribution of the student population: 'For many, many years I have had the possibility through my work of living in contact with young people and of absorbing through them the signs of change and progress in life, a breath of air which has been renewed and extended daily. It is a contact from which I have received more than I have given.'[7]

Almost ten years on he would try once more to listen and to bring the dissenting voices into an open atmosphere of democratic free speech. In March 1977, following a series of attacks on DC offices, he warned: 'In this difficult moment of national life, intolerance and violence serve only to aggravate the situation and obscure our horizons. Too often the origins and nature of violence are mysterious. But we can be sure that any form of violence, when it goes against our basic liberties, is inconceivable and inadmissible'.[8] In a climate of liberty, Moro affirmed, nothing need be excluded, whereas in one of violence, all could too easily be lost.

By the end of the year, Moro's view of Italian political evolution became more clearly defined: the post-war years of reconstruction and recovery had been a 'first phase' in which the DC had had absolute control and domination. Then followed the 'second phase', the years of the centre-left coalition, which by common consensus were definitively over. In January 1976 Socialist Secretary De Martino had stipulated that his party would not actively support another DC government without the active representation of the Communist Party. And at the end of 1977 Ugo La Malfa, Republican party Secretary, publicly affirmed the need to form a 'government of national solidarity' which would include the PCI. Ever since the elections of 1976 from which the PCI and the DC had emerged as 'joint winners' Moro had believed that a new political equilibrium had to be recognized. This consisted of an acknowledgement by all the democratic parties of certain areas of compatibility and others of incompatibility, which he referred to as the 'indifference of the political forces.' Only once this recognition had taken place could the consequent 'third phase' commence. In Moro's mind the third phase had two distinct parts; the first was determined by the immediate need to overcome the present crisis of governmental stalemate, allowing the formation of a government which would endure until the presidential elections of December 1978. This would give the various political forces a breathing space from which could come the second stage — the creation of a basis of government by which right and left could alternate within an agreed programme of continuous progress, permitting the desperately-needed social, judicial and economic advances to take place. An agreement had to be reached between all the democratic parties which would be 'limited, but adequate to win national consensus on the major objectives of economic revitalization and development, of social progress and of the realization of the democratic order.'[9]

In an interview with *La Repubblica*'s editor Eugenio Scalfari in February 1978 (but published posthumously) Moro gave this idea its most lucid elaboration: 'Then I believe that there should be a second phase, not too far off, with the entering of the PCI into government. I know very well that it will be a tense moment to overcome. We have to overcome it. . . We [ie the DC] are no longer able to "hold on" to the country by ourselves in these conditions. Great national solidarity is necessary. I know that Berlinguer thinks and says that in this phase of Italian life it is impossible for one of the two largest political parties to be in opposition. . . On this point his and my viewpoint are absolutely identical. . . The period of emergency will ultimately be followed by one of alternation, and the DC will be relieved of the necessity to govern at all costs.'[10]

Moro has been attacked on the grounds that the historic compromise was a short-term strategy of mere opportunism, and that if elected President, his politics of conciliation would gradually fade out. However, his critics underestimate the fundamental coherence of his lifelong convictions, based on a fusion of strongly spiritual values with an acceptance of practical realities, and on an unswerving belief in the need to widen the scope of democratic consensus. 'Success relies on consensus. A democrat can promote it with all his might, but can never demand it', he wrote in 1969.[11] And answering the rhetorical accusation of excessive political pragmatism, he assured his party colleagues in 1978, 'I do not believe that politics is a matter of pure expediency; it has elements of expediency, but it is not pure expediency; politics is also idealistic'.[12]

The kidnap of Guido De Martino (son of the former PSI leader) in the spring of 1977 and the murder of Carlo Casalegno, Deputy Editor of *La Stampa*, in the autumn had a profound effect on Moro. The risk to his own safety was a fact of life with which he had learned to live. He received the standard quota of anonymous letters common to all public figures, and even his daughter Maria Fida recalls that from 1969 until 1977 she received an average of one letter per week threatening her father with death. However, the risk to his family which the De Martino kidnap brought home was perceived as a new and growing threat. By 1977 no one within the parameters of power could feel safe. The Moro family members were provided with bodyguards and Moro's office in Via Savoia was fitted with bullet-proof glass. Under pressure from his wife and from his escort chief, Leonardi, Moro put in a request for a bullet-proof car as additional security. Strangely, although Moro assured his family and Leonardi that the official request had been made, neither Prime Minister Andreotti nor Interior Minister Cossiga recalled having heard of it, nor of any particular fears Moro had for his safety. When the car was not forthcoming Moro did not insist and let the matter drop, feeling that if he himself had the benefit of greater protection his family would be correspondingly more vulnerable.

In retrospect, a number of strange occurrences could have alerted Moro and his entourage to heightened danger. Some were noted; at other times, passing observations were half forgotten until afterwards, when family, friends and colleagues began the uncomfortable process of guilty recall.

Oreste Leonardi in particular was increasingly worried about Moro's safety, and according to his wife was losing both sleep and weight over this at the beginning of 1978. Twice, all four tyres of Moro's car had burst while the vehicle was in motion. Nicola Rana, Moro's private secretary, had his car tampered with ten times within the space of two months. Leonardi was convinced that Moro's movements were being observed, and had some grounds for believing that subversive elements from outside Rome were present in the capital, but he was unable to gain any satisfactory response when he requested further details from a superior.

One day in late November 1977 the Chairman of *Corriere della Sera*, Franco di Bella, arrived in Via Savoia for a meeting with Moro. As his car pulled up outside, Di Bella caught a glimpse of what he believed was a revolver gleaming in the hand of a waiting motorcyclist. Yet when the man was later traced no evidence could justify his detention. On another occasion in February 1978, a man by the name of Franco Moreno was seen gazing intently into the gardens adjoining Moro's office for hours. Investigations subsequently proved that Moreno had links with subversive organizations and had a criminal record of drug smuggling. Immediately after Moro's kidnap he was arrested, but was released two days later for lack of evidence against him.

After Christmas 1977 the parliamentary crisis deepened to the point where Andreotti was compelled to offer his government's resignation. Discussions and negotiations lasted for a period of two months, one of the most delicate periods politically in the Republic's history. As Moro, party Secretary Zaccagnini and the left of the DC worked to break down the Christian Democratic party's natural resistance to co-operation with the Communists, Enrico Berlinguer and union boss Luciano Lama continued their struggle to gain the confidence of the PCI and the unions.

With the possibility becoming ever more likely that the Communist party might enter the parliamentary majority, the United States lost few opportunities to voice its concern, generally through its ambassador to Italy, Richard Gardner. Aldo Moro became angry at the blatant attempts to interfere in another country's affairs, and prepared an article for publication in the Milan newspaper *Il Giorno* in mid-January, but in the end his press secretary Guerzoni dissuaded him from making such an unguarded response, and the piece did not appear. But Moro's public pronouncements spoke for themselves. In a speech to a joint meeting of DC Senators and Deputies on 28th February, he again stressed the need for the political forces to act together to overcome the crisis. It was not yet possible, he explained, to include the Communist party 'in full equality, in full political solidarity with other parties' due to opposition from inside and outside Italy, but it was possible and crucial to transform the government of 'non-opposition' which had been in power since 1976 on the basis of abstention, into a system of 'positive adhesion.' Only by acting altruistically and in agreement upon a common goal could the political forces overcome the crisis, which threatened the ultimate well-being of the whole nation: 'I believe in the state of emergency, I fear the state of emergency. . . I believe we all ought to be concerned about certain possible forms of impatience and anger which could explode in society in the face of a situation which needs to be corrected. . .'[13] The careful avoidance of repressive polemic and the willing assumption of the need and responsibility to resolve the crisis of the left were, ironically, the hallmarks of Moro's last public speech.

In early March, the continuous round of inter-party consultations moved ponderously towards its conclusion, as the framework for a government of national solidarity began to take shape. Aldo Moro declined Andreotti's invitation to preside over the new government, feeling that the latter's premiership over a parliamentary majority which included the PCI would be viewed, particularly abroad, with somewhat less disfavour than his own. Presentation of the new government to Parliament was scheduled for Thursday, March 16th, 1978.

References

1. Letter No 38 from prison, printed in *Relazioni di Minoranza della Commissione Parlamentare d'Inchiesta sulla strage di Via Fani, sul sequestro e l'assassinio di Aldo Moro e sul terrorismo in Italia*, Vol. secondo, Roma, 1983.
2. Problemi dell'Università, Studium, Bari, 1942.
3. Italo Pietra: *Moro, Fu Vera gloria?*, Garzanti, Milan, p. 51.
4. M. Slater: *Italy: Surviving into the 1980's*. Southern Europe transformed. Harper & Row, London 1984, p. 69.
5. Aldo Moro, *l'Intelligenza e gli avvenimenta*, Testi 1959–1978, Garzanti 1979, p. 292.
6. Comm. Parl. Vol. V, Roma, 1984, p. 5–6.
7. Aldo Moro, *l'Intelligenza e gli avvenimenti*, Testi 1959–1978, Garzanti, 1979, p. 216.
8. *Il Popolo*, 7/4/1977.
9. *Il Popolo*, 19/11/1977.
10. *La Repubblica*, 14/10/1978.
11. *L'Intelligenza e gli avvenimenti*, p. 213.
12. *ibid*, p. 385.
13. *L'Intelligenza e gli avvenimenti*, p. 388.

3
MYTH AND REVOLUTION

What is terrorism? The inevitable subjectivity which governs any interpretation of this phenomenon makes one look instinctively for a lowest common denominator to link groups whose activities span the world and whose diverse ideologies encompass the extremes of political and religious fanaticism. Common to all terrorist organizations is the use of violence as a means to a political end, but given that this is applicable to such diverse groups as Second World War resistance fighters, Central American guerrillas and the Italian Red Brigades, it advances our quest for a definition only marginally.

By common consensus we do not call 'terrorists' those who use force in their rejection of manifestly unjust or intolerable conditions. Any definition must be reached by looking at the process by which the authority being rebelled against has acquired its control, and at the methods by which it maintains itself in power. If power has beeen acquired, for example, through the invasion of territory, or through the military seizure of power leading to a one-party dictatorship, then we do not call that government 'democratic' or 'legitimate.' We could then define terrorism as the threat or use of violence by a non-elected group to intimidate the legitimate authorities of the state in furtherance of the group's political aims.

Italy is a democracy; every parliament since 1948 has been

elected legitimately, on the basis of universal adult suffrage. It would seem obvious, therefore, that anyone who tried to cause the downfall of such a regime would automatically be acting undemocratically, against the wishes of the majority. However, matters are not so clear cut in Italy, where the practice of democracy or legitimate government has at times become blurred around the edges. In moments of crisis the ponderous bureaucracy of Italian institutional life and the immobility of legal and parliamentary procedures have encouraged groups or individuals to short-circuit standard democratic channels and to solve immediate problems with immediate, arbitrary solutions. Moreover, certain corrupt elements of state power have used state protection to thwart democratic procedures and institutions. It is now publicly admitted that the Italian state has provided cover for illegal and subversive operations through its security services; it has used high level 'messenger boys' to negotiate undercover deals with foreign governments, business consortia and criminal organizations with whom the State does not officially wish to dirty its hands.

In 1981 a raid on the Tuscan home of Licio Gelli, Grand Master of the secret masonic lodge Propaganda 2 (P2) revealed a membership list that included government ministers, generals, judges, senior civil servants, chairmen of private and state-owned industries, security service chiefs, editors and bankers. A Parliamentary Commission would subsequently report that P2 had contacts with overseas security services and that it was linked to right-wing terrorist attacks, in particular to the Bologna station massacre. The report of the Independent Left to the Parliamentary Commission of Enquiry examining the kidnap and murder of Aldo Moro and his bodyguards included the observation that 'More or less significant traces of direct action or of involvement of the [security] services are to be found in practically all the judicial decisions affecting acts of terrorism (especially right-wing) from the massacre of Piazza Fontana up to that of Bologna station,'[1] a period of eleven years. If Italy has never quite deserted the ship of democracy, there have certainly been times when only a skeleton crew has been left at the helm.

European terrorism generally falls into one of three categories, namely nationalist terrorism, as practised by groups such as the IRA and ETA, where violence is used to intimidate the state authorities into granting political concessions based on cultural, religious or ethnic criteria; right-wing or neo-fascist terrorism, whose aim is to terrorize the inhabitants of a democratic state into accepting a government of rigid military discipline which denies the individual's right to criticize or oppose; and left-wing or revolutionary terrorism, which has as its objective the violent overthrow of the capitalist state, the seizing of power by the proletariat and the setting up of a socialist regime along Marxist-Leninist lines. There can also be ideological overlaps and even positive co-operation between the three.

In all cases, success for a terrorist group depends not so much upon military victory over the state, but rather upon the degree to which it can rally popular enthusiasm and media coverage for the fight against the power of the state within the area of its potential support. Recognizing its resources to be puny in comparison with those at the state's disposal, the organization looks for the weak links in society, the grievances of a particular group, the critical moments of an unstable government — points of insertion from which the state or its representatives can be manipulated towards the achievement of the group's aims, with the eventual transformation, via publicity and propaganda, of its minority status into a mass popular movement.

The political analyst Philip G. Cerny suggests that the conflict between terrorists and society sets a 'two-fold trap' into which either side may fall. Democracy may become a victim of its own liberality if the terrorists succeed in 'forcing the authorities to break their own contract, to reveal the underlying authoritarianism of the political bond, and thereby to demystify "democratic" capitalist society and catalyze a popular search for alternatives. The potential power of these groups seems to lie not in their threat to overthrow society by force of arms *per se*, but in their ability to symbolize the fragility and vulnerability of the social order and to force that order to subvert itself by eroding the liberal and democratic values upon which its own legitimacy is based. If a strong authoritarian potential is latent in a society with a liberal-democratic order, then the danger to liberal democracy is that it will be subverted through its own forms and institutions as the objective of social survival takes priority. This danger exists most strongly where the process of modernization has been controlled, overtly or covertly, by a coherent set of elite groups whose position derived originally from a pre-modern — feudal or dynastic — social order, but who have been able to transform and reinforce that position in the context of industrial capitalism.'[2]

The deliberate erosion of democracy can be a preliminary step in terrorist tactics, so that the subsequent repression of political and social freedom will in turn lead to a popular revolt and eventual revolution. However, the risk or trap here for the terrorists is that of total annihilation. If the state is considered a repository of individual freedom and security, public opinion will rally to the collective defence of its institutions, and terrorism will become, according to Cerny, 'the eschatological myth of capitalist society, evoking an existential dread, the fear of the collapse of the social order itself. . . In this context, terrorism becomes a myth that can be used for the purpose of social control. It becomes embedded in the catch-phrases of the media and the rhetoric of the politicians. In an age of limited wars in far-away places, it fulfils the function of a war-in-microcosm, increasing social solidarity.'

Many aspects of Cerny's excellent analysis shed light on Italy's vulnerability to terrorism at the end of the 1960's. It was a society undergoing a constant process of self-discovery, experimenting with the freedom that economic prosperity had brought, yet still linked by administrative and religious tradition to the antiquated power structures of the past. Politically immature, its governing class was more concerned with controlling the mechanisms of power than with identifying or resolving the tensions inherent in the rapidly developing nation. The very qualities which had helped to lift Italy out of its post-war morass — personal initiative, energy and self-advancement — were also the driving force behind the creation of apparently impermeable spheres of influence and power, together with a sensation of impunity amongst those who moved within them. The poor, the young and the uneducated were excluded from the corridors of power and, not surprisingly, resented it.

Revolutionary terrorism has elements in common with anarchism, but should never be confused with it: it implies a political strategy, set within a framework of tactics and objectives agreed in precedence by those who practise it. Despite the frequency of epithets such as 'mindless violence' and 'blind aggression', terrorism has its own morality, its specific justifications which must be studied and taken seriously if the phenomenon is to be understood. The arguments or justifications for terrorism may certainly be considered fanatical or specious by some, but they are far from being mindless. Those who have confronted Italian terrorism directly are the first to discredit the notion of the bloodthirsty desperado as often portrayed by the media. Judge Rosario Priore, who has conducted hours of painstaking interrogations with terrorist suspects, sums up the typical terrorist as a person whose ideas are meticulously worked out through careful analysis and serious reflection, for whom everything is seen in terms of politics, someone who above all is 'well-prepared.'

A Milan lawyer who has defended left-wing terrorists and has himself been at the receiving end of death threats stressed that three characteristics common to all the terrorists he had met were 'great intelligence, great openness and great generosity, with sometimes a bit of exhibitionism.' The intelligence, he reasons, is evident in their analysis of sophisticated economic and social theory and is necessary to live the double life between society and secrecy. Openness and generosity are required in that, despite the associations of a certain glamour or excitement, groups such as the Red Brigades sincerely believed that they were conducting a battle against oppression and suffering on behalf of the proletariat, putting their own powers of communication at the service of these beliefs in an attempt to persuade or convert their contemporaries. For this reason, the lawyer explains, the families of terrorists are frequently confused and devastated when a son or daughter is arrested. Their family behaviour has been loving, kind and generous — apparently incompatible with the ferocious image of the terrorist revolutionary. The respected journalist Giorgio Bocca — a former partisan leader and currently foremost Italian chronicler of the more recent armed struggle — firmly rejects the 'them and us' theory of contemporary terrorism, or that the typical terrorist is either sick, mad or monstrous. Furthermore, in arguing that the 1986 presidential amnesty be extended to include terrorist as well as common crimes, he suggested, 'I think in a way we are all responsible for what has happened. The Italian left bears great responsibility; the Communist party has very great responsibility'.[3]

Many of those on the left who had participated in the partisan struggles during World War II had fought for a utopian vision of post-war Italy which by no means corresponded to reality. They had hoped that the idealism and enthusiasm which inspired the resistance movement would be transformed into a revolutionary surge capable of sweeping through the entire nation and installing a socialist state based on Marxist/Leninist principles. Instead, the idealists watched with dismay and some self-reproach as their dream faded. Disappointment became embedded in the spirit of the 'missed revolution', the 'betrayed resistance movement' whose aims had somehow been pushed aside. Simultaneous fears that a new fascist regime could arise from the debris of the old were harboured by many, including millionaire publisher and eccentric Giangiacomo Feltrinelli, whose personal politics lay somewhere between communism and anarchism. Feltrinelli had led a privileged and cosseted, but lonely childhood. During the war he had believed fervently in the need to fight fascism and had tried to join the ranks of the partisans, but was restrained by his over-protective family. After the war he expended considerable energy, political zeal and personal finance on the setting up of a left-wing publishing house and on the establishment of an organization known as Partisan Action Groups (GAP), whose function was to maintain constant alertness for the possibility of a right wing *coup d'état*, and to crush it should it materialize. The hard core of GAP was composed of partisan veterans, many of whom had not handed in their weapons when the fighting was over, and who kept them in readiness for the predicted right-wing offensive. Feltrinelli's contacts included the KGB, Che Guevara and Fidel Castro, whose formidable support he expected to enlist should the *coup* take place. He was killed in 1972 whilst laying an explosive charge under a high tension electricity pylon; some suggested he had blown himself up accidentally, others that the security services had murdered him as a powerful and influential Eastern-bloc agent. The latter theory gained credibility in May 1986 when a former head of Italian counter espionage admitted in a highly controversial interview that 'Feltrinelli's death fitted in very conveniently with the operations in progress'.[4]

Those of the *'resistenza tradita'* did not expect to survive solely on memories of partisan heroics and thwarted revolutionary bravado; their legacy had to be passed on to the next generation and fully understood, it had to find a contemporary echo in the new industrial society. In an Italy caught up in the inexorable process of industrialization, automation and, in Marxist eyes, exploitation, the inevitable focus of revolutionary ambition became the worker, or *'operaio.'* Consequently, ideological and intellectual aims began to coalesce with the more immediate aims of the workers whose conditions of employment, housing and welfare were largely being neglected. A small but influential group attempted to refound the Communist party along strict doctrinal lines — the Italian Marxist Leninist Communist

Party had little following amongst workers, but its idealogues were sincere in their championship of the proletariat; they promoted the factory worker to the forefront of revolutionary struggle, and made none of the compromises of loyalty to state institutions adopted by the official PCI.

The factory worker became crucial firstly by virtue of his symbolic role at the heart of industrial society. Whereas once he had been an integral part of a professional unit, had been trained in specific skills and could feel some pride in his achievement, the increasing automation of factories, their expansion as part of anonymous multinational empires, and their apparent indifference to employee welfare now rendered the individual labourer unimportant, his personal contribution irrelevant and his work routine tedious and repetitive. Although 'exploitation' had existed before, it had been at a simpler level — the 'oppressor' had forced the labourer by economic superiority to work in his factory. But because the worker was skilled, he had confidence in the knowledge that he and his companions had the ability to take over and run the factory should the opportunity arise. Now, however, the power structures of multinational management and the computerized technology of robot-operated production lines were destroying this conviction, and with it the pride and self-respect of the worker, whose status passed from that of skilled labourer to mass labourer — the lowest of the low. Increasing dissatisfaction was nourished in the late 60's by the emergence of new political groups which in turn led to the diffusion of widely read and influential publications. An organization called *Potere Operaio* (Worker Power) and the publications *Quaderni Rossi* and *Classe Operaia* were amongst the most significant. Direct inspiration to the workers to bring about the revolution was derived not only from the experience of the Russian revolution but also from the countries of the Third World, whose struggles were highlighted by Feltrinelli's Third World review, 'Tricontinental.'

France is traditionally credited with responsibility for the wave of student revolts which swept Western Europe in 1968, yet by early 1967 Italian universities were already coming under strong pressure to change. Pisa university was occupied in February during a conference convened by university rectors to discuss reforms. Later that year, Milan students protested angrily about a proposed increase in enrolment fees. The numbers of students attending university in Lombardy had risen from 10,000 to 50,000 without any significant increase in accommodation provision, lecture halls or staff levels. Examination systems were outmoded, and teaching techniques were too rigid to cope either with the practical needs of the students or with the questioning of authority and desire for self-determination which characterized the new generation.

Other elements helped to unify student protest during the late 1960's: the foundation of the University of Trento gave Italy its first sociology faculty, and consequently brought together students with a propensity for radical — even revolutionary — thought from all over the country, providing a more concentrated intellectual impetus and focus to revolt than was present in the more traditional universities. The model of the Chinese revolution and the works of Mao Tse Tung were even more of an inspiration to students in quest of an ideology than those of the Russian revolutionaries. The Vietnam war had united the whole of the Italian left in common cause against American imperialism, and particularly incensed the students, whose contemporaries across the Atlantic were being conscripted to fight. A rift did occur, however, between the PCI, whose call for a 'free Vietnam' was at odds with the extra-parliamentary left, or '*Movimento*', who urged a 'red Vietnam.'

Those who participated directly in the experience of 1968 continually stress the physical nature of the mood which led them to demonstrate their need for change. Giorgio, whose political convictions subsequently led him to take up the *lotta armata*, talks of the 'political and cultural effervescence' that awakened a whole generation to a world of intellectual and sensual stimulation. Such a world had little to do with the formal education of school or university, but emerged from the works of Marx and Mao, from the lyrics of Bob Dylan songs, from the writings of George Jackson and other black power American writers, from Jack Kerouac and the Beat Generation, from the movies of Sam Peckinpah, and even from the cult of excitement and adventure contained in the classic adventure tales. 'If you can combine Lenin with Treasure Island,' Giorgio assured me, 'you'll begin to tell our story.'

Protest was gradually extended to any form of authority in any sphere. The university was seen as an instrument of state power, wielded in the interests of subversion and indoctrination. The sole preoccupation of the ruling élite, or oppressing class, was to maintain itself in power by any means, thus any deviance from the rules laid down by it was merely the violation of an arbitrarily imposed code of morality. To disrupt or overthrow such a code, even by violence, was seen as justifiable.

Italian revolutionaries tackled the problem of violence by creating the categories of 'defensive violence' and 'offensive violence.' To use violence to protect oneself against that of apparently fascist policemen, employers or industrialists who, it was maintained, frequently could and did use violence themselves, was considered legitimate, although indiscriminate violence was generally condemned. The principle of 'militant antifascism' was used to legitimize retaliation against what was seen to be the status quo: society was *itself* violent, fascist atrocities were still being practised, if not so overtly, then covertly, against migrant workers, especially factory employees, against the poor, the sick, the elderly and against women. Even objectively, Italy was still a country of violence. Fascist squads had been responsible for the deaths of some 300 workers during the 20 year period after the war. Violence was seen as a part of everyday life — not a deviation from the norm but as the norm — hence the conviction that it was necessary to fight like with like. And when students began to arm themselves with bricks, stones and petrol bombs, far from innovating a pattern of social behaviour, they felt they were merely confirming what had always existed. As Giorgio pointed out, 'It was accepted that the revolution would be born violent.'

The simultaneous creation of an individual mythology, parallel and complementary to the abstract ideology of revolution, exaggerated the symbolic weight of violence and death. It served to bridge the gap between intellect and imagination, providing a highly personal interpretation which shielded those who sought to use violence from reality and nourished their illusions. The importance of Mao Tse Tung in the creation of revolutionary mythology lies not so much in the theory, which Mao adapted directly from Marx and Lenin, but rather in the imaginative, mythological framework within which his utterances were set. Mao was convinced of the inevitable duration of the revolutionary process. He believed it 'cannot be other than protracted and ruthless. . . It is wrong to think that the forces of the Chinese revolution can be built up in the twinkling of an eye, or that China's revolution can triumph overnight.'[5]

In this respect, Mao was especially revered for his imaginative, deeply spiritual approach to sacrifice and death. One of his more famous maxims, adopted enthusiastically by Italian practitioners of the *lotta armata*, helped them to cope not only with the prospect of dying themselves, but also with the morality of committing murder: 'All men must die, but death can vary in its significance. The ancient Chinese writer Szuma Chien said, "Though death befalls all men alike, it may be heavier than Mount Tai or lighter than a feather." To die for the people is heavier than Mount Tai, but to work for the fascists and die for the exploiters and oppressors is lighter than a feather'.[6]

By attributing spiritual significance or weight to dying, Mao thus glorifies or immortalizes the heavy death, and at the same time absolves the murderer or perpetrator of the light death from moral guilt and responsibility.

The noble aspect of death, this spirit of revolutionary romanticism which has been ascribed to Mao as 'the hero's quest for doing more than the possible, risking and courting death in order to alter the meaning of both life and death'[7] links up Mao and the myth of religious martyrdom to another, more frivolous, interpretation of heroism which both reinforces and trivializes individual commitment: the old-fashioned adventure of the nineteenth century novel, the quiet bravery of the Hemingway hero and the violence and disregard for death of the American cult western. These were the raw materials from which an entire revolutionary culture was forged, in which the Italian militant saw himself in the role of pirate, cowboy or Robin Hood as, gun in hand, he leapt to the defence of the poor or the underprivileged. Admittedly with some self-irony, he saw himself as a conquering hero.

The guerrilla groups of Latin America also occupy a position of honour in Italian revolutionary mythology, for the simple reason that they successfully practised the techniques they preached. Carlos Marighella's 'Minimanual of the Urban Guerrilla', published by Feltrinelli in 1970, effectively served as the first practical text book for the emerging militant organizations. In it the Brazilian Marighella defines the qualities necessary for the urban guerrilla, who was 'characterized by his bravery and decisive nature. He must be a good tactician and a good shot. The urban guerrilla must be a person of great astuteness to compensate for the fact that he is not sufficiently strong in arms, ammunition and equipment'.[8]

Despite the inevitable technical inferiority experienced by the small organization which takes on a more powerful adversary, Marighella considered the urban guerrilla morally superior in that he 'defends a just cause, which is the people's cause. This moral superiority is what sustains the urban guerrilla. Thanks to it, the urban guerrilla can accomplish his principal duty, which is to attack and to survive.'

Marighella also had a precise idea of the urban guerrilla's longer-term goal: 'within the framework of the class struggle, as it inevitably and necessarily sharpens, the armed struggle of the urban guerrilla points towards two essential objectives: (a) the physical liquidation of the chiefs and assistants of the armed forces and of the police; (b) the expropriation of government resources and those belonging to big capitalists, multinationals and imperialists, with small expropriations used for the maintenance of individual urban guerrillas and large ones for the sustenance of the revolution itself.' Kidnapping, according to Marighella, was 'capturing and holding in a secret spot a police agent, a North American spy, a political personality, or a notorious and dangerous enemy of the revolutionary movement . . . is used to exchange or liberate imprisoned revolutionary comrades, or to force suspension of torture in the jail cells of the military dictatorship.' The liberation of prisoners was 'an armed operation designed to free the jailed urban guerrilla . . . the urban guerrilla who is free views the penal establishments of the enemy as the inevitable site of guerrilla action designed to liberate his ideological brothers from prison.'

Marighella followed his own advice when he participated in a spectacularly successful political kidnap — that of the United States Ambassador to Brazil, C. Burke Elbrick, whose release was obtained only after the liberation of 15 political prisoners and the publication of the terrorist group's entire manifesto.

Another South American example was of particular symbolic importance: the kidnap in Argentina in May 1971 of Stanley Silvester, British Honorary Consul and head of the Swift de la Playa meat packing plant. In return for Silvester's release, the terrorist group demanded that the company reinstate 300 sacked workers, improve conditions in the plant, provide medical attention, distribute $50,000 of food to specified working class districts, reduce work quotas, and publish its manifesto throughout the media. All these demands were met, and the hostage was liberated a week later.

Two factors lent this kidnap a special significance: it was the first time a terrorist organization had forced an international company to change working conditions and provide relief for the poor; secondly, it was realized that while diplomats were deliberately selected for their loyalty and devotion to patriotic duty and were rewarded with due privilege and honour, a company employee lived in a foreign country simply to do a job, and could not be expected to martyr himself on the altar of a profit-making multinational organization. From then on, big business was almost bound to pay a ransom for the release of a kidnapped employee if it wished to maintain an image of staff care and protection.

From the spring of 1968 onwards, the focal point of anti-authoritarian protest ceased to be the university campus and moved to the factories where serious attempts were made to unite middle-class student rebellion with working-class grievances. The attempted fusion was only partly successful. Although united in their condemnation of the exploitative capitalist state, a difference of approach separated bourgeois youth from working-class labourer: the students claimed to despise bourgeois values, the acquisitive habits and cult of consumerism characterized by the economic prosperity of the '60's, whereas the workers believed that these were positive benefits which were desirable and should be universally available, and not just for those who could afford to acquire them by the exploitation of others. Inevitably, the students could only partially identify with the labour struggles in the factories. If for them to protest and demonstrate was an expression of emancipation and exuberance, for the worker a protest entailed a day's less pay for a hungry family, the possibility of being arrested or injured and therefore of being unable to work, and the certainty of being marked down as a trouble maker by an employer, who could make life even more difficult. Giovanni Casucci, a labourer at the Alfa Romeo car company, who later joined the Red Brigades, recalls the results of his political militancy with bitterness, when after a protest at an arbitrary increase of working hours, he was abruptly moved to the paint spraying department of another plant, presumably as punishment, where 'the environmental conditions were extremely dangerous, caused by the use of paints and by the presence of other sources of atmospheric pollution, with complete disregard for adequate safety measures.'[9]

If student/worker collaboration never fully took off in 1968, positive co-operation undoubtedly occurred, especially in the north where the working class had a stronger tradition of revolutionary ideology, and was more prepared to harness itself to the student cause, stimulated by the hope of mutual advancement through defiance of a common enemy. But the binding force was not strong enough, and in the absence of a strong left-wing party prepared to assume leadership of the common struggle, the students' revolt perforce made way for the real battle to come — the workers' fight for better wages and conditions.

From the time democracy was restored in Italy, trade union affiliation closely followed political party alignment. However, the unions were external to the workplace and had no specific rights to legislate from within, or even to hold meetings during working hours or on working premises. Additionally, ideological differences prevented the harmonization of a common approach to management, and hampered attempts to promote the workers' demands for reform. Significantly, these did not simply relate to the basic elements of salary, working hours etc, but were designed to create overall improvements in the quality of life and especially to provide parity of treatment in areas of social welfare. Union leader Pierre Carniti describes the three central aims of the workers' struggle as being the effort to bring a proper dignity, or 'citizenship' of work to society; the satisfaction of an ever-increasing need for security; and equality of treatment.[10] Many working-class Catholics, stimulated by shared grievances and the new political atmosphere of Catholic/Marxist compromise, suddenly awoke to political consciousness and discovered a common cause with their Marxist brothers.

Throughout 1968 and 1969 strike followed strike, violent clashes occurred frequently between police and activists at factory gates and on marches. Individual acts of brutality, of reprisal between striker and non-striker, were commonplace. In July 1969 a demonstration in Turin led to a fight involving demonstrators and police in which 70 were injured and 19 arrests made. Events came to a head when the metal mechanics' contract came up for renewal in October: 50,000 were mobilized on the streets of Milan in support of their claims. Later that month one demonstrator was killed and 125 injured in a battle which was allegedly fomented by fascist squads. A national strike followed, bringing out an estimated five million adherents. Finally, in May 1970, a Statute of Workers' Rights was passed which improved wages and conditions and recognized the right of elected Factory Councils to exist within the work place.

The practical results of the so-called 'Hot Autumn' were felt almost immediately: wages rose by nearly 20% in 1970 alone, and by 1974 the number of hours worked had dropped by 12%. Overall, the cost of labour in Italy increased by 28% in the years 1970–1973.[11] In contrast with the student struggles of 1968 which had achieved little beyond a thorough shakeup of a creaking, anachronistic education system, the workers' struggles of 1969 proved that acquisition of tangible material benefits could be fought for and won by the masses for the masses. For the Marxist/Leninists, the elements were coming together for the material construction of a truly working class party within the factory system — the vital core of the inevitable revolution.

Given the accumulation of left-inspired protest throughout Italy in 1968 and 1969, a strong reaction from the neo-fascist right was perhaps inevitable, both to demonstrate the 'validity' of the might-is-right thesis, and to point to the need for repressive action on the part of the state to control civil unrest and 'get the country back to work again.' This was probably the immediate aim of the bomb attack in a bank in Piazza Fontana, Milan, on 12th December 1969, which caused 16 deaths and 88 injuries. The longer-term objective was to destabilize Italian democracy by means of a programmed 'strategy of tension' whereby the fear of terrorism would encourage the civilian population to opt spontaneously for the relinquishment of certain freedoms in exchange for the physical security provided by a military dictatorship.

Initial claims that the bomb was the work of left-wing terrorists were encouraged by President of the Republic Saragat, whose irresponsible remarks gave state backing to the immediate arrest of a well-known anarchist, Pietro Valpreda. Subsequently, the speed with which the arrest was effected led to rumours that the explosion had been carried out by a person or persons wishing to put an end to the politics of the centre-left. To general disgust, the bloodshed and misery was manipulated by both sides of the political spectrum in a bid to gain support. The right tried to make the government look weak and ineffectual in the face of left-wing subversion, and claimed that only a firm, authoritarian regime could restore the necessary civil order to a lawless country. The left threw the accusation back to land on the shoulders of the neo-fascists, and attacked them for the propaganda attempt to insert the massacre into the pattern of working class struggles and to rouse opinion against the proletarian cause. The DC denounced the 'opposing extremes' and tried to rally a broad consensus of opinion around a fear of both. The accusations against Valpreda could not be proved, and two neo-fascists, Freda and Ventura, as well as a security services agent by the name of Giannettini were subsequently arrested.

The consequences of the Piazza Fontana massacre were devastating: the short term horror at the loss of innocent life was real enough, but for many the long term implications were psychologically traumatizing. Nearly all the 'first generation' of left-wing terrorists will point to December 1969 as a turning point, a decisive moment in which political commitment was made, when the urgency of the need to act was concretized, when the fear of fascism was first experienced as a physical revulsion. Following on from the 'missed revolution', the political disillusionment with PCI reformism and DC patronage, militant anti-fascism now went on to the attack. The 'final justification' had arrived. There was a vacuum to fill, a role to play. The Red Brigades were born.

One factor which distinguishes terrorism from all other forms of politically inspired protest is the strategic use of violence. It is the crucial factor which alienates those who practise it from those who reject it. Those who practise terrorist violence do not do so mindlessly, but on the basis of a series of convictions which in their eyes justifies its use.

How *did* the Italian revolutionary movement justify the morality of killing judges, policemen, politicians? And in particular, how did the factory picket or student with brick and petrol bomb turn into a gun-toting terrorist, trained and willing to shoot in cold blood? The development of the armed struggle in Italy from the relatively low level of violence of the *'propaganda armata'* to the use of revolvers and sub-machine guns in the 'guerrilla offensive' was a gradual process and needs describing in detail, but a preliminary look at the development of violence may be helpful.

The violence which erupted on the picket lines and during the demonstrations of 1968 and 1969 was considered by many to be justifiable retaliation in self-defence against a more powerful oppressor, the self arrogation of a proletarian right, emphasized and exaggerated to maximum symbolic potential. However, Marx and Lenin had also laid the moral foundations for the act of murder when performed in the interests of revolutionary justice. To see how this was translated into practice it is necessary to reduce society to a series of symbols: if the world is divided clearly into oppressed and oppressors, the source of evil can be identified as an avaricious and anonymous enemy — one who is responsible for all the sufferings of the poor, the unemployed, the underpaid and the homeless. The state, then, is an organized power structure which provokes endless suffering, illness and death on a national and even international scale. The enemy may comprise not only politicians but anyone who contributes to the oppressive powers of the state — journalists, policemen, prison officers, judges and lawyers. A Milan lawyer told me of the death threat he had received which accused him of being 'a lawyer of the state . . . part of the army of oppression.' Unable to wage open warfare

against such an army, the terrorist's solution is to opt for the
myth of collective intimidation, or 'get one and educate a
hundred.' This abstract, anonymous way of fighting the state
is the urban guerrilla's moral solution to the act of murder. He
or she is able to concentrate collective anger and hatred for a
general enemy on to the personage of a single victim whose
identity resides solely in his function, whose death, according
to Mao, will be 'lighter than a feather.' Within the given
function, selection of the individual victim depends upon
more specific criteria, such as the supposed neo-fascist
inclinations of a particular judge or the reputation of a prison
officer for cruelty — traits intended to highlight the inherent
baseness of the function.

Adriana Faranda* helps to illustrate the symbolic and
personal aspects more clearly, but admits there were 'many,
many contradictions' for those who practised terrorist
violence. In one sense, violence was removed to 'a level of
extreme abstraction . . . which serves to project a series of
responsibilities on to an entire category of people.'

But co-existing with the abstract level was a personal
component — 'people's unhappiness, deaths at the
workplace, homeless earthquake victims, young people dying
of heroin because someone allows it to happen . . . and our
own companions killed in demonstrations by the police.' On
this basis, to attack another human being was both to strike a
blow at a symbolic enemy and to discharge a 'burden of
passion.' The Red Brigades fully recognized that their
attempts to replace the existing society with an ideal model
of their own construction would lead to violent battles with
the defenders of the old order, but felt that 'the purifying
blood bath was a necessary price to pay for the utopia of
tomorrow. . . . But despite the impulse of anger it [ie
violence] is something from which you feel estranged,
something which you are obliged to use but which you don't
like. At the moment of going to attack someone there is a part
of you which you have to silence, to mutilate, which rebels

* For the full text of this interview see Appendix II

and says no!'

The fear of taking life is not easily overcome. Terrorists admit that at the moment of killing they simultaneously experience a part of themselves as dying. Sociologist Franco Ferrarotti suggests that at the moment of death a murderer feels an identification with his victim, since the point of murder is also the moment at which the tables could be turned and the murderer become the victim. Yet the fear induced by the act of murder can be absorbed within an overwhelming sense of power, even exhilaration. If we accept that anger at perceived injustices and hatred for those deemed responsible can be catalysts for violence, the exercise of violence can be seen as both a liberating and a purifying experience. This idea is evoked by Mao Tse-tung in an essay entitled 'War and Peace', in which Mao praises revolutionary war as 'an antitoxin which not only eliminates the enemy's poison but also purges us of our own filth.'[12]

We can find direct confirmation of the exhilarating effect of violence from some who have practised terrorist violence in Italy, such as Bruno Laronga of *Prima Linea*: 'The exercise of violence . . . had a fundamental role in my life, made me feel a complete person, capable of determining my own space. I was at the age when every empty day seemed frighteningly lost.'[13]

It seems that the terrorist's ability to use violence depends largely upon the existence of two factors: hatred and anger directed towards an enemy who is anonymous rather than personal, and a dread of emptiness and futility which are temporarily banished by the exercise of violent action. Violence helps the individual to escape the irrelevance of his existence, fills the emptiness of his life, and provides him with the heady experience of power over himself and over others. Without passion, boredom, contempt, dissatisfaction, are all that are left — ordinary, everyday emotions experienced by ordinary, everyday people. As Alessandro Silj observes, 'Anger is an indispensable premise in the birth of any attempt at liberation. Without anger there is only resignation.'[14]

The catalyzing force of anger and of hatred is therefore the power which unleashes and concentrates violence, which permits the terrorist to shoot in cold blood, either to wound or kill. Terrorists are not inhuman, they do not enjoy watching others suffer and die, but they deliberately condition themselves to overcome their natural inhibitions with the protective belief that the validity of their goal justifies the violent means necessary to achieve it. The arrogance that accompanies this assumption allows the terrorist to feel almost superhuman — he can leave his routine, dull persona behind, creating a new reality in which he is free and untrammelled, and in which his violence finds its moral justification through the symbol and the symbolic gesture, the enemy's 'light death' or the hero's *bella morte*. By shrouding their acts of violence in symbolic significance, terrorists are able to elevate them to the status of noble, heroic, even religious acts, conferring legitimacy upon them and upon themselves.

The student revolts of 1968 and the workers' struggles of 1969 and 1970 coincided with another movement whose aims were emancipation, equality and freedom from oppression: the impact of the women's liberation movement was felt not only in its insistence upon parity in legal rights, social status and employment conditions, upon freedom of choice in birth control and abortion, but also within revolutionary movements in Italy and elsewhere. Although the myth of the female terrorist forms no part of the revolutionary culture created by the terrorists themselves but has been imposed from outside, it nonetheless seems apt to examine its validity or otherwise in the context of this chapter.

Two characteristics are traditionally associated with the female terrorist, firstly that her political commitment to revolution is a direct result of sexual discrimination and oppression, and secondly that she is more ruthless and fanatical than her male counterpart.

Certainly the countries of the Middle East, where female emancipation scarcely exists, have provided female terrorists of exceptional sacrificial devotion and fanaticism — witness Leila Khaled, responsible for the hijacking of an aeroplane during a flight between Tel Aviv and London in 1970, and founder member of the all-female 'Fatima Brigades' — the valkyries of the Islamic revolution. Other examples of female prominence can be found within the IRA, and within the Red Army Faction in Germany, in which female membership was once estimated to be as high as 50%.

The Dutch industrialist Tiede Herrema, held prisoner by IRA members Eddie Gallagher and Marion Coyle for 31 days in the autumn of 1975, affirmed that as pressure mounted on the kidnappers, Marion Coyle gradually assumed both psychological and material control by taking possession of the gun and by dictating conduct towards both hostage and negotiators. Whereas Herrema was able to establish some sort of dialogue and rapport with Gallagher, Coyle remained aloof and unapproachable throughout, despite the enforced intimacy imposed by siege conditions. During the final moments of the kidnap, as police prepared to storm the house in which they and Herrema were cornered, it was Coyle who remained defiant and aggressive, her companion crouching terrified on the floor, passively awaiting capture.

Undoubtedly, the traditional madonna/mother image of wifely virtue and cow-like docility have made emancipation more difficult for the Italian woman, and may go some way to explain female participation in terrorist activities. Most Italian women who have espoused politically inspired violence will admit to a strongly developed sense of repression and exploitation which is partly, but by no means entirely, experienced as a sexual phenomenon. They have certainly had cause for complaint: when one remembers that an Italian could legally beat his wife until 1975 and that, as Peter Nichols reports, 'In December 1966, the ninth section of the Civil tribunal in Milan (Milan, not Naples or Palermo) ruled that a wife's behaviour in forcing her husband to wash plates and carry out other domestic tasks gravely injured his dignity and was a just cause for granting a legal separation, there being no legal recourse to divorce', then one realizes that the feminist cause in Italy has lagged some way behind that of Britain or America. Until 1969, Nichols continues, 'a woman's adultery was punishable with up to three months imprisonment, and could be cited as grounds for a legal separation. A man's adulteries were only punishable if it could be proved that he had a lasting relationship with a woman which was cause for public scandal.'[15] However, one must beware of drawing too close a connection between repression and reaction, since the percentage of women in West German terrorist organizations has been higher than in Italy, and female emancipation has also been greater. Nor does the Italian female terrorist appear to fit into any particular sociological or psychological grouping: social backgrounds vary from the aristocratic to the working class, with a strong middle class component drawn from the teaching profession and the universities. The intellectual level has tended to be high.

To examine female terrorist participation it is important to distinguish between those who join organizations through personal ideology and commitment and those who join in support of a husband or boyfriend whose commitment they come to adopt. (The reverse of this situation, that the male joins to support his female partner, is rare.)

Adriana Faranda does not believe that motivation can be separated into 'male' and 'female' but, if anything, considers the men in the Red Brigades to have been 'more rational, whereas the women had a more emotional, almost maternal involvement in the injustices they saw around them'. There is, however, one substantial difference that she observed within the BR — 'women always remain hostile to any type of power whatsoever . . . even when talking about the seizure of power, there is always a trace of recalcitrance, almost an identification of the evils of humanity with the very existence of a power exercised over others . . . it's something they always feel, continually.'

In the Red Brigades, where female membership averaged 10%, there was no division of roles or responsibilities on grounds of sex, although Faranda remarks that during her period of militancy (1976–79) no woman ever reached the Executive Committee, the top of the BR hierarchy. 'I can't say there was any real discrimination, but I felt that the men were listened to more. Also, if any uncertainty or doubt were shown by a woman, it would seem more serious.'[16] Perhaps to dispel any doubts over the issue of motivation and to avoid the customary dominant male hierarchy, several all-women groups were formed within the loose ambit of the *Prima Linea* organization, usually concentrating on targets of special relevance to the feminist cause.

With seven years experience of terrorism from the other side of the fence, Milan Public Prosecutor Armando Spataro rejects the idea that characteristics and motivations differ significantly between the sexes, and dismisses the myth of the female terrorist, about whom, he claims, much banal exaggeration has been made. His colleague in Rome, Rosario Priore, concedes that women revolutionaries may be more tenacious, and believes them to be, if anything, better prepared ideologically, perhaps more dedicated and more prone to sacrifice.

Some guide as to whether female terrorists are indeed more loyal might be found within the statistics which distinguish repentant terrorists (ie those who give information leading to the arrest of others) from the dissociated (those who confess their personal responsibility but remain silent as to the actions of their companions). From these figures no such trend emerges: in July 1986 out of an estimated prison population of 880–890 left-wing political prisoners, approximately 10% were women. The same percentage was maintained in the numbers of male and female '*dissociati*' in provisional liberty. Yet out of a total of approximately 340–350 '*pentiti*' the female percentage rises to 23%, or an estimated 80–90 women. No proof here that the female suffers in silence or that her loyalty surpasses her male companion's.

The driving force of the female terrorist seems to conform largely to that of the male, though perhaps with less of the accompanying myth construction. More dogmatic, stripped of the elements of fantasy, heroism and the *bella morte*, her idealism may be rawer, more acute and more passionately felt. As regards the central issues, they are united in their profound sense of injustice, in their hatred for a society which seems to have caused misery and inequality, and in their conviction that a solution can be found through violent revolution. Thus the mythical female terrorist seems, in Italy at least, to be a more a creation of the media than a creature of reality.

But just what was that reality, and how did it react with or absorb the world of myth? How did militant anti-fascism become an 'attack on the heart of the State', *propaganda armata* turn into guerrilla warfare?

REFERENCES

1. *Relazione della Commissione Parlamentare d'Inchiesta sulla strage di Via Fani sul sequestro e l'assassinio di Aldo Moro e sul terrorismo in Italia: Osservazioni dell'onorevole Stefano Rodotà alla Relazione di maggioranza* (Gruppo Misto — Independente di Sinistra) pp. 174.
2. Philip G. Cerny: *Terrorism, A Challenge to the State*, Martin Robertson, Oxford, 1981, *ed.* Juliet Lodge, pps. 91–93.
3. Giorgio Bocca, in interview with Liisa Liimattainen of Finnish television in 'Post terrorismo', January, 1986.
4. General Ambrogio Viviani, interviewed by Romano Cantore & Carlo Rossella, Panorama, 18/5/1986.
5. Selected works of Mao Tse-tung, Foreign Languages Press Peking 1967, Vol II, pp. 316.
6. Quotation from Chairman Mao Tse-tung, quoted by Robert J. Lifton: *Revolutionary Immortality, Mao Tse-tung and the Chinese Cultural Revolution*, Pelican books, 1970, pp. 66.
7. Lifton, op. cit., pp. 81.
8. *Minimanual of the urban Guerrilla* by Carlos Marighella: Appendix to Urban Guerrilla Warfare: Robert Moss, Adelphi Papers No. 79, The International Institute for Strategic Studies, 1971.
9. *Frammenti di lotta armata e utopia rivoluzionaria, CONTROinformazione*, Milan, 1984, p. 9.

10. *Antigone*, Anno II, numero 7, May–June 1986, p. 4.
11. M. Slater: Italy: Surviving into the 1980's. Southern Europe transformed. p. 73.
12. Quoted from 'Quotations from Chairman Mao Tse-tung' in Lifton, op. cit., pp. 67.
13. Giorgio Bocca, *Noi Terroristi*, Garzanti, Milan, 1985, pp. 193.
14. Alessandro Silj, *Mai Più Senza Fucile*, Vallecchi, Firenze, 1977, p. 118.
15. Peter Nichols: *Italia, Italia*, Fontana/Collins, Glasgow, 1973, pp. 31.
16. Interview with Gabriella Parca, *Il Giorno*, 15 February, 1985.

4
ARMED PROPAGANDA 1969–1977

I   1969–1974

The origins of the Red Brigades can be traced back to the formation of two groups in late 1969 and 1970. The first, called the '*Collettivo Politico Metropolitano*' was founded by Renato Curcio and Margherita Cagol with contemporaries of theirs from the Sociology faculty of Trento university. Renato Curcio was born illegitimately in 1941 and was brought up by his mother and her family, his wealthy father providing money for his upkeep but remaining physically and emotionally at a distance. Renato's replacement father figure was represented by his mother's brother Armando, who fought and died with the partisan forces. In a letter to his mother from prison in 1974 Curcio evoked the enduring spirit of his idol: 'His bright, ever-smiling eyes looking far off towards a society of free, equal men. I loved him like a father. And I picked up the gun which death alone, meted out by the murderous hands of the Nazi fascists, had wrenched from him. What more can I tell you? My enemies are the enemies of humanity and of intelligence. Those who have built and are building their wretched fortunes on the material and intellectual misery of the people. Whose hands have locked the door of my cell.'[1]

On leaving school, Curcio worked for some time as a bell-boy in a Milan luxury hotel before enrolling for a diploma in Chemistry at a college in Albenga. From there he obtained a scholarship to study sociology at the new faculty in Trento, beginning his degree course in the autumn of 1964. Margherita (Mara) Cagol came from a much more conventional middle class background and was of good catholic stock. Born in Trento, her mother worked in a pharmacy, her father owned a perfumery.

Their first experience of direct confrontation with authority occurred in 1967 when, during an anti-Vietnam demonstration, police were called to the university premises. Along with others, they were dragged into vans, taken to police headquarters where they were interrogated and photographed, and files were opened on their activities. Although his political consciousness was aroused by what he considered imperialism, exploitation and oppression, Curcio did not immediately envisage the tactics of guerrilla warfare as a suitable or useful weapon in the Italian struggle for proletarian self-realization; rather they were the choice of 'a petit bourgeois in search of excitement, not a proletarian revolutionary.'[2] The couple's political energies were concentrated to a large extent on a publication called *Lavoro politico* (Political work) in which theories and examples of revolutionary activity were analyzed and explained. The failure of the May 'revolution' in France in 1968 prompted Curcio and his fellow authors to consider more deeply the framework within which the revolution would have to occur: 'This is not a revolutionary but a pre-revolutionary moment. . . . It is foolhardy to pretend or make people think that the seizure of power and the realization of an egalitarian society is a quick and easy task: on the contrary, we must continually stress that it will be long and difficult. We have before us not the Cuban but the Chinese model, that is, the organization of the happy isle is not possible within two years of struggle, but it is possible after 40 years of resistance.'[3]

The months between the autumn of 1968 and the summer of 1969 when they left Trento were spent by Curcio and Cagol in a general quest for political solutions and in a drive towards commitment and action. Curcio briefly joined the Italian Marxist-Leninist Communist party, but this seemed too ideological, not concerned enough with reality and practical struggle. They also came to believe that it was the industrial metropolis rather than the university campus which would be the battlefield of revolutionary struggle. The couple then married (a church wedding) and moved to Milan where they formed the 'Collettivo Politico Metropolitano', later to be called 'Sinistra Proletaria'. In February 1971, following the occupation of some empty houses in Milan, Curcio and the by then pregnant Mara were forcibly ejected by the police, had their names taken and their apartment searched. She lost the baby, and Curcio lost his job at the publishers Mondadori when news of the event reached his employers. Discussion at this time within Sinistra Proletaria centred on the validity of using violence as a means to a political end. Curcio and Cagol made their choice, transferred to an address without informing their families, and made their leap of commitment to clandestinity and the armed struggle.

The other founding element of the Brigate Rosse emerged in the town of Reggio Emilia from the dissatisfaction and dissent of members of the Federation of Young Communists (FGCI) with the emergence of a reformist, conciliatory spirit inside the parent party. Amongst these was Alberto Franceschini, born in 1947 of working class parents with a strong Communist tradition. Both Alberto's father and grandfather had worked for the 'Reggiane', an engineering and construction company which was the largest industrial employer in the area. Franceschini's grandfather had spent 13 years between prison and domiciliary confinement for his overt opposition to fascism, and his father, after capture as a partisan, was deported to Auschwitz. Alberto followed the family commitment to communism but was also concerned to bridge the gap between catholicism and communism which, he considered, were both crucial elements in the path to revolution. Indeed, in the area of Reggio Emilia the links between the two were strong. Because there was no university in Reggio Emilia, youth protest found its voice either through the FGCI or through the catholic youth groups. Franceschini studied engineering at Parma and then Bologna universities until 1969, when he left to devote himself full time to political activities. When in that year he was suspended from the FGCI for his unorthodox views, he and about 20 other dissidents (including his younger companion Roberto Ognibene) formed themselves into the *Collettivo politico operai studenti* (CPOS), generally known as the 'Apartment group' from their regular meeting place. The founding premises of the group were threefold — the 'betrayal' of the official PCI, the need to rediscover the principles of Marxism/Leninism, and the historic necessity of bringing about the collapse of the bourgeoisie.[4] Just as Renato Curcio and Mara Cagol found their political voice through '*Lavoro politico*', Franceschini wrote first for '*Alternative*' and later for a publication called '*Reggio 15*'. In an account published in '*Reggio 15*' of a round table discussion held in July 1968 his views were already concise: 'The most important single aim after the seizure of power is to continue the revolution, to prevent the bourgeoisie from taking power back under different forms, and to ensure that the socialist society is truly democratic, not in the bourgeois sense of the word, by means of these pseudo-representative institutions, but democratic because all the elements of production have real power.'[5] The only efficient means of realizing such a society, he concluded, was to build up a revolutionary party of the working class.

When the *Gruppo dell'appartamento* of Franceschini and Ognibene joined up with *Sinistra Proletaria* in Milan in 1970 to form the Red Brigades, the nucleus of the 'fighting communist party', their aims were identical: to educate, organize and encourage the working classes to throw off the oppressive rule of capitalism by an armed proletarian revolution. This, the BR were convinced, could only be

achieved by the gradual destabilization of the bourgeois state
and the dismantling or 'disarticulation' of its institutions.

In addition to the Red Brigades, other revolutionary
groups began to coalesce in Northern Italy around 1969–70.
Feltrinelli's GAP was largely, although not entirely, com-
posed of former partisans. Amongst its younger members was
Mario Moretti, a former student of Milan's Catholic
University. After the death of his father when he was a baby,
Moretti was supported by a rich, aristocratic Milanese family.
On completing his studies, he was offered a job in the firm Sit
Siemens, with a strong recommendation from his teachers,
who felt able to assure his future employers of his 'excellent
political and religious sentiments.'[6] One year later Moretti
disappeared from his old life to follow his political goals, first
entering GAP and then an organization known as *Superclan*
(an abbreviation for *superclandestinità*; the group dispersed
to Paris after 1972) before he joined the Red Brigades.

By early 1970 a broad spectrum of political organizations
had formed within the New, or extra-parliamentary Left, all
in one way or another sharing the aim of a proletarian
revolution as a common goal. Their origins derived from four
basic sources — the spirit of the 'betrayed resistance
movement', which was in turn closely linked to disappointment in the reformist tendencies of the PCI; the student
protest movement of the late 1960's, and an intensification of
militancy within a section of the workers' movement
following the struggles of the 'Hot Autumn.' All represented
political traditions or ideals which for different reasons now
found themselves without a coherent political mouthpiece.
The resistance legacy was partly represented by GAP, partly
by an organization known as the XXII October Group, which
contained former communists as well as a common criminal
element. Groups like *Potere Operaio*, *Lotta Continua*
(Continuous Struggle) and *Manifesto* were centred on
eponymous publications, and were consequently able to
reach an audience and gain public attention far in excess of
their actual membership.

Some groups, like *Manifesto*, took a positive stand against violence and relied upon peaceful and legal methods of change, whilst *Potere Operaio*, *Avanguardia Operaia* (Workers' Vanguard) and *Lotta Continua* sat awkwardly astride legality and illegality. There was a great measure of fluidity between the concepts of 'social insubordination', 'mass illegality' and 'new spontaneity'; between urging non-co-operation with factory management and discipline, and the encouragement of direct acts of sabotage and rebellion. The popular slogan, *'prendiamoci la città'* ('let's take over the city'), was symbolic of the general mood of self-determination, freedom and defiance of authority which characterized the times. The city was seen as the centre of exploitation and of capitalist repression, but also where it was at its most vulnerable, where its resources could be expropriated and recycled, where the state could be attacked. But in their unequivocal commitment to the use of violence against the state as practised by an armed, clandestine vanguard, the *Brigate Rosse* stood alone.

The first requirement, according to the BR, was to abandon ideas of glorious spontaneity in favour of a sound, structural organization based on specialized 'nuclei' to deal with the complexity of industrial, political, social and military problems. It was essential to have a solid social basis in order to stimulate sympathy and to encourage mass participation, without which the revolution could not take place. The first institutions to come under attack were the factories, symbols as they were of oppression, capitalism and the dehumanization of the individual, and whose influence was all too evident in the 'ghettos' of the industrial triangle of Milan, Genoa and Turin. Life itself was portrayed as 'all factory': 'outside the factory there's still more factory — the city factory'.[7]

The streamlining of industry which was taking place at this time was an obvious point of insertion for the fledgling BR, whose main task was to become involved in the labour struggles from within, and to set up cells or centres of resistance in the Milan factories such as Pirelli, Sit Siemens and IBM. Their first opportunity came in 1970 when the giant tyre company Pirelli made large numbers of workers redundant. The BR set fire to directors' cars and damaged company property. This was followed in 1971 by an arson attack on some Pirelli trailers parked in the factory grounds: an act which made national headlines and put the new organization officially on the map. Between 1970 and 1972 the Red Brigades carried out a series of sporadic attacks of this nature, injuring no one and achieving little beyond the satisfaction of disrupting production, angering their employers and drawing attention to themselves by their actions and by their subsequent publicly expressed claims of responsibility, the major vehicle for their revolutionary propaganda. In these early days they and their actions were possibly known to the local PCI and union leaders who, despite their official condemnations, preferred to turn a blind eye to their 'misguided comrades', faithful to the old Mafia spirit of '*omertà*', or conspiracy of silence.

In September 1971 the BR published their first 'theoretical resolution' in which their political analysis was clearly laid out: the opposing forces of reaction and revolution were both seen as being involved in a process of reorganization. In the first instance the state was restructuring itself and its institutions along a 'reactionary and violently anti-proletarian perspective'[8] which was a prelude, or first stage before the full forces of repression could take over. These two stages were subsequently referred to as '*gollista*' from the French experience under De Gaulle, and '*golpista*', characterized by the military coup d'état, or '*golpe*'. In order to oppose this transformation and bring about a successful counter attack, the left had to move quickly, firstly to organize itself, for it was in a retarded position vis à vis the State, and then to act. According to BR theory, the left had to mobilize its forces in a two-fold operation, consisting of an initial stage of political preparation, agitation and propaganda, followed by guerrilla warfare and armed insurrection. In order to take on the power of the State, the revolutionary movement had to meet two conditions: '1) achieve parity with State power at every level (free political prisoners, carry out death sentences on murdering policemen, expropriate capitalists etc) and naturally demonstrate its capacity to survive at these levels; 2) create an alternative centre of power in the factories and in the working class districts.'[9]

The propaganda value of kidnap for ransom, political concessions, or simply for publicity purposes was well known to the *Brigate Rosse* from their studies of the Tupamaros group in Uruguay. Their own first venture into this field took place in March 1972, with the kidnap of Idalgo Macchiarini, a director of Sit Siemens in Milan. He was detained for half an hour and photographed under the adopted BR logo of a five-pointed star in a circle, a gun pointing at his head and a sign around his neck pronouncing him to be a 'fascist, tried by the BR. . . . The working classes have taken up arms, for the bosses it's the beginning of the end.'[10]

Having consolidated a firm base in Milan, the BR next sought to extend their influence into the heart of Italian industry, the Fiat car works in Turin. Occupied intermittently during 1972 and 1973, a high degree of political militancy existed already inside Fiat, and the sight of workers marching in factory courtyards, their faces concealed behind red handkerchiefs or balaclavas was a common one. However, the workforce was quite different in calibre from that in the Milanese homeland of the *Brigate Rosse*. A large proportion of the Fiat workers were immigrants from southern Italy and had none of the traditions of political action, partisan idealism or organized industrial rebellion. Nonetheless, Turin was the obvious place for the BR to set up their second column, and Fiat the natural point of insertion.

In mid-1972 Mara Cagol and Renato Curcio left Milan for Turin, where they built up a column of ten members. At this time, a significant change took place within the organization, enforced by necessity rather than choice. BR member Marco Pisetta, who had been at Trento with Curcio and Cagol, was captured in a 'safe house' in Milan in March, and by June had turned police informer. Secrecy suddenly became imperative for those whom Pisetta could betray, and a new division arose between 'regular' and 'irregular' members of the

organization. The former were full time BR activists who for
reasons of notoriety were forced to change their names and
abandon the trappings of their former lives, such as jobs,
family and friends. They were paid a wage by the organization
out of funds generally acquired from bank robberies.
Irregular members held down ordinary jobs but in most cases
used the place of employment to recruit sympathizers and
encourage disruption from within, and also assisted those
forced underground with accommodation and other needs.

In February 1973 the atmosphere at Fiat was tense due to
wage negotiations with the metal mechanics, one of the
largest and most militant groups within the factory, whose
strike had given the major impetus to the 'Hot Autumn'.
Simultaneously, an MSI conference was taking place in Rome
under siege conditions, and frequent demonstrations
disrupted its progress. Against this background, the BR
kidnapped again; this time a right-wing union official in Fiat,
Bruno Labate. His detention was of short duration, but the
manner of his release was more spectacular than that of
Macchiarini — he was chained, shaven-headed and
trouserless, to a lamp post at the factory gates. Their third
victim was an Alfa Romeo manager in Milan, Michele
Mincuzzi, kidnapped in Milan on 28th June and released after
a brief interrogation, a propaganda poster tied to his back.

As Italy suffered the first effects of soaring oil prices,
unemployment and inflation, the BR in Turin began to plan a
daring, high profile action to enhance their status in the eyes
of the workers and attract attention to their aims. Fiat gave
them their opportunity when, following a 30% drop in car
sales, 600 workers were made redundant. This time the
kidnap victim was Ettore Amerio, Vice Chairman of
Mirafiori and Personnel Director of the Fiat group. He was
seized on 10th December 1973 and kept a prisoner for eight
days, during which time negotiations were conducted on the
company's side through the Turin newspaper *La Stampa*, and
by the BR distribution of leaflets indicating their demands.
The simultaneous diffusion of propaganda leaflets in Milan,
Genoa and Porto Marghera (near Venice) provided a mis-

leading but impressive show of strength from an organization whose full time membership was only around fifteen.

After much bargaining, Fiat eventually re-instated the workers and the hostage was freed. The Red Brigades had not only won a symbolic victory over the 'oppressors', but had demonstrated a bargaining power superior to that of party or union, and in doing so, had gained particular prestige in the eyes of many workers. Not surprisingly, they became inundated with requests for action against this or that employer in a variety of factories, many wildly unrealistic and purely opportunist in nature.

Seen from the outside, the BR presented a somewhat ambiguous image: they were judged variously by the press as bandits, drug-crazed delinquents, and even tools of neo-fascist subversion, part of the 'strategy of tension.' Even within the New Left there was some doubt as to the value of their actions, and they were criticized by both *Lotta Continua* and *Manifesto* for the risk they ran of alienating working class consensus by criminalizing political dissent.

From 1973 the BR began to redefine and harden their opposition to the State. They believed that Italy had sold out to big business, that all political and economic decisions were guided by capitalist, US-dominated conglomerates in the interests of their allies, the ruling Christian Democratic élite. For the BR, police, judiciary and government were all seen as collaborating in the restructuring of the country and in the jealous protection of their imperialist interests. The BR, however, were determined that the proletarian revolution could happen, but only 'over the lifeless corpse of the old society; the corrupt and violent bourgeois state, its putrid, sick, syphilitic ruling class.'[11] Hatred for this society deepened. Guns were no longer carried for symbolic value as had been the case hitherto, but could 'justifiably' be used to wound and kill.

The BR's unequivocal assumption of a direct and violent confrontation was beginning to fragment the New Left, such that the blurred boundaries between methods and aims amongst the different extra-parliamentary groups were no longer sufficient to distinguish them. Positions had to be more clearly defined. *Potere Operaio* was dissolved and its membership was either diffused into other organizations, such as *Autonomia Operaia*, or drifted back to the historic left of traditional Italian communism. For those who chose to remain on the side of the *lotta armata*, the debate centred not so much on whether or not there could be a revolution, but on how and when it could be brought about.

Lotta Continua carried on a further two years, the only major organization of the extra-parliamentary left to survive a long period of both legal and illegal operations. One area of LC's concern, the material, political and psychological conditions of Italy's prison population, evolved between 1972 and 1974 into an organization in its own right, known as *Nuclei Armati Proletari* (Armed Proletarian Nuclei). Unlike the BR, which emerged from distinct historical and political traditions, NAP was more practical than intellectual, and saw its role as a rallying point for the outcasts or dregs of society, the 'underproletariat', for whom no unified political structure had hitherto existed, and who had felt themselves rejects and misfits. The aim in uniting this section of the population was to restore self-respect to those living in conditions of excessive misery and desperation, provide them with a political identity and, by channeling their anger and energy, to stimulate practical opposition to the state which was seen as responsible for these ills.

Originally based in Naples, the organization eventually put down roots in Florence and in Milan. Although similar to the BR in their determination and in their commitment to the armed struggle, in discipline, organization and idealism the latter considered NAP sloppy and even dangerous.

1974 gave proof of an intensification and a new focus of attack within the *lotta armata*: two NAP members lost their lives in a gun battle with police in Florence, the BR killed for the first time, and they made their first direct challenge to the power of the State by kidnapping one of its prominent employees.

Genoese judge Mario Sossi had been responsible for

prosecuting eight members of the XXII October Group for the murder of a bank messenger during a robbery. Sossi was a known right-wing sympathizer, and a typical representative of 'bourgeois justice.' The BR assumed that his influential position would make Sossi party to high-level governmental activities, and hoped that, under the strain of a kidnap of some duration, he would be willing to expose the extent of DC control over Genoese business and commercial transactions. They intended to question him on Italy's links with foreign security services, such as the CIA, and in particular to confirm their suspicions of Italian involvement in the *coup d'état* in Chile. They also wanted to interrogate Sossi on matters closer to home: they suspected security services agent Guido Giannettini of having planted informers in extremist organizations of both left and right and believed Giannettini had infiltrated spies into the XXII October Group, whose arrest and trial had in their view been framed by falsification and distortion of circumstantial evidence.

The potential gains from Sossi's kidnap were matched in significance by the importance of its timing; a propaganda technique of increasing importance to the BR. It was planned for April 18th, anniversary of the Christian Democrat landslide victory of 1948. It was also the day Fiat Chairman Agnelli would become President of the Italian Employers' Association. Political tension was running high over the retention or abolition of the law legalizing divorce; Amintore Fanfani was conducting the anti-divorce campaign as a full-blown political issue, hoping to use it as a rallying point for national and family unity around the centre-right coalition.

The BR point of view, expressed in a document of April 1974, was that if the DC, 'at the forefront of the neo-gaullist forces, were to win the referendum, the plan of institutional reform would receive a huge push, and would immediately become a platform (to) re-establish the complete dominance of the bourgeoisie.' Henceforth the scope of the attack was to be widened and deepened: 'It is time to overcome the traditional limitations of militant anti-fascism. It is right and necessary to attack fascists with every means and in every place . . . in order to win today, the masses must overcome the spontaneous phase and organize themselves on the strategic terrain of the struggle for power. And the working class will only take power by means of the armed struggle'.[12]

Sossi's kidnap was therefore intended as an attack on behalf of an oppressed proletariat on capitalism, on an unjust judiciary and on the State, whose internal divisions were to be manipulated and exaggerated in the project of 'disarticulation.'

The operation came close to being a spectacular success for the BR. Contrary to their expectations of a hard, resilient interlocutor, Sossi sobbed, pleaded and talked continuously during the 35 days of his detention. Confirming many of the BR's existing suspicions, he revealed details of extensive corruption implicating the political head of the Genoese police force and Interior Minister Taviani in illicit arms deals. Acting as BR 'legal adviser' in negotiating his own salvation, to their advantage he wrote to the chief public prosecutor of Genoa, Francesco Coco, begging him to suspend 'useless and harmful enquiries' as to his whereabouts, and to aquiesce to the BR demands — the release of the 8 members of the XXII October Group, including their leader, Mario Rossi. The slogan of the moment was '*Fuori Rossi o a morte Sossi!*' (Rossi out or Sossi dies!)

Sossi's pleas and the BR stipulations produced precisely the intended results — total confusion, disarray and disagreement. The judiciary called a temporary halt to their enquiries in deference to the prisoner's request, but on the authority of General Carlo Alberto Dalla Chiesa, the carabinieri continued to carry out house searches, road blocks and routine investigations.

On 10th May riots broke out in Alessandria prison, and 17 hostages were held at gun point by 3 prisoners. Dalla Chiesa took a determined line and ordered the immediate suppression of the revolt, which was summarily crushed. However, four of the hostages were murdered by their captors and two of the three rebels killed, the other wounded.

News of the carnage at Alessandria served to terrify Sossi

even more, and on May 15 he appealed to President Leone to release the XXII October Group from prison. On the 19th, a sensational interview appeared in the weekly magazine *L'Espresso* between an emissary of the Red Brigades and journalist Mario Scialoja. In the interview the BR representative explained the strategy behind the kidnap. Sossi was 'a target of proletarian hatred', a 'fanatical persecutor of the revolutionary left' and 'an ideal instrument for all the dirtiest tricks.' The BR saw the present crisis in Italy as one of bourgeois hegemony over the proletariat, therefore, 'the task of the revolutionary forces must be to deepen this crisis and to lead it to its furthest point, building up the politico-military instruments necessary to open up the road to revolution. . . . The masses are at the basis of everything, therefore they must be united, mobilized and armed.'[13]

On May 19 the BR issued their ultimatum — Judge Sossi would be released 24 hours after the departure of the 8 prisoners for either Cuba, Algeria or North Korea. Despite the attempts of Dalla Chiesa and numerous politicians to prevent the bargain, the majority of magistrates had more interest in protecting their colleague than the security of the state, and on the 21st the Genoa Court of Appeal granted provisional liberty to the XXII October Group, and ordered the release of their passports. The prisoners were initially to be transferred to the Cuban embassy in the Vatican City before leaving for Cuba itself.

But behind the scenes furious negotiations were being pursued. It was rumoured that Interior Minister Taviani was bringing pressure to bear on PCI leader Berlinguer, who in turn appealed to Soviet leader Brezhnev, who prevailed upon Castro not to accept the Italian refugees from justice. Whatever the truth of the speculation, Cuba withdrew its offer of hospitality, under pressure from Chief Prosecutor Francesco Coco the release order was reversed by the Court of Cassation and, the drama over, Sossi was released on May 23rd. Although materially they had gained nothing, in propaganda terms the BR had clearly won a substantial victory — they had made an impact on the world's superpowers, they were popular heroes in the eyes of their admirers and emulators, and, more significantly, they were rapidly becoming a myth to themselves. Later, Sossi himself would provide more fodder for the BR propaganda machine, declaring in an interview that they were 'extremely organized, and there must be many thousands of them. They've got huge files from here to there, everything is filed, catalogued, recorded, they're informed to the highest degree.'[14]

The kidnap undoubtedly had a dramatic impact on Italian public opinion, which was split down the middle over the issue of whether the life of a man, and in particular that of a state employee, was a negotiable instrument in bargaining with terrorists on a principle of national security. It caused a surprising show of solidarity from Genoa trade union leaders, who for the first time called a general strike in support of a prominent public figure of the right-wing establishment, and finally it forced the left to state its position on the issue of terrorism.

The Communist party newspaper *Unità* took the view that the BR could not possibly be a left wing, armed revolutionary group, and considered them to be puppets of neo-fascist strategy; the director of *Manifesto* suggested it did not matter whether the BR were 'red' or 'black' (ie neo-fascist) since they simply 'did not exist' politically. On the whole, however, the New Left gave the action cautious approval.

BR operational capability expanded considerably after the Sossi kidnap. Instead of individual groups or columns working sporadically, using weapons, money and manpower as best they could, a centralized bureaucratic structure developed to provide a comprehensive framework of funding, control and strategy. The organization was divided both vertically and horizontally by virtue of geographical location and organizational function. Each column of tactical and operational necessity centred on a city, and was divided into brigades of regular and irregular members, usually working within a particular area or workplace. A new structure of 'fronts' was created to deal with the requirements of an increasingly militarized, secret organization. A logistic front was set up to deal with practical issues such as the provision of arms and training in their use, the procurement of vehicles and false number plates, location of temporary bases and longer term accommodation, and the falsification of documents and official stamps. The careful development of the logistic front and skills such as photography, printing and forgery meant that the BR were dependent neither on the criminal underworld nor on other organizations less secure than their own for their essential services.

Two further subdivisions were created, namely a front for the maintenance of grass roots support in factories and amongst the workers generally, and a counter-revolutionary front, devised to provide an intelligence service for the organization, and to prevent security leaks and infiltration. The leaders of each column and each front automatically sat on the 'Strategic Directorate', which was supposed to meet regularly, debate courses of action and elect the ultimate BR authority; the 'Executive Committee' consisting of 4–5 members. In short, a comprehensive, efficient and highly militarized machine was constructed.

The carefully planned measures of compartmentalization and discipline by which the BR now defined themselves came too late to prevent infiltration of the organization. Ex-priest Silvano Girotto's reputation for revolutionary activity in Bolivia had earned him the nickname 'Father Machinegun' and also an introduction to BR circles through the former partisan leader Lazagna, through whom Girotto made known his request to join the group. In reality Girotto was a Dalla Chiesa pawn, an integral part of the general's highly trained, unorthodox anti-terrorist squad which, set up in the wake of Sossi's kidnap, was under intense pressure from the authorities to produce concrete results.

On 8th September Renato Curcio and Alberto Franceschini fell neatly into the trap laid for them, agreeing to a meeting with Girotto at a specified mountain rendezvous. Surrounded by Dalla Chiesa's men, they put up only token resistance and were easily captured.

In October the net closed again around the original leadership of the *Brigate Rosse*. A base at Robbiano de Mediglia near Milan was discovered and observed for a number of days, and when searched, revealed extensive BR archives and documentation. Thus when Roberto Ognibene returned one day, he too found a carabinieri patrol lying in wait for him. In a bid to escape, the 20-year old Ognibene shot and killed Marshall Felice Maritano. For this young revolutionary, freedom and political militancy concluded with a 28-year prison sentence. By the end of the year, nine of the BR founding membership were behind bars.

The hardening of left-wing terrorist determination in 1974 coincided with the re-appearance of neo-fascist violence. On 28th May, five days after Sossi's release, a bomb went off during an anti-fascist rally in Piazza della Loggia in Brescia. Eight died and 104 were injured. In retaliation, the BR raided MSI headquarters in Padua and shot dead two party officials. The prior intent to murder was denied, but the responsibility claim which immediately followed the attack was unequivocal — this was an act of revenge on the neo-fascists for the Piazza Fontana and the Brescia bombs. The document henceforth empowered the revolutionary forces to use the 'armed justice of the proletariat' to respond to 'fascist barbarism.'

Undeterred, the far right struck back again in an indiscriminate act of *'stragismo'*. This time a bomb exploded on the crowded Italicus train on 4th August killing 12 and injuring 105. Strangely enough, a series of chance delays and hindrances prevented one passenger from taking the Italicus on that hot August day, one passenger whose death could conceivably have served a purpose. His name — Aldo Moro.

Social and political upheavals throughout the year had led to increased governmental instability and the downfall of the Rumor government. Aldo Moro was invited to form his fourth administration at the end of November, and appointed as his coalition deputy Ugo La Malfa. Corruption within the security services, the oil industry and the world of finance, political scandal and the breakdown of law and order had all contributed to the depletion of national morale and international status. Major changes were inevitable and imminent.

II 1975–1977

By 1975, public opinion and political allegiances had begun a swing back towards the left, both in Italy and abroad. A *coup d'état* in Portugal in 1974 had made way for a Socialist government; the regime of the Greek colonels had fallen, and in May 1975 the United States abandoned Vietnam to Communist forces. With the exposure of corruption in the security services, the neo-fascist right was deprived of state cover for its subversive actions, and the threat of a *coup d'état* in Italy was effectively over. In the administrative elections of 1975 the PCI made sweeping gains and a number of regional governments came under joint PCI/PSI control. After his personal failure over the divorce campaign and with the DC losing ground to the left, Fanfani resigned as party Secretary to be replaced by Benigno Zaccagnini, a close collaborator of Aldo Moro. Together, Moro and Zaccagnini drew the DC gradually leftwards towards an understanding with the PCI. Thus in parliamentary terms, if the years 1969–1974 were characterized by 'opposing extremes', the period from 1975–1977 can be described as one of 'converging parallels'.

Central to the policies of the Moro/La Malfa government was the restoration of public confidence in the state and in its ability to maintain public order. The Reale Law, passed in May 1975, provided for increased police powers to hold and question subjects, implement telephone taps and search premises, and relaxed controls over the carrying and use of firearms by police officers. After the wave of neo-fascist violence, the law met with relatively little resistance from guarantors of civil liberties on the parliamentary left.

The *Brigate Rosse* were also compelled to re-organize themselves in the years 1975–77. Despite the influx of new support after the Sossi kidnap, the overall strength of the organization had been severely sapped by the wave of arrests in 1974. Under Mario Moretti and Franco Bonisoli, a new style of leadership emerged, based on painstaking preparation, rigorous discipline and careful, even pedantic, political analysis, which contrasted with the more traditionally based ideological communism of the first generation. And if the achievements of Dalla Chiesa and his men had given the public at large the impression that the BR were finished, the successful attempt in February 1975 to spring Renato Curcio from Casale prison may have been a sign that the members themselves saw their original leadership as indispensable.

While the boldness of the action seemed excessively risky to the Moretti faction, to the 'old guard' BR the rescue bid was seen as the restoration of a father to the bosom of his family. In fact, the operation was a relatively simple one, as the administration at Casale allowed prisoners considerable internal freedom, and on the day that Mara Cagol arrived at the prison gates with a pile of laundered clothing for her husband, Curcio was ready and waiting. A revolver whipped out from the laundry temporarily immobilized the unsuspecting guards and, in the meantime, the rest of the commando team found and liberated their leader.

In April 1975 the BR published their official 'strategic resolution', in which for the first time the enemy was clearly identified in a single, homogenous image. The object of attack was now the 'Imperialist State of Multinationals' or 'SIM', a combination of foreign, (in particular US) domination with capitalist exploitation. In other respects, the BR line remained unchanged, 'namely that of a converging attack on the heart of the State . . . the maximum disarticulation possible both of the regime and of the State'. Furthermore, the BR were careful to distinguish between the vanguard, as they considered themselves, and the potentially revolutionary masses from which the fighting communist party was to be formed. The vanguard had by definition to lead from the front, had to be armed and clandestine, but at the same time had the task of educating and encouraging the masses to build up the organization necessary for a successful revolution: 'It is not a question of organizing the class movement within the area of the armed struggle, but of entrenching the organization of the armed struggle and the political realization of its historical necessity within the class movement.'[15]

Despite the confident rhetoric, the BR were operationally insecure. The kidnap of wine millionaire Vallarino Gancia which took place on June 4 was intended as a fund raising exercise, but the inexperience of the kidnap team led to an unmitigated disaster for the BR. Gancia's 'prison' was a farm house which had been used for some years as a rural hideout for the group, whose faces were known in the area. Furthermore, the hostage was carelessly guarded and, on the 5th, when a carabinieri patrol encircled the building, an attempt by the *brigatisti* to shoot their way out resulted in the death of one officer, the wounding of two others and the death of Mara Cagol. The BR paid a posthumous tribute to their founder member, their first martyr killed in action: 'Let all sincere revolutionaries honour the memory of Mara, reflecting on the political lesson she gave by means of her choice, her work, her life. Let a thousand arms reach out to pick up her gun. . . . Mara is a flower which has bloomed, and the Red Brigades will continue to cultivate this flower of liberty until victory comes.'[16]

In the south, NAP too was active, kidnapping Judge Guiseppe De Gennaro in an attempt to win improved prison conditions for three of their companions. Simultaneously a well co-ordinated revolt by the NAP prisoners in Viterbo prison led to the seizure of hostages and stronger bargaining power of the terrorists. When their communiqué was read out over national radio and the three prisoners transferred nearer home, De Gennaro was released. Despite this victory, NAP became increasingly self-destructive and inefficient, and by 1976 the majority of its membership was

either in prison or dead. Those who escaped either fate sometimes joined forces with the BR, and in the spring of 1976 a
number of attacks on carabinieri barracks in various parts of
Italy were claimed jointly by BR and NAP. If NAP's organization was loose and chaotic, their strong emphasis on prison
activism may have had increasing appeal for the BR as their
own numbers in prison grew. Indeed, Renato Curcio's respite
from prison was brief; he was re-captured in January 1976 in
Milan along with Nadia Manovani, another BR regular.

For the next few months the BR lay low, intent upon
reorganization and rebuilding. Proper columns were formed
in Turin under the leadership of Franco Bonisoli and Raffaele
Fiore, and in Genoa by Rocco Micaletto and Riccardo Dura
with some former members of *Lotta Continua*. The Milan
column, probably the weakest due to arrests and the
proliferation of other militant groups, was run by Lauro
Azzolini and Walter Alasia.

Another Milan organization emerged at this time, originally from *Potere Operaio* and then via *Senza Tregua* known
as *Prima Linea* (Front Line). PL's first actions were rooted in
militant anti-fascism and in the still-frequent battles between neo-fascist and left-wing youth. Violence inflicted by
both sides provoked continual acts of retaliation during
the notorious 'April days' in Milan in 1976, culminating
in the fatal stabbing of a young left-wing student which
was followed two days later by the murder of an MSI councillor.

In the meantime, economic and social difficulties were on
the increase in 1976: inflation was running at nearly 20%, the
lira had reached an all-time low and unemployment,
particularly amongst the young, was steadily increasing.
Confidence in the state was dealt two further blows by
revelations made in the United States, firstly of CIA funding
of Italian institutions considered 'pro West', with the DC
clearly in the front line, and secondly of bribes to the tune of
$78 million paid out by the Lockheed Corporation to two
successive Italian defence ministers, Christian Democrat Gui
and Social Democrat Tanassi, to 'encourage' the Italian

government to purchase Hercules aircraft. Furthermore, the mediator of these deals, mysteriously referred to by the code name 'Antelope Cobbler', was rumoured to be a former Prime Minister of Italy. His identity was not discovered, but speculation raced around the names of Moro, Leone and Rumor.

Two successive Moro governments were brought down in January and April 1976 by disagreements between the DC and the Socialist party. The PSI was becoming suspicious that Moro's overtures towards the Communists were becoming too exclusive, and finally they broke with the DC over the abortion issue, on which they could not back the government's negative line. Following the second withdrawal of PSI support, Moro resigned on 30th April, President Leone dissolved parliament and a general election was called.

After months of inactivity, the BR chose the object and timing of their next action with calculated precision. The trial of the captured BR leaders for, amongst other crimes, the kidnaps of Labate, Amerio and Sossi, opened in Turin on 17th May. Given the calibre and numbers of *brigatisti* present in the court room, the period of silence must have suggested the virtual extinction of the organization. Yet the defendants' defiant behaviour was far from passive, as was evident from the statement read out to the court: 'The "accused" have nothing to defend themselves against, whilst on the contrary the "accusers" have to defend the criminal, anti-proletarian practice of the infamous regime which they represent. . . . Lead the attack to the heart of the state!'[17]

As well as denouncing the judicial system to which they were being subjected, the BR bitterly condemned the reformist, compromising tactics of the PCI, which in their view 'can only represent an internal solution to the imperialist counter-revolution. At best, the historic compromise will be a rubber bullet in the guns of the fuzz.'

The political forces were in the midst of pre-election fever, heightened by the general assumption that the PCI stood to make considerable electoral advances. The BR aim was to exploit the atmosphere of tension and uncertainty by dividing political opinion, to isolate the Communist party from its potential block of new voters and in so doing to win the party back from the historic compromise to consciousness of its true revolutionary purpose.

The victim of the attack was selected with equal care in the person of the Chief Prosecutor of Genoa, Francesco Coco, whose stubbornness had been instrumental in blocking the release of the XXII October Group two years earlier. On this occasion the BR chose not to kidnap, but for the first time to murder in cold blood, gunning down Coco and his two bodyguards in the centre of Genoa. The responsibility claim blamed Coco for his refusal to grant a release order for the XXII October Group, and also for having omitted to bring criminal proceedings against the builders of a Genoese apartment block which had collapsed in 1970, killing 18 people.

Inevitably, attention turned immediately to the flesh and blood *brigatisti* in the Turin courtroom. Jubilantly, they too claimed responsibility for the three murders:

'Yesterday, 8th June 1976, an armed nucleus of the Red Brigades executed state pig Francesco Coco and the two mercenaries paid to protect him . . . this action opens up a new phase in the class war which aims to dismantle the apparatus of the State, attacking the men who are identified with it and who direct its counter-revolutionary drive.'

Rejecting any inference that in killing Coco's bodyguards they had murdered two oppressed members of the proletariat, the BR claimed that they were not 'sons of the people' but 'two thugs in the service of the counter-revolution.'[18]

The assumption of co-responsibility threw court proceedings into disarray and caused the trial to be postponed until the following year. By their own standards, the BR had triumphed over the state and passed judgement on its judges.

If such can be considered a success, the same could not be claimed for the aim to disrupt electoral events. The results of the 20th June election gave the Communist party 34.4% of the vote, against the DC's 38.8%, an increase for the PCI of

40% in the space of four years. For the first time the total strength of the right, excluding the MSI, was equalled by the combined forces of the left. It was the Socialists who emerged as principal losers, taking only 9.6% of the vote, a failure which led to the replacement of PSI secretary Francesco De Martino by the younger, more abrasive Bettino Craxi. For the first time, too, the New Left had been represented, in the shape of the Proletarian Party of Democratic Unity (PDUP), but to the disappointment of its followers the new party only polled 1.5% of the vote.

The principles of the historic compromise passed overnight from intellectual theory to virtual necessity. As Aldo Moro pointed out, the election results had produced joint winners in the DC and the PCI, both of whom were in a position to paralyze the workings of the other unless some co-ordinated policy agreements were reached. After weeks of consultation within the six parties of the 'constitutional arc' Giulio Andreotti succeeded Aldo Moro as Prime Minister to preside over an all-DC government, held in power by the abstention of the PCI, the PSI, the Liberals, the Social Democrats and the Republicans, otherwise known as the government of 'non-sfiducia', or non-opposition.

1976 ended with the BR losing another of their regular members in December when Walter Alasia, cornered in his Milan home by carabinieri, shot and killed two officers before being killed himself.

1977 was, like 1968, a year of excess and social eruption, during which numerous groups which had swirled and flowed from one idea to another, from one course of action to another, suddenly exploded into activity. Yet almost a decade had elapsed, and there were significant differences. Whereas the student rebellion and the 'Hot Autumn' had had positive goals and a distinct revolutionary perspective, the '77 Movement' was less directional, more uncertain and for this perhaps more desperate and anguished. According to one former *Prima Linea* member, there were basically three contributing elements — the various organizations of the New Left in a state of movement and flux, a working class minority seeking to extend its activities beyond the confines of the factory, and 'a mass of young people face to face with instability and unemployment, dissatisfied with their education, moving angrily out of the metropolitan ghettos, driven by the instinct to re-appropriate everything from which they felt excluded, and with a burden of aggression which frequently found its voice and its example in "provocation" and in the exultation of violent action.'[19] Unable to discern legal means of changing the status quo, the *Movimento* seemed to be legitimizing itself, making 'irrational choices' based on 'existential needs and a desire to participate'. The journalist Giorgio Bocca talks of the dual aspirations of the '77 Movement' as being 'the existential and the insurrectional', and those who took part in it stress the desire to live *'fuori e contro'* — outside and against the traditional patterns of life and work.

These assertions demonstrate the essential difference between the two major Italian revolutionary groups of the 1970's. In contrast to the BR's commitment to seize power, PL's aim was rather to break down existing power structures, to push the masses as far as was possible to the point of no return, where revolution would spontaneously occur, and to show them that from then on they could control their own destinies.

Within a few months the adherents of the new 'Movement' leapt from a few hundred to four or five thousand, with a cushion of sympathizers of between fifteen and twenty thousand.

The city was still the heartland of action, the seat of power where the rich were richer, the poor poorer and where crime, drug trafficking and the black economy in goods and services could flourish. With this in mind, *Prima Linea* and other Milan groups formed 'proletarian bands' and 'district squads' — armed vigilante groups which patrolled the streets in the working class districts and urban hinterland of Milan. Their attacks on police stations and carabinieri barracks were a deliberate affront to the official forces of law and order whose authority they despised and usurped. They saw themselves as taking the protection of the exploited into their own hands, for example by raiding bars in which heroin was dealt or offices where black economy work was distributed at below subsistence rates to those who were in no position to complain, such as immigrants without papers, women who could only work irregular hours, or those without the education to seek an alternative.

By 1977 the carrying of firearms had become commonplace amongst members of the *Movimento*. Guns could still be purchased relatively easily over the counter using a forged or stolen licence. In other instances, they were stolen from shops, armouries or from security guards. Even if in many cases guns were used primarily to intimidate and threaten, the principle that they could be used was tacitly accepted. Few actually condoned the tactics of cold-blooded elimination of one's opponents as increasingly advocated by the Red Brigades but many more were reluctant to withdraw from what they considered was a 'historic right', embedded in their working class heritage, to use violence as an ultimate means of self-preservation. The phrase '*né con lo Stato né con le BR*' ('neither for the state or for the BR') expressed an attitude common amongst those who distrusted the ability or the sincerity of the state to defend the freedom and the rights of the man in the street, yet who could not support the violent excesses of terrorism.

1977 is often referred to in Italy as 'the year of the P 38' from the commonly carried hand gun of that name, yet another equally appropriate description would be 'anti-PCI' year, in the course of which the New Left definitively turned its back on the traditional left.

Following the PCI's public adherence to the government's austerity policies, the party and union representatives came under increasing attack. On 18th February, Communist trade union leader Luciano Lama was scheduled to speak in Rome university in the course of a student occupation. He was whistled, booed and eventually driven off university premises in a blatant anti-Communist party demonstration, the first public display of hostility between opposing forces of the left.

In the riots that followed Lama's expulsion, a severe head injury received by a demonstrating student was the excuse for a massive response, and violent battles continued until March 6th when the university was closed down.

Three days later the Lockheed scandal became the focus of attention, when a combined sitting of both parliamentary chambers met to consider whether or not to strip former ministers Gui, Tanassi and Rumor of their parliamentary immunity, thereby compelling them to face conventional court proceedings on charges of corruption and the acceptance of bribes. On this occasion, Aldo Moro made one of the worst tactical blunders of his career, taking it upon himself to defend Tanassi, his DC colleague Gui and almost in the same breath the DC itself, throwing a protective cordon around the party and challenging the public's right to expect accountability from its ministers.

Parliament did find enough evidence to deny immunity to Gui and Tanassi, and they were sent for trial in the High Court (Gui was eventually acquitted, Tanassi found guilty). Mariano Rumor escaped the fate of his colleagues thanks to the casting vote of the Socialists. In protest against this, a large and violent demonstration took place in Bologna on 11th March, during which Francesco Lorusso, a former leader of *Lotta Continua*, was killed. The next two days can only be described as a period of mass insurrection, in which tens of thousands took to the streets. Riots occurred in Bologna, Milan and Rome; in Turin a brigadier of the carabinieri was killed in retaliation for the death of Lorusso. In Bologna groups of *Autonomia*, far-left militants, confronted PCI demonstrators in scenes of angry violence, and in the course of the day the PCI was actually compelled to call for police protection against left-wing extremists. After the death of one policeman and the wounding of a further three at the end of April, Interior Minister Cossiga proclaimed a one-month ban on street demonstrations in Rome. Defying the ban, the Radical party called for a celebratory march to commemorate the third anniversary of the divorce referendum on 12th May. A young female student, apparently quite extraneous to the demonstration, was killed in what quickly became a full-scale riot, and in the inevitable backlash a police officer was murdered.

Francesco Cossiga attempted to tighten up on law and order, but admitted in a candid interview that the State had made many mistakes in its handling of the street violence. Not only did he confirm his belief in a national strategy of violent protest, Cossiga also described the hypothesis that it was supported or controlled by foreign security services as 'very likely', fuelling uncertainty and speculation even more. And in response to the accusation that Italy's own security services 'until recently were more intent upon subverting the state than defending it', and that consequently they were currently 'in a state of complete lethargy', Cossiga could only reply: 'Indeed, until a few years back there was, let us say, some corruption and degeneration. And now it seems as if they are having some difficulty in being operational. I believe that when the corruption was ascertained, politicians should have had the courage to dissolve the services and recreate a whole new organization from top to bottom. Instead . . . some sections were amputated and a few individuals were sent home, leaving the basic structure intact. It was an error.'[20]

Humble and sincere talk, but hardly likely to inspire a new wave of public confidence or deter an ardent band of determined revolutionaries!

Parallel to the huge upsurge of spontaneous and not-so-spontaneous street aggression, the Red Brigades were proceeding with their own plans, now in virtual isolation. In early 1977, with the Milan column in difficulties and a column in Rome still not properly functional, Genoa and Turin were the main centres of operational capability. The first major BR action of the year was the kidnap in Genoa of shipping magnate Pietro Costa. A payment of 10 billion lire (approximately £4.5 million or $8 million) was demanded for his release. Eventually the negotiators contrived to bring the sum down to that for which he was insured, namely 1.5 billion lire. The ransom was paid and Costa released.

Another kidnap occurred in April whose circumstances are to this day obscure, that of Guido De Martino, a PSI official in Naples and son of the former national party leader. In the days following the kidnap various responsibility claims appeared, none of which was verifiable, but after 40 days De Martino was released on payment of around a billion lire. NAP, the only known political organization capable of operating in Naples denied its involvement, yet an organized crime racket might well have looked to a wealthier source of ransom. However, De Martino senior was by no means a poor man, and, using his political contacts, was able to raise the necessary sum to have his son released.

De Martino admitted the defeat implicit in his decision to pay, but summed it up as one between 'saving a life and paying a political price or else losing that life for the sake of principles.'[21] Not surprisingly, De Martino would himself support the attempt to negotiate with the *Brigate Rosse* for Aldo Moro's release less than a year later, no doubt recognizing the echo of his own anguish in Moro's plea from prison that 'even principles have to take account of reality.'[22]

The kidnap of the Socialist leader's son, and the climate of left-wing political extremism in which it occurred, produced a new sense of fear amongst parliamentarians, who now realized not only that they themselves were at risk, but that their families were equally vulnerable. Aldo Moro was not alone in insisting upon bodyguards for his family; most prominent politicians took to travelling escorted and in bullet-proof cars. Office buildings and political headquarters were fitted with armoured glass. The era of '*democrazia blindata*' or 'armour-plated democracy' had arrived.

Reclaiming the limelight, the Red Brigades attacked next in Turin, scene of the postponed trial of the 'historic leaders.' On 28th April, just five days before the trial was due to open, they dealt another blow to the State's legal system, and once again succeeded in paralyzing its course. Fulvio Croce, President of the Association of Turin lawyers, was shot dead. In earlier BR days, Croce's record as a partisan might have saved him, but the new generation was merciless. Croce was 'guilty' because of the office he held and because amongst his responsibilities was the organization of lawyers appointed by the state to defend the *brigatisti*, who had themselves refused such provision.

Croce's murder caused uproar and panic within the legal profession and amongst the general public, making the formation of a jury impossible and causing the trial to be postponed for a further eleven months — until in fact the first week of March 1978 — just days before the kidnapping of Aldo Moro.

Maintaining an astonishing momentum, the BR mounted an unprecedented series of attacks on those they considered most representative of SIM (Imperialist State of Multinationals), either as representatives of justice, of law and order or of industry. In most cases victims were shot in the legs as an admonishment, a warning or simply to instil sheer terror. Three Fiat managers in Turin were kneecapped in as many weeks, and on three successive days in June 1977 the media came under attack, when Vittorio Bruno, deputy editor of the Genoa publication 'XIX Century' was shot in the legs, followed by Indro Montanelli, founder of the Milan daily paper *Giornale Nuovo*, and Emilio Rossi, head of national television news. A similar fate was in store for local Christian Democratic councillors around the country, and for Remo Cacciafesta, Professor of Political Science and Economics at Rome University.

Unprepared and unable to identify the sources of spiralling violence, the forces of law and order reacted in an *ad hoc*, spasmodic fashion, making numerous arrests only to release suspects for lack of evidence. The Red Brigades continued their systematic wounding of public figures into the autumn. On 17th November Carlo Castellano, a communist manager employed by the Ansaldo company in Genoa was shot in the legs. Castellano was typical of the 'new breed' of PCI — loyal to Berlinguer and the historic compromise, he had been instrumental in forging a deal between workers and management over the introduction of nuclear power into the factory.

However Castellano got off lightly compared to the previous day's victim, Carlo Casalegno, deputy editor of the Turin paper *La Stampa* who was shot four times in the face and neck, and would die two weeks later of his injuries. *La Stampa* had been singled out because it was seen as an organ of the capitalist press controlled by Fiat boss Gianni Agnelli, and Casalegno in particular because the BR objected to the disparaging tone in which he referred to their revolutionary ideology.

The original plan had been to wound rather than kill Casalegno, but the responsibility claim which followed the shooting reported that the decision to kill him was taken to show solidarity with the three members of the Baader-Meinhof gang, whose deaths in Stammheim prison on 18th October had been claimed as suicide by the State and murder by many on the left.

The Casalegno drama and the way it was handled by the media provoked a storm of polemic, and led to accusations of sensationalism and distortion within the media. On the day after the shooting, random interviews at the Fiat factory gates revealed a general indifference to Casalegno's fate, even if by and large the workers disapproved of the BR tactics. A strike called in protest against the shooting had evinced scant enthusiasm, partly because one had taken place a short time previously, but also, it was claimed, because Casalegno had never been known to champion workers' rights in any dispute. The main grievance was that the strike had only been called because Casalegno was an important man, whereas, *'per i pezzi di merda non si fa sciopero'* — 'no-one strikes for shits like us.'[23]

Throughout the months of 1977, the Italian Communist party continued steadily along the path of political conciliation. In March, the attempt to win respectability was internationalized when Enrico Berlinguer met his counterparts in Spain and France to proclaim the principles of 'Euro-communism', by which potential voters in those countries were given assurances of West European Communist commitment to the ideals of economic and political freedom. Later in the year, Berlinguer reassured those who feared for their religious autonomy, recalling Togliatti's conviction enshrined in the PCI's constitution since 1946, that membership of the party should depend on acceptance of 'a political programme, independent of religious faith and of philosophical convictions', and that Marxism should be 'understood and employed critically, not accepted and read dogmatically like an immutable text.'[24] When in December Berlinguer pledged his party's loyalty to the EEC and to NATO, the PCI's transformation seemed virtually complete.

As the year ended with the traditional left making overtures towards the centre, thousands on the far left stood poised on the brink of terrorism. Acts of violence had risen by almost a thousand within a year. In the space of two weeks in January 1978 the BR kneecapped a Fiat manager in Turin; a manager of SIP, the national telephone company, in Rome; a DC official in Genoa, and a Sit Siemens department head in Milan. And as the re-opening of the BR trial in Turin approached, the forces of law and order came in for special attention: Riccardo Palma, a Court of Cassation judge with responsibility for prison reforms was murdered on 16th February, as was Rosario Berardi, a carabinieri official who had investigated BR activities, on 10th March.

With the Costa ransom money carefully invested in weapons, safe houses and other funds for the revolutionary vanguard, the Red Brigades saw their opportunity to launch an all-out attack on the 'heart of the state'. And that heart, they believed, was beating in Rome.

References

1. Reproduced in Alessandro Silj, '*Mai Più Senza Fucile*', Vallecchi, Firenze, 1977, pp. 57, from extract of an interview

from magazine '*Gente*', of August 1975.

2. Reproduced in *Silj*, op cit pp 46.
3. *Silj*, op cit, pp 47.
4. '*S'avanza uno strano soldato*', Liano Fanti, Sugerco Edizioni, Milano, 1985, pp 111.
5. Liano Fanti, op cit, pp 122.
6. '*Operazione Moro*', Giuseppe Zupo, Vincenzo Marini Recchia, Franco Angeli, Milano, 1985, pp 23.
7. '*Noi Terroristi*', Giorgio Bocca, Garzanti, Milano, 1985, pp 136.
8. Reproduced in '*Storia del Partito Armato*', Giorgio Galli, Rizzoli, Milano, 1986, pp 33.
9. Giorgio Galli, op cit, pp 34.
10. Galli, op cit, pp 38.
11. Giorgio Bocca, op cit, pp 69.
12. Reproduced Giorgio Galli, op cit, pp 71.
13. '*L'Espresso*', 19/5/1974.
14. '*Corriere della Sera*', 28/5/1974.
15. Reproduced in Giorgio Galli, op cit, pp 96/97.
16. Galli, op cit, pp 100.
17. '*Criminalizzazione e Lotta Armata*', Collettivo '*Libri Rossi*' *Editoriale*, Milano, June 1976, pp 46–48.
18. '*Criminalizzazione*'. . . pp 51–52.
19. '*Una premessa d'obbligo*', Bergamo, pp 13.
20. '*La Repubblica*', 26/5/1977.
21. '*La Repubblica*', 17/5/1977.
22. Letter No 20 to Francesco Cossiga, reprinted in Comm. Parlamentare . . . Vol II, pp 106.
23. '*La Repubblica*', 18/7/1977.
24. '*La Repubblica*', 13/10/1977.

5
ROME — THE HEART OF THE STATE

Adriana Faranda was born in Messina, Sicily, on 7th August 1950 into a prosperous middle-class household. Her father was a lawyer, her mother was a housewife. Adriana was the second child, born between two brothers, and enjoyed a happy childhood; family bonds were close, in true southern Italian tradition, but not suffocating. Signor Faranda was interested in the emancipation and development of the woman's role, and positively encouraged his daughter in her scholastic pursuits. In fact, one of the few family rows Adriana remembers centred on her desire to attend art college against the wishes of her father, whose ambitions on her behalf were for an academic course of study and a professional career. Partly to appease her father, who by 1967 had suffered a series of heart attacks and required constant nursing, Adriana bowed to his wishes, and applied for entry to the Arts Faculty at Rome university.

In 1968 Signor Faranda died, and Adriana began her university studies clad in mourning, the slightly built, dark-haired beauty conspicuous amongst the T-shirts and faded blue jeans of her contemporaries.

Her first political steps were based on purely peaceful methods of protest — rallies, marches and the distribution of propaganda leaflets — all part of a newly-discovered spirit of collective commitment which satisfied both her need to feel 'involved' and her developing social conscience. However, disillusionment followed the autumn of 1969 when, she recalls, friends who had set off on a demonstration with peaceful intentions ended the day either in prison or in hospital. It seemed as if dissent was becoming a punishable offence. Adriana Faranda began to look towards a more drastic form of protest. It was not enough to modify or correct certain injustices in society, because society itself was too degenerate, too corrupt to be worth correcting. Everything was seen in terms of absolutes, with 'this desire to transform everything radically', to which it seemed there was only one solution: 'I became convinced that to bring about a radical transformation the only possible way was through revolution, which necessitated violence'.[1]

She joined *Potere Operaio* in 1970, and in that same year married a fellow revolutionary in the organization, Luigi Rosati. Their daughter Alexandra was born in 1971. For a year or two Adriana Faranda's political activities were circumscribed by her young child, but her sense of discontent remained. The marriage gradually fell apart.

Valerio Morucci, the son of Rome caretakers, also entered the Arts faculty of Rome university in the infamous year of 1968, one of some twenty students of that intake who subsequently joined a terrorist organization. Morucci was constantly looking for a positive role to play. An addict of the American gangster movies, his revolutionary aspirations were reinforced by a mixture of escapist fantasy and existential searching. His portrayal of the early 1970's is similar to Adriana Faranda's in that the period was dominated by the unresolved conflict between the need to transform society and the lack of political will to tackle the country's pressing social and economic problems. He too concluded that the armed struggle was the only viable means of realizing the total changes that he thought necessary. Morucci was also a member of *Potere Operaio*, in which he represented the 'hard liners', the armed, semi-clandestine wing. After *Potere Operaio* folded, his militant activities continued, despite his arrest in 1974 on the Swiss border on the charge of trying to smuggle arms into Italy: he was later released.

In 1975 Morucci and Faranda came together as a couple, the young woman increasingly leaving Alexandra to the care of her own mother as her political commitment intensified. Both were active in a group called the *Formazioni Armate Comuniste* until the autumn of 1976, when Mario Moretti offered them the command of the nascent Rome column of the Red Brigades. This was a gamble on both sides.

Mario Moretti was aware of the problems of building a stable organizational structure in Rome, quite a different task from recruitment in the industrial heartlands of Milan, Genoa and Turin. Whilst the existing columns had a strong core of ex-PCI, partisan ideology rooted in working-class traditions, the extremist groups in Rome on which Moretti could draw were essentially middle-class, had no entrenched tradition of political militancy, and were not concentrated in factories but were diffused and fragmented within the Roman suburbs such as Tiburtina and Centocelle. Two earlier attempts to set up a Rome column had been made, but had failed. The first, in 1971–1972, collapsed because those who wanted to join the organization were unprepared to accept the discipline upon which the BR insisted: the mentality of the would-be recruits was one of indiscriminate street violence rather than that of carefully planned revolution. The second attempt was initiated in 1974 by Alberto Franceschini, who spent some time in Rome attending meetings of NAP and *Autonomia Operaia* assessing potential resources and recruitment possibilities. Later that year, however, Franceschini's arrest put an abrupt end to these plans.

When he arrived in Rome in late 1975, Mario Moretti knew exactly what the purpose of the Rome column was to be, and it had little or nothing to do with the labour struggles or factory disputes of the capital. Moretti was a committed militarist; under his guidance the BR had undertaken a strictly controlled campaign of selected attacks against key figures of symbolic weight and prestige — a policy which was to be brought to fruition by the new column. From its very inception this group had but a single purpose in Moretti's mind — to bring the attack to the heart of the state with a campaign of terror against the representatives of state authority.

Valerio Morucci on the other hand, had built his experience on a broader basis of medium level actions, operating from within a specific group or area of dissent rather than as part of a highly specialized military commando. Although a devotee of military action, he was not accustomed to the BR's rigid compartmentalization and discipline. Yet for Morucci the BR represented 'solidity' and success. They were the only group which seemed to bridge the elusive gap between aspiration and action which had plagued him throughout his political militancy. He admits now he was 'dazzled' by what appeared to be a highly efficient, committed and successful organization which offered him the genuine possibility of realizing his political ambitions. However, his companion had some misgivings about joining, concerned as she was about ideological differences between her own political commitment and the BR's adherence to Marxist/Leninist doctrine which seemed inflexible, dogmatic and too single-minded. But she too admits she was fascinated by the group, believing the BR offered the only realistic opportunity to bring down the state. She affirms, 'even if the political policy was already defined, Valerio Morucci and I were convinced that it was susceptible to change.'[2]

In September 1976 the couple made their leap of commitment and joined the BR as full-time members of the new Rome column. Morucci was immediately co-opted on to the Logistic Front, where his skill and knowledge of arms was put to use.

In addition to Morucci and Faranda, Moretti recruited elements of other militant groups such as Barbara Balzerani and Anna Laura Braghetti, formerly members of the Tiburtina branch of *Potere Operaio* known as the *Tiburtaros*, (from Tiburtina and Tupamaros), some from a group called

Viva il Comunismo and others from *Comitati Comunisti Centocelle*. By March 1977 he was supervizing the training of six regular and around twenty irregular members. They progressed by degrees, starting with small robberies, break-ins and arson attacks on cars. In April they were joined by Prospero Gallinari, one of the original Reggio Emilia founder members, whose escape from Treviso prison in January reinforced the column's experience and expertise.

The huge influx of funds from the Costa kidnap was invested in a systematic programme of expenditure: Adriana Faranda, Gabriella Mariani and Anna Laura Braghetti each purchased an apartment in Rome; a house was rented at Velletri, just outside the city, large enough to accommodate all 14 members of the Strategic Directorate who would meet there for a year and a half to discuss tactics and targets; Enrico Triaca, an irregular member of the organization, was instructed to acquire a renovated printing press and to move the existing printing facilities to a new office in Via Foà, a short distance by car from the flat Mario Moretti and Barbara Balzarani shared in Via Gradoli.

In the meantime attacks were stepped up, with the shooting of Remo Cacciafesta in June and of Mario Perlini, a leading figure in the politico-religious organization *Comunione e Liberazione* in July. The column members joined in political demonstrations held throughout the country, but were careful not to draw too much attention to themselves; preferring to leave the area of overt militancy to the members of *Autonomia Operaia*. In November 1977 the BR published a 'strategic resolution' in which their analysis of the 'crisis of imperialist countries' was explained. The document referred to the six-party agreement holding Andreotti's government of non-opposition in power as 'the best guarantee for the construction of the police state; it represents the highest point in the creation of consensus for the project of the imperialist restructuring of the State.' SIM (the Imperialist State of Multinationals) was 'the most efficient instrument for introducing new levels of exploitation of the working class and, more generally, for continuing the process of oppression of nations all over the world'. Within this vision, the DC was 'the guarantor and effective controller of SIM.'

And the response to this state of affairs? The BR document spelt out its message loud and clear: 'ATTACK, HIT, LIQUIDATE AND DEFINITIVELY ROUT THE CHRISTIAN DEMOCRATIC PARTY, AXIS OF THE RESTRUCTURING OF THE STATE AND OF THE IMPERIALIST COUNTER-REVOLUTION'.[3] The politicians were warned.

Throughout 1977 the regular members of the Rome column had devoted themselves to a study of the key men within the party. They concluded that the essential qualities of the DC were personified by three individuals, namely Amintore Fanfani, former Prime Minister and currently President of the Senate, Giulio Andreotti, then Prime Minister, and Aldo Moro, former Prime Minister and President of the Christian Democratic Party.

Extensive enquiries were made into the movements of all three men. No detail or moment of their lives was passed over. They were observed at work, at leisure, at official functions and with their families. Fanfani was ruled out first as a potential victim: his movements were too irregular to permit the efficient planning of a kidnap, he could not be relied upon to follow any specific routine or even reside regularly in the same place, and he was too well protected. Andreotti was the next to be struck off the list — his house in the Corso Vittorio was guarded by a minimum of ten armed police, and he never travelled without two escort cars and a couple of motor cycle outriders. By comparison with his colleagues, Aldo Moro was a soft touch. The timing and route of his journey to work each day varied only slightly, and he made use of only one escort vehicle. Finally and fatally, neither Moro's car nor that of his bodyguards had any protective armour.

In symbolic terms Moro was the ideal and obvious choice: he represented both the continuity and the authority of the DC. The BR were convinced Moro as future head of state would strengthen presidential powers in a Gaullist-style 'Second Republic', with the inevitable reinforcement of DC control over the capitalist, multinationalist society. He was the pivot around which the DC rotated; in Valerio Morucci's words, 'the political godfather . . . with the maximum and most direct responsibility for the essential political choices.'[4]

But how precisely would Moro's kidnap bring about the destruction of SIM, the smashing of the Christian Democratic party, the end of the historic compromise? The answer lies in the conditions the BR intended to lay down for Moro's freedom. The kidnap of Judge Sossi in 1974 had taught them a number of valuable lessons. Firstly, they had discovered that even an apparently strong, resilient public figure could turn into a whimpering, terrified and co-operative kidnap victim, willing to expose fraud, implicate colleagues and admit to state corruption. On this count Moro was potentially a gold mine — he had been at the heart of Italian politics for thirty years, his terms of office as Prime Minister and Foreign Secretary had made him party to European and NATO policies at the highest level, and his central role within the DC ensured he would be *au fait* with all the political intrigues and scandals of post-war Italy. If he chose to talk, Moro could provide the BR with enough material to expose and humiliate the State at every level.

Sossi's kidnap had also transformed the liberation of political prisoners from an abstract ideological goal into a concrete possibility. Still smarting from the criticism that they had climbed down too easily in 1974 with the simple release of their hostage, the BR were determined that the government would have to make considerable concessions to have Moro safely returned. And once again the timing was crucial — after the postponement of the 1977 trial caused by the murder of Fulvio Croce, the 'historic leaders' were once again coming up for trial in Turin, amidst a near hysterical atmosphere of obsessive security and nervousness on the part of judges, jury and witnesses, many of whom were too terrified to appear in court at all, for fear of reprisals against themselves or their families. The kidnap of Moro at this particular moment would permit the BR to conduct their own 'people's trial' in tandem with the official Turin version, thus parodying the state judicial system and demonstrating the existence of a parallel form of justice. And at the conclusion of the people's trial, an exchange of prisoners could be demanded, an act of political mediation which, if realized, would involve the state's acknowledgment of an autonomous political alternative to itself.

Still with the Sossi case in mind, the BR recalled the tension and dissent which had divided the politicians, the legal profession and the general public over the issue of negotiations, and reasoned that such contradictions as would arise within the state over Moro would be even more bitter and intense, given his higher political office and his long and distinguished contribution to government. If the DC refused to negotiate, internal tensions might cause the party to split; if it did give in to blackmail, the humiliation which it would suffer and the corresponding prestige gained by the BR might still lead to its eventual collapse. Naturally they hoped for the latter response, and on this basis projected the next stage of their ambitions.

If the DC government was shown to be a shambles, the working classes might finally recognize the state for what it was, namely a cardboard castle built upon the deception, exploitation and injustices of capitalist oppression. Then, realizing that revolution was within their grasp, they would follow the strong and decisive leadership of the BR and topple the bourgeois state in favour of a proletarian dictatorship. And not only the masses, but also the other revolutionary groups of the left would be forced to acknowledge the undisputed authority of the *Brigate Rosse* in their capacity as the revolutionary vanguard. The Communist party would be isolated entirely from the mass movement, and its aspirations to be a party of the people held up to ridicule.

In the late autumn of 1977 the Strategic Directorate of the BR met and voted in favour of the kidnapping of Aldo Moro. The Executive Committee endorsed the decision in December and 'Operation Fritz' was officially launched. The code name, taken from the characteristic *frezza* or tuft of white hair at the front of Moro's head, would lend an almost childlike air of frivolity to the undertaking.

The net tightened around Moro. A *brigata universitaria* was formed, led by Antonio Savasta, with the task of following Moro's movements around the faculty of Political Science where he held a professorship. Some of Moro's colleagues were also watched, such as his friend and assistant Franco Trittò. Other members of the *brigata universitaria* saw to the provision of vehicles, were instructed to look out for cars with particular characteristics, but were kept in ignorance of the purposes of their researches. The mosaic of Moro's life, his family, his colleagues and his friends was put under the microscope. All his movements were observed, his arrival and departure from home and office were noted and telephone calls made simply to ascertain his presence. The scope of the project now necessitated the participation of the whole column, although each *brigata* only knew a small part of the overall plan.

Two crucial decisions of location had to be made: where the hostage could be seized with the minimum of risk, and where he could be kept in safety while negotiations proceeded. The Rome column members tended to live under assumed names in small apartments scattered around the capital, where they maintained distant but polite relations with their neighbours and led apparently conventional, unremarkable lives. Mario Moretti and Barbara Balzerani lived in Via Gradoli in the northern part of the city, Adriana Faranda and Valerio Morucci in the district of Ostiense, and Prospero Gallinari and Anna Laura Braghetti in a first floor apartment in Via Montalcini, in the south-west of Rome, where they posed as engineer Altobelli and wife. This last apartment was probably the safest refuge for a number of reasons: it had been acquired in July 1977, but due to legal delays the deeds were still in the name of the former proprietor in the spring of 1978.

Only telephone and electricity bills were sent to 'the
Altobellis.' Via Montalcini was situated in a quiet residential
area of broad, leafy avenues. Access to the building was
controlled by entryphone rather than by a porter. Each flat
had a garage with an electronic locking device, from which an
internal door led into a hallway, which in turn gave direct
access to the living quarters. Within the first floor flat of 8,
Via Montalcini a partition was built separating the main living
quarters from a windowless boxroom. It is now assumed that
this boxroom was Aldo Moro's prison. (There is still no
absolute proof for this assertion, but it has been confirmed by
Valerio Morucci and Adriana Faranda. Rosario Priore,
instructing judge in the Moro trial, made an inspection of the
apartment and is convinced that it was indeed where Moro
was held.)

Having established a suitable hiding place for their
prisoner, the BR's attention turned to where and how to
effect the kidnap. Savasta reported that the university
campus was not a suitable place for the snatch, as Moro was
always surrounded by his bodyguards and the numbers of
people continually milling around would increase the
possibility of wounding bystanders. Their studies of
Tupamaros kidnaps, their own experiences, and the 1977
kidnap of West German industrialist Hanns-Martïn Schleyer
had provided useful precedents in proving that a potential
victim was at his most vulnerable while in transit, when he and
any bodyguards would be in a restricted, well-defined space
with little time or space to react.

Aldo Moro was a man of routine: almost every day at
approximately 9 am he would emerge from his fifth floor
apartment in the Via del Forte Trionfale, where his
bodyguards would be waiting for him. He would invariably
have five bags accompany him, two of which were locked into
the boot of his car, the other three kept by his side. Of these,
one contained a selection of medicines and a blood pressure
counter, another held the day's newspapers, which Moro
would peruse on the way to work, and the third, official and
private documents. He always occupied the seat directly

behind the driver in the official Fiat 130, which was always followed directly by the escort vehicle. Every morning, with rare, enforced exceptions, Moro would make one scheduled stop en route, at the nearby church of Santa Chiara, where he would pause for ten minutes in prayer and contemplation. Two members of the escort would remain with the vehicles, two would position themselves at the church entrances, while the fifth would accompany him to his usual pew — at the front right-hand side of the church below the altar.

There were very few possible variations to Aldo Moro's route to the centre of Rome. The most frequently used was that which began in Via del Forte Trionfale, continued into Via Trionfale, Via Fani, Via Stresa and into Via Camillucia, where the church of Santa Chiara was situated. The junction of Via Mario Fani and Via Stresa offered the BR the possibility both of a successful ambush and a suitable escape route. In February 1978 it was selected as the most favourable point to launch the key operation of the BR's 'spring offensive.' The ambush was planned down to the last detail and rehearsed as far as possible. Raffaele Fiore and Rocco Micaletto, the column leaders, in Turin and Genoa respectively, came south in early March to reinforce the group, taking part in the painstaking hours of target practice on deserted stretches of beach to the south of Rome. Cars and vans were stolen, number plates were changed, and weapons were assembled, cleaned and oiled, including the four pistols Mario Moretti had bought in July 1977 in an armoury not far from Aldo Moro's office in Via Savoia.

The Bar Olivetti on the corner of Via Stresa and Via Fani had gone out of business some months before, and the shrubbery around it offered good protection for one element of the commando team. Material stolen from a tailor's shop in Ostia, near Rome airport, was used to make up uniforms similar to those worn by Alitalia personnel. On 10th March Adriana Faranda purchased four matching caps. The area was popular with airline staff, and the sight of four young people in uniform would raise no eyebrows. Who would ever suppose that in the large leather holdall carried by each

nestled a sub-machine gun instead of the personal
requirements for a few days' flying?

Daily life in the Via del Forte Trionfale and in Via Fani was
scrutinized with scientific precision. In mid-March a number
of events occurred which seemed of small significance at the
time, but which would eventually emerge as integral parts of a
carefully mounted and meticulous operation. Around 8 am
on March 14th, 15th and 16th, a couple was noticed
embracing affectionately on the corner of Via Fani and Via
Stresa; only later did the witness match the face of *brigatista*
Lauro Azzolini to that of the early morning Romeo. A spate
of dangerous driving was reported to police in the area — cars
were seen carrying out risky manoeuvres at high speeds — but
no one was apprehended. And the inhabitants of Via Fani
could hardly have been expected to notice that the street
cleaners wearing the official uniform of the *Nettezza urbana*
were different from usual, and were excessively zealous,
cleaning up the street on days when their presence was not
recorded in any official roster of duties.

A strange and to this day unexplained event occurred on
the evening of March 15 in the town of Siena, some 150 miles
north of Rome. A blind man, Guiseppe Marchi, was taking
his dog for a walk. As he went, his white stick tapped a parked
car, whose occupants were talking both in Italian and in a
foreign language which Marchi could not identify. However,
he heard quite clearly the end of the conversation, which was
in Italian: 'They've kidnapped Moro and killed his
bodyguards.'

Immediately Marchi went home where he and his wife
switched on the television, expecting to hear more details, but
to their surprise the event was not mentioned. Later, Marchi
paid a visit to his local bar and told his story to a circle of six
companions, who promptly laughed uproariously and
accused him of telling yet another of the tall stories for which
he had earned the nickname 'Beppe the liar'. In less than 24
hours the sceptics would be forced to take their unreliable
friend more seriously.

To have Moro's kidnap coincide with the presentation to

Parliament of the 'government of national unity', the first
for thirty years to have active PCI support was undoubtedly
the BR's aim, yet any number of unpredictable factors could
have prevented their plans from coming to fruition on that
precise day. The *Brigate Rosse* could only aim for the 16th
March, and hope that luck would be on their side. It was.

The most memorable day in the history of post-war Italy
begins in the most unmemorable of places. Shortly before
dawn in Via Brunetti, near Piazza del Popolo, Rome,
someone quietly slits all four tyres of a small van owned by
Antonio Spiriticchio, a flower seller. Like Aldo Moro,
Spiriticchio is a man of habit. Every morning at the same time
he goes to the flower market, fills up his van and drives to his
usual position on the corner of Via Fani and Via Stresa. He
frequently notices Aldo Moro's official car driving past
with the accompanying escort vehicle, and sometimes
acknowledges the convoy with a friendly wave. But on March
16th his thoughts are far from friendly as he curses the vandals
who have ruined his morning's business, and sees to the
replacement of his slashed tyres.

For Aldo Moro the day is a crucial one, for it represents the
culmination of months, even years, of preparation and effort,
but in practical terms the day's programme is much the same
as usual. After morning mass he will go to the Chamber of
Deputies in the Palazzo Montecitorio for the presentation of
the fourth Andreotti government at 10 am, followed by a
meeting with some of his politics students with whom he will
discuss the morning's proceedings. From Montecitorio he will
drive to the Political Science faculty where at noon he is due
to look over some student theses. A light lunch, a brief stroll
in the park for his daily exercise, and on to his office in Via
Savoia. In many respects, a normal day.

The joy of Moro's life is his two year-old grandson Luca.
The adoration is reciprocated, and Luca loves nothing more
than to go for a ride with his grandfather in the big car, often
accompanying him to church before being dropped back

home to his mother. On 15th March Maria Fida, Luca's mother, is suffering from acute back pains, and leaves him to stay overnight with his grandparents. She goes to collect him in the morning about 8.15, still in pain, but determined that she will take Luca to watch the firemen's display as she has promised. Grandfather Moro is reluctant to let Luca go, asking her several times if Luca might not ride with him as far as Santa Chiara, then be brought back. But Maria Fida is stubborn, and some strange instinct makes her insist on keeping Luca by her side. Even Luca himself, excited by the prospect of the treat ahead, for once pushes his grandfather away in his own eagerness to be off. 'Go away', are the last words Moro hears from his grandson before he descends to join his waiting bodyguards in the courtyard below. It is a grey, overcast day threatening rain.

Today's escort team are almost all old friends, and Moro greets them as such. Driving the official Fiat 130 is Lance Corporal Domenico Ricci, aged 44, from the seaport of Ancona, married with two children. Beside him sits the head of the squad, Turin-born Oreste Leonardi, who at 52 has been Moro's faithful shadow for 18 years. Moro takes up his usual position behind the driver with his papers and briefcases. Driving the accompanying Alfetta 1800 is an officer of the civil police, or *Polizia di Sicurezza*, Giulio Rivera, who is the baby of the group at 23. With him travel fellow PS colleagues Francesco Zizzi and Raffaele Iozzino, both aged 25. All three are southerners of peasant stock, proud to hold positions of such responsibility at this early stage of their careers. For Zizzi it is the first day of guarding Aldo Moro.

Shortly before 9 am Moro climbs into the car, his head soon bent deep over his newspapers as Ricci weaves his way through the Rome traffic. The convoy proceeds along Via Fani and slows down for the right turn into Via Stresa. It is 9.02 am. A Mini traveller is parked just in front of the junction, preventing Ricci from entering the right hand lane. It is parked illegally, but this is scarcely a matter for surprise in Rome, where parking is determined by the laws of possibility, not by those of the land.

A white Fiat 128 estate car with a diplomatic number plate suddenly accelerates past both cars, then stops and reverses abruptly, ramming the 130 from the front. Rivera tries to avoid a collision but the Alfetta's brakes are faulty and he bumps the 130 from behind. Ricci raises his arms in anger, starts to gesticulate to the driver of the 128, but before he can complete the action two occupants have leapt out of the vehicle and are shooting at the 130 from both sides.

The four Alitalia pilots have emerged from the cover of the shuttered Bar Olivetti, having drawn their weapons from their leather bags and are shooting to kill, two going for Moro's car, two for the occupants of the Alfetta. Other assailants appear as if from nowhere, a motor cyclist in a balaclava covers the lower end of Via Fani and an armed woman with police diversion signs stands at the junction, ready to shoot at anyone who dares to approach. No one does.

Leonardi tries to protect Moro, leaning over the back seat to push him on to the floor of the car away from the hail of bullets, but is shot in this position: his final act of loyalty. A number of close range shots to the head finish off Leonardi, Ricci and Rivera. Iozzino opens a car door, leans out and manages to fire a few shots but he too is gunned down and dies. Only Zizzi survives the assault, but will succumb to his wounds during an emergency operation at a nearby hospital.

Aldo Moro is hauled from his car, bundled into a waiting Fiat 132 and driven off at high speed, followed by others of the commando team in a blue and a white Fiat 128 which have been parked in readiness. The motorbike roars off with its balaclava-wearing driver and one passenger, who fires at another motorcyclist riding up Via Fani on his way to work. A former police officer who has witnessed the last moments of the attack gives chase, unaware of the identity of the hostage, whom he perceives only as a figure squashed between two uniformed men who are pressing something white to his face. But within a few minutes the fugitives are lost in the heavy morning traffic.

The 132 takes its cargo only as far as Piazza Madonna del

Cenacolo, where the hostage is dragged out, put into a
waiting Fiat van and driven off. The 132 is abandoned. The
van winds a skilful course through a maze of streets until it
turns into the underground car park of the '*Standa*'
supermarket in the Via dei Colli Portuensi. Moro is loaded
into a wooden packing case, into another Fiat van and driven
to his destination. Five men lie dead or dying. For the sixth
the ordeal is only just beginning.

References

1. Interview with Adriana Faranda by Gabriella Parca, *Il Giorno*,
   13/2/1985.
2. Interview Faranda/Parca, *Il Giorno*, 13/2/85.
3. *Atti della Corte*, reproduced in '*Il Mandarino è Marcio*, Mimmo
   Scarano & Maurizio De Luca, Editori Riuniti, Rome, 1985,
   pp. 172.
4. *Commissione Parlamentare d'Inchiesta sulla strage di Via Fani,
   dul sequestro e l'assassinio di Aldo Moro e sul terrorismo in
   Italia*, Vol X, pp. 631.

6
KIDNAP — ACTION AND REACTION

'I came upon a scene of immense confusion which we ourselves created.'
General Pietro Corsini, Carabinieri Commander, commenting on his arrival in Via Fani on the morning of 16th March, 1978[1]

Thursday, March 16

A small crowd began to gather, although fear kept many away. After the first cries of shock and panic a strange hush fell on the street. But the silence was only temporary. Within a few minutes, Via Fani and the surrounding roads were swarming with hundreds of police and carabinieri. All access routes were now made impassable by the jam of blue and white vehicles, a siren wailing on each. At 9.24 orders went out to put road blocks around the city, and to make special checks at stations, airports and frontier posts.

At 9.25 the national radio station GR 2 interrupted its morning broadcast with the following announcement: 'We interrupt our programme to give you a dramatic piece of news which seems incredible but which unfortunately appears to be true, although it has not been officially confirmed. The Honourable Aldo Moro, President of the Christian Democratic party, was kidnapped a short time ago by a terrorist commando. . . . We must also add that Moro's escort team consisted of five men: they are all presumed dead.'[2]

One of the first to arrive on the scene was Signora Eleonora Moro, alerted by a terrified young policeman who had traced her to the nearby church of San Francesco. Most eye witnesses were of the opinion that Aldo Moro had not been injured in the ambush, and with this the Signora was given some comfort. But her concern was not limited to her husband's plight. 'It may sound bad, but I know what I'm saying: I suffer more for these dead men than for the fate of my husband: They were good, fine boys', she murmured, as she knelt to pray for them.[3]

Nor did the practical details of the ambush escape her notice — Signora Moro observed that on the blood-drenched floor of the official car there were two clear marks where Aldo Moro's bags had stood. A former nurse, she knew that blood from a wound does not immediately gush, but takes some time to flow. Therefore, as the ambush had lasted a mere three minutes from start to finish, she deduced that the two bags had been snatched after, not during the attack. But by whom?

At 10.08 came the first responsibility claim, to the ANSA press agency in Milan: 'Red Brigades here. This morning our organization brought the attack to the heart of the state. You'll hear from us again as soon as possible. Moro is only the beginning.' At 10.10 the second call came, to ANSA in Rome, followed shortly afterwards by calls to newspaper offices in Turin and Rome. The message was substantially the same — 'We have attacked the heart of the state. The hostage is in our hands. Long live the Red Brigades.'[4]

At Palazzo Montecitorio, the Chamber of Deputies was buzzing, with almost all the 600 deputies gathered for the debate on the new government. The news flashed through the debating chamber like lightning, provoking incredulity, horror and anguish. Some deputies wept openly, others sat immobilized by shock and grief.

Word reached Prime Minister Giulio Andreotti 'like a bolt from the blue'[5], during the swearing in of a number of new under-secretaries in his official residence at Palazzo Chigi. Immediately he summoned the members of the interim government, the leaders of all the principal political parties and the three trade union chiefs. A brief cabinet meeting was followed by a round of inter-party consultations, culminating in a series of hastily taken but unanimous decisions: the party secretaries agreed on the convening of emergency debates in both parliamentary chambers to facilitate the immediate formation of a government invested with full authority and such emergency powers as were deemed necessary. The union leaders Lama, Macario and Benvenuto decided to call a nationwide general strike from 11 am until midnight of that same day, and a joint policy towards the terrorist challenge was adopted: 'By that same morning the majority parties . . . agreed with the Prime Minister on a policy of decisive rejection of any attempt at blackmail on the part of the Red Brigades'.[6]

Whilst Francesco Cossiga met with the senior law enforcement officers to initiate investigations, Andreotti briefed the assembled party and union leaders on the conclusions of the morning's meetings. As these broke up, the deputies left Palazzo Chigi for Montecitorio. PCI members Berlinguer and Pajetta defiantly shunned the official cars and bodyguards waiting outside to make the short journey on foot through the jostling, excited crowds. Meanwhile in Parliament, eulogies were being heaped on the heads of Moro and the murdered bodyguards. Ex-President Saragat called the attack 'an outright act of civil war', a judgement with which Republican Ugo La Malfa concurred, and for which La Malfa urged the immediate restoration of the death penalty. MSI Secretary Giorgio Almirante agreed, and proposed that Francesco Cossiga resign forthwith, to be replaced by a military Minister of the Interior. But in general, the need to protect democracy with democratic methods prevailed over panic measures of repression. And by evening, both Houses of Parliament had approved the creation of a government of national solidarity, an all-DC government with the active support of the Communists, Socialists, Social Democrats and Republicans. With an overwhelming vote of confidence Parliament gave a first, unhesitating response to the terrorist challenge.

As the hours passed, more details began to emerge about the terrorist commando. A total of 250 witnesses contributed to an overall view of the day's proceedings. Luciano Infelisi, deputy procurator of Rome, was entrusted with the judicial enquiries. It was ascertained that a total of 91 bullets had been fired, of which 49, from an unidentified weapon, had been fired with special accuracy. Of the firing group, thought to number 6 or 7, all but one had their faces uncovered, the exception being the balaclava-wearing motorcyclist. At least one woman, a blonde, was reported to have participated in the action, although some said there was a second. One of the terrorists had been heard to exclaim in a foreign language, but again there was disagreement: some said the oath was in French, some in German, some were sure it was in neither of the two.

In the course of the day a total of six telephoned responsibility claims were deemed authentic amidst the inevitable profusion of hoax messages. In Milan a woman received a call asking her to give a message to *Corriere della Sera* from the Milan, or 'Walter Alasia' column of the BR. The message called the police operations 'ridiculous', since Moro was already out of the country, and promised photographs to prove it. A call came through to a Rome press agency in the name of the Baader-Meinhof group. 'Aldo Moro ist mit uns', it declared.

In the evening Giulio Andreotti appeared on national television to make an appeal for calm and order, and to ask the public to collaborate with investigations in every possible way. At first there were grounds for hoping that the gunmen would be caught. On the evening of the 16th the names and photographs of some 20 suspected terrorists were issued by national police headquarters. In reality, two of the 'wanted' men were already in prison, two were one and the same person, one was a police informer and two were in self-imposed exile in France, where a journalist from the weekly magazine *L'Espresso* was subsequently able to interview them. Nonetheless, included in the list were Mario Moretti, Rocco Micaletto, Prospero Gallinari and Lauro Azzolini, all of whom had indeed been in Via Fani that morning. Two others on the list were regular BR members and a further two had recently left the BR to join other armed revolutionary groups; thus police intelligence, even at this early stage, had a solid basis to work on.

Throughout the country the unions obeyed the strike calls of their leaders, abandoning offices, schools and factories to participate in mass demonstrations. Estimates put the figures as high as 200,000 in Rome, 80,000 in Milan and 50,000 in Turin. But public opinion was infinitely more sympathetic towards the murdered bodyguards than to the fate of Aldo Moro. Vittorio Alfieri of the BR 'Walter Alasia' column recalls the scene in the Alfa Romeo factory at Arese: 'The remarks most common in the discussions were more about the attack itself. The men of Moro's bodyguard were quite a separate issue from Moro. The bodyguards will quickly be forgotten, but Moro on the other hand. . . .'

Then, as factory machinery was switched off for the national strike, a note of paradox crept in. The workers did not approve of the BR action, nonetheless 'they wondered why they should go on strike for Moro, when until yesterday they had to strike *against* him and his government.' Alfieri's position can scarcely be considered impartial, yet there is no doubt that at the time of his kidnap Moro was not a well-loved public figure. He was generally thought to be aloof, intellectual and a man without much warmth or human feeling. Many were heard to say that the risk of kidnap was simply the price to be paid for the power, prestige and rewards provided by the upper echelons of political life. However, there was surprise at the choice of Moro, generally considered to be above the corruption and intrigues of which Andreotti, Fanfani and other DC politicians were suspected.

Some even wondered whether Andreotti, whose national and
international allegiances were always viewed with suspicion,
had had a hand in the matter, as part of a move to rid Italy of a
personal and political rival. Such rumours were common, as
were jokes such as this one, overheard on a Rome bus during
the kidnap: 'Andreotti is sitting in his office on the morning of
16th March. As his secretary enters he asks her the time.
Before she can answer the telephone rings. She listens for a
moment, then white as a sheet, she stammers, "Aldo Moro
has been kidnapped". Andreotti replies, "Oh, it must be 9.15
then."'

Friday, March 17

Giulio Andreotti's first task was to form a crisis committee
whose exclusive function was to take the strategic decisions
affecting the political aspects of the kidnap. In addition to
Andreotti himself the Interministerial Committee for
Security (CIS) consisted of the Ministers of the Interior,
Foreign Affairs, Finance, Defence and Industry; the heads of
the civil and finance police and of the carabinieri; the heads of
the Security Services SISMI and SISDE and of their
co-ordinating committee; to this group were added a
representative of President Leone, and another minister who
attended in the capacity of a Moro family friend.
Simultaneously a political committee was established to
co-ordinate police and judicial enquiries, and relations
between the police forces and the security services.

Road blocks around Rome and throughout the country
were extended, and orders were given for two helicopters to
comb the city during the hours of daylight. Controls at
airports, railway stations and ports were intensified, public
telephone boxes were kept under random surveillance and
known centres of left-wing sympathy such as factories,
universities and colleges were infiltrated in an attempt to pick
up clues and rumours.

But from the start the BR succeeded in outsmarting their
pursuers. In addition to the white Fiat 128 used to cause the

collision in Via Fani, three other cars had been positively identified as used by the terrorists. Between 16th and 19th March all three were found carefully parked in the same street — Via Licinio Calvo, less than a mile from the scene of the ambush. The 132 into which Moro had been bundled was found later the same morning, the other white 128 was found on Friday 17th at 5.15 pm and the blue 128 at 9 pm on the 19th. In the two 128s were found police sirens and wire cutters which had been used to cut away a chain barring the entrance to one of the streets on the escape route. On one vehicle there was a large, bloody hand print. It was not that of Aldo Moro.

On Friday afternoon Andreotti chaired the second meeting of the five majority party leaders, with Cossiga also present. Unanimously they decided that whatever the demands of the terrorists, they would adhere to a line of the utmost firmness. Measures for increasing penalties for terrorist crimes and upgrading police powers were discussed.

Saturday, March 18

Police house searches began in earnest, in particular in the residential district surrounding the Moro family apartment in the Monte Mario area of Rome. In this zone, if house occupants were absent, police were instructed to break in and carry out an inspection, after which an officer was to be posted outside until the occupants returned. However, in most cases this did not happen, and the police simply went away when door bells were not answered. It certainly was not done at 96, Via Gradoli, the flat rented by Mario Moretti and Barbara Balzarani under the name of Borghi. When no one answered the door, a few enquiries with neighbours established that the couple were 'quiet people', and no further action was taken. But one of the tenants of the apartment block took the opportunity of the police visit to report some strange sounds which had come from the building on the evening of 15th March which, she claimed, sounded like morse code.

At around midday, an anonymous telephone message reached the offices of *Il Messagero* newspaper in Rome. A communication from the *Brigate Rosse* was to be found on top of a photo booth in a pedestrian subway in the Largo Argentina, a few yards away from the DC headquarters. When the journalist arrived at the designated spot he found an orange envelope containing a polaroid photograph of Aldo Moro sitting under a BR banner, together with the BR's 'Communication No 1.' In it the BR gave a clear account of the aim and motivations for the kidnap: Moro had been captured because he was 'the most faithful executor of the directions issued by imperialist centres', of which the Christian Democratic party was 'the central and strategic force'.[8] Moro was to undergo a 'people's trial' in which his personal responsibilities would be assessed and judged. The BR warned the proletariat not to heed the propaganda of the government 'counter-revolution' and promised that all proclamations in their name would be made public, as would the results of Moro's trial. Finally, they promised that all their messages would be typed on the same typewriter. The photograph of Moro showed him without jacket or tie and his shirt crumpled, but otherwise apparently unharmed.

In the Basilica of San Lorenzo, Rome, the state funeral took place of Iozzino, Ricci, Leonardi, Zizzi and Rivera. Between fifteen and twenty thousand mourners lined the funeral route and clustered silently round the church. For once, the DC banners with cross and shield fluttered in sympathy beside the hammer and sickle insignia of the PCI. Demonstrations continued throughout the day. In the evening two young students were shot dead in Milan by neo-fascist vigilantes.

After the funeral the Moro family returned to their fifth floor retreat in Via del Forte Trionfale to wait for news, while outside, an encampment of reporters settled into position. One daughter, Anna, who was pregnant and in need of rest, returned to her home and husband. Maria Fida, still suffering from disc problems in her back and almost immobilized with pain, kept vigil with her husband in their apartment opposite the family home, and tried to avoid Luca's persistent questioning as to where his grandfather was. Giovanni and Agnese remained at their mother's side. Telephone and television were their principal links with an outside world for which they themselves had become the centre of attention.

Sunday — Friday, March 19–24

A period of anxious expectation and wild speculation: the report that one of the terrorists had exclaimed in a foreign language was the basis of numerous rumours involving the Baader-Meinhof group, the infamous and ubiquitous Carlos, not to mention Czechoslovakia, Israel, Libya, and of course the long arm of the KGB. The Baader-Meinhof theory was reinforced by superficially plausible circumstantial evidence: the military expertise of the attack in Via Fani was considered to have all the hallmarks of a sophisticated, highly trained terrorist team hitherto not seen in Italy. In particular, the technique of the ambush closely resembled the kidnap of Hanns-Martin Schleyer in September 1977. The announcement that an identikit picture of one of the BR assassins of Marshall Rosario Berardi, murdered on 10th March, corresponded to the militant left-winger Brunilde Petramer immediately fuelled the Italo/German co-operation theory. Petramer, an Italian from the former Austrian province of Alto Adige, was captured on 22nd March and succeeded in establishing an alibi for the 16th, but the associations with her Germanic name once made were not easily relinquished. Finally, a mini-bus with a German number plate had been spotted heading northwards from Rome on 16th March with a number of young men inside. The vehicle's number plate proved to be false, and was eventually traced to the German terrorist Willi Stoll.

Apart from speculation as to the provenance of the kidnappers, the two other topics of greatest general interest were Moro's physical and mental condition, and the demands likely for his release. Previous kidnap victims such as Ettore

Amerio and Mario Sossi were invited to explain what Moro
would undoubtedly be feeling, and the nature of the mental
torture to which he would be subjected. It was generally
agreed that drugs might be used either to tranquilize him or to
make him talk.

The issue of media coverage was given full and careful
consideration both by the politicians and by the press itself in
anticipation of the inevitable dilemma between the duty to
inform and the risk of enhancing or aggrandizing the terrorist
image by affording publicity to their acts and their ideology.
The politicians had appealed for caution, discretion and a
sense of responsibility on the part of the media, but had not
attempted to impose direct legislation or censorship. *La
Stampa* speculated on the possible effect of simply ignoring
any messages from the kidnappers, whereby if a telephone
call gave details of where a document could be found, the
response would be, 'No thanks, we're not interested', and the
telephone put down. Such an attitude, however appealing in
the abstract, could hardly prevail in the certain knowledge of
five deaths and the possibility of a sixth. *La Repubblica*
carried out a survey of 11 newspaper editors to establish what
line of action would be taken if the terrorists produced a
'confession' from Moro which admitted the DC's
involvement in neo-fascist subversion. Six said they would
publish, with an accompanying 'explanation' as to terrorist
methods, three said they would not print it, and two did not
know, but would agree a line with other editors should it
happen.

On the 21st, fifteen of the original Red Brigades members,
including Curcio, Franceschini and Ognibene made their first
court appearance in Turin. Curcio attempted to read
out a prepared statement, but the judge, who insisted on
reading the document himself first, refused to give it a public
hearing. Shouts, jeers and catcalls from the chained-up
prisoners resulted in their all being led out of the courtroom
and back to their cells, but not before Curcio shouted
triumphantly, 'We've got Moro in our hands!'

By Tuesday the government had put together a package of

stronger anti-terrorist legislation which increased penalities for kidnapping and gave police wider powers of search, arrest and phone tapping. The law also compelled those who had sold or rented property since 1977 to report details of the change of occupation to the authorities. This was a skilful move by the government, based on the supposition that the money the BR had received from the Costa kidnap in 1977 had been invested in property — an accurate assumption.

On Friday 24th a former Christian Democrat mayor of Turin was shot in the legs. The attack was claimed by the Red Brigades.

Saturday — Tuesday, March 25–28

On Saturday the BR announced the delivery of a second Communication at specified points in Genoa, Milan, Turin and Rome. Most of this was devoted to a long attack on the DC, which had turned Italy 'from the state as expression of the parties, to parties as pure tools of the state', and to Aldo Moro's thirty-year association with his party.

The logical conclusion of Moro's political career, the presidency of the Republic, would invest him not only with the powers of head of state, but also of the judiciary and of the armed forces, an invincible position from which, the BR believed, the DC could complete the restructuring of the Imperialist State of Multinationals. The protest demonstrations against terrorism organized by Berlinguer and by the union leaders were denounced as 'counter-revolutionary manoeuvres', encouraged by 'traitors, spies of the regime'. The document concluded with a salute to the young Milanese boys, killed by 'thugs of the regime.' But there was no mention of a ransom demand, no ultimatum. Moro's trial was continuing.

As far as investigations were concerned, the police manhunt had proved so far to be inconclusive and ineffectual. Franco Moreno had been arrested on 18th March but released two days later. Brunilde Petramer's arrest had led nowhere; the house search of a Roman member of *Auto-nomia Operaia*, Lanfranco Pace, on the 23rd had revealed an old BR document of 1972, but nothing which, according to the authorities, could either justify his arrest or lead to the ringleaders of Via Fani. However on the 25th the police received a tip-off — an anonymous telephone call to the Minister of the Interior's special investigative force gave the names of five individuals whose movements 'should be watched', and who might lead to the *Brigate Rosse*. No addresses were given, but indications such as car number plates and places of work left little room for doubt. Amongst the five was Teodoro Spadaccini, irregular member of the Rome column.

One man who took a back seat during the turbulent events of late March was President Giovanni Leone. Under a cloud of suspicion for his possible involvement in the Lockheed scandal, Leone's fate was very much in the hands of his fellow DC colleagues, and rather than take a potentially unpopular initiative in the matter, he preferred to let the government be seen to take all the decisions. For this he was much criticized, especially by Arrigo Levi, editor of *La Stampa*, who proposed that Leone be asked to abdicate from the presidency in favour of the absent Aldo Moro. The proposal caused a stir for a few days but was not pursued.

Wednesday — Sunday, March 29–April 2

On the evening of the 29th, telephone calls to newspapers in Milan, Rome, Genoa and Turin gave the whereabouts of another message from the BR: Communication No 3. The document began with the affirmation that Moro's interrogation was proceeding with his 'complete collaboration', and that all the revealed material would be made known to the revolutionary movement, which could use this for its own best interests. 'Nothing will be withheld from the people', it announced proudly. This document was directed specifically at the masses, who were urged to continue the revolutionary initiative set in motion by Moro's kidnap. It was also an appeal to the far left to support and increase the armed offensive against the State.

The same day, three letters written by Aldo Moro were delivered to his office in Via Savoia — one was addressed to Nicola Rana, Moro's secretary, one to Moro's wife, and the third was to Francesco Cossiga. Moro obviously believed the letter to Cossiga would remain strictly private, but the BR deceived him, and left copies of it with their third Communication, defending their decision with the assertion that secrecy was the trademark only of the 'Demo-Christian Mafia'.

The tone of Moro's letter to Cossiga was clear, calm but quite determined: 'Although I know nothing either of how my capture occurred or of what has happened since, that cannot be discussed — I have been told with the utmost clarity — as President of the DC, I am considered a political prisoner, undergoing a trial whose aim is to ascertain my thirty-year responsibilities (a trial in the political sense, but which is becoming ever more demanding). . . . In truth all we leaders are being taken to task and it is our collective work which is under attack and for which I am now having to answer. . . . I find myself under a total and uncontrolled domination, subjected to a people's trial which can be stepped up at any moment . . . with the risk of being expected or compelled to talk in a manner which could be unpleasant and dangerous in certain situations.'[9]

Full of similar veiled threats and warnings, Moro's letter went on to argue that his release was vital, not only in his own interest but also in that of the State, which could suffer 'certain and incalculable harm. . . . The sacrifice of innocent people for the sake of an abstract legal principle is inadmissible.' Moro then went on to cite cases in which political prisoners had been released or exchanged, and suggested that the state might find an intermediary to bargain on its behalf — 'I think a cautious step from the the Vatican (or even others, who?) could be useful.' Before a final greeting of affection to his colleague, Moro concluded with another warning 'An attitude of hostility would be an abstraction and an error.'

The letters to Rana and to Noretta, his wife, (only published later) were short and affectionate, although in Rana's there was a specific warning not to allow his office or his telephone to be kept under surveillance, since 'an accident could bring everything crashing down with incalculable damage.'

A number of references in the letter to Cossiga confirm that Moro was indeed deprived of news of the outside world, and suggest he may even have believed there were other kidnap victims beside himself. It is also clear that Moro had had some dialogue with his captors and had gained at least a partial understanding of their position and of their release terms. There is no hint that at this stage Moro felt his life to be seriously threatened, but he did believe that the government had to be frightened into taking decisive action by the threat of his being compelled to divulge information damaging to national security.

Reactions to the publication of this letter were dramatic: a meeting was hurriedly called, first of the DC national committee, and then of the government. Public opinion was divided over what the government should do.

The Vatican newspaper *l'Osservatore Romano* took the initial viewpoint that the letter was a hopeful sign that Moro's release could be obtained; the Milan daily *Il Giorno* began by running the headline, 'Negotiations? Top secret', but in later editions it was changed to 'No negotiations with the BR'.[10] Acting swiftly and decisively, the DC and the government had resolved the issue quite simply — there was to be no giving in to blackmail, no negotiations with terrorists; Moro's suggestions were quite out of the question.

But the DC could not stifle Moro nor could it ignore his requests for negotiation. A solution had to be found. This time the press found it for them. How could a politician of Moro's calibre be so base, consider himself so self-important as to expect the country to throw up its legal and democratic principles for his sake? The idea was preposterous, Moro's mind must have been adversely affected by his ordeal, or his letter must have been written under coercion from his captors. Besides, he had not even mentioned the fate of his poor bodyguards whom he must have realized were dead. On the 30th, *La Repubblica* was without a doubt. 'These words are not his', it announced.

It continued, 'if the fact of having written the letter proves that Moro is alive, the style and content of the message suggests that Aldo Moro has been subjected to such pressures that the word torture, even if understood as persistent and forceful psychological conditioning, is not exaggerated or far from the truth of the matter . . . Moro's suggestion of an exchange of political prisoners, if accepted and carried out, would signify his political end . . . by making an unacceptable distinction between the victims of common crime and those of political motivation, Moro would, in fact, in exchange for his physical freedom, be signing his own death warrant as a politician and as a statesman'.

Corriere della Sera too speculated that the letter must have been written by a man 'rendered powerless by the isolation of a cruel imprisonment'.

The view that Moro, albeit material author of the letter, was 'not himself' for a variety of reasons, was almost unanimously endorsed by the Italian press. As Alessandro Silj writes, 'Right from the very first letter, so much was said and written to deny their [ie the letters'] validity that in fact the operation "Moro isn't Moro" took place in the space of only two days, the 30th and 31st March, and would condition every future comment on successive messages.'[11]

Calligraphic experts studied Moro's handwriting, cryptologists combed his sentences for hidden meanings, psychiatrists and psychologists analyzed his possible mental state. Moro's sentences were taken apart syllable by syllable. Much was made of the repeated use of the word 'sotto' (under), which, it was suggested, could imply Moro thought he was underground, in a cellar or possibly — in a submarine.

Meanwhile, his family and friends despaired. Their viewpoint, that Moro's arguments were fully coherent and in keeping with his usual sense of balance and reasonableness, was completely ignored. On the one hand, they believed Moro was trying to gain time, hoping that a period of token discussions would allow the police to find him; on the other they felt Moro was only arguing for himself what he had urged in other kidnap cases, namely that humanitarian considerations should always prevail over 'reasons of state' when human life was at stake. Instead, what Silj calls the 'progressive demolition/removal' of Moro's character had begun, and once in motion could not be halted.

On Thursday 30th Adriana Faranda and Valerio Morucci's names appeared on the list of BR suspects wanted in connection with the murders and kidnap in Via Fani. Morucci had been identified as one of those in the commando team, and Faranda as the purchaser of the pilots' caps.

On Friday it began to look as if the Pope was responding seriously to Moro's suggestion of intervention. Publicly acknowledging the request, l'Osservatore Romano announced that the Vatican was 'not indifferent' to the idea of mediation, although some further clarification would be needed before anything could be done. Although few people knew of it, there was a precedent for papal intervention with regard to political detainees which dated from 1944.

A young Catholic professor by the name of Giuliano Vassalli had been captured, tortured and condemned to death by the Nazis, but his life was saved at the last minute after an appeal from Pope Pius XII. Moro certainly knew of this. A delegation from the Christian Democratic party went to the Vatican for consultations. These were of course private, but the contents of the meeting could be deduced from the subsequent announcement: the Vatican reluctantly felt unable to mediate directly to save Moro, but it encouraged all individual or collective efforts to do so. The DC was clearly worried that as an old friend of Moro and his wife, Pope Paul might become involved in joint negotiations with the family which would exclude the government and leave it humiliated. As if in compensation for his withdrawal, the Pope's Sunday address from St Peters contained an appeal to 'the unknown authors of the horrifying episode' to release their hostage.

Meanwhile in Turin the 1978 Socialist party conference had opened up under the slogan 'Overcome the Crisis' — in the circumstances, entirely appropriate. Inevitably the theme of terrorism dominated those of economic and political development. In the course of the five-day conference, a Socialist lawyer by the name of Giannino Guiso approached Party Secretary Bettino Craxi. Guiso was legal counsel for Renato Curcio and a number of other Red Brigades prisoners who, he suggested, might be willing to co-operate in some way in possible negotiations for Moro's release. Guiso had talked to his clients, who had assured him that whatever happened, the Moro affair would not end in the same way as the Sossi kidnap, that is with the unconditional release of the hostage. This time the government would have to negotiate if it wanted Moro back. Guiso took the fact that Moro was permitted to write letters as an encouraging sign that there was some room for mediation, but, he warned, it was necessary to act quickly, for the sluggish methods of political bargaining were far removed from the immediacy of terrorist demand and response.

Monday — Wednesday, April 3–5

Another meeting took place between Cossiga, Andreotti and the five coalition party secretaries. For the first time there was a hint of a break in the unanimity of the so-called 'line of rigour' adopted hitherto. After his discussions with Guiso, Craxi was beginning to believe in the need to find some opening, some way of engaging the *Brigate Rosse* in dialogue with the government. He did not disguise his new attitude, announcing to the press at the conclusion of the meeting, 'To negotiate does not mean to yield.'

But of the assembled politicians he alone held this view.

There were certainly justifications for the hard-line approach: Giulio Andreotti recalls the fear that the whole episode might cause an extreme reaction in military and right-wing circles, provoking a *coup d'état* and the installation of a military regime. Undoubtedly, after the murder of the police and carabinieri bodyguards, the forces of law and order would have reacted strongly to any obvious climb-down on the part of the government. Furthermore, given Italy's record of right-wing terrorism, the hypothesis that the Moro affair could be exploited by the right and thus become the crossroads between two forms of extremist violence could not be dismissed lightly.

A flurry of police and carabinieri activity took place on Monday, centering on a round up of *Autonomia* members thought to have contacts and sympathies with terrorist groups, in particular former members of *Potere Operaio*. Homes were searched and around 30 arrests were made. A similar operation was carried out on 6th May, resulting in the arrest of a further 23 suspects. On both occasions all those detained were released a few days later for lack of incriminating evidence. But Morucci and Faranda were known suspects; they were both ex-members of *Potere Operaio* and were also known to have kept contact with former companions such as Lanfranco Pace and Franco Piperno. Pace's house had been searched previously but, strangely enough, neither his nor Franco Piperno's movements were watched, nor were any detailed investigations carried out as to these contacts. If they had been, events might have turned out differently.

On Tuesday, the BR broke their six-day silence, announcing the distribution of Communication No 4, to which was attached a 'Resolution of the Strategic Directive', a document of some 60 pages. A letter to DC Secretary Benigno Zaccagnini was also delivered the same day, a copy of which was left at the Milan office of *La Repubblica*. The letter to Zaccagnini was essentially an appeal to all the DC leaders, on whom Moro called to take responsibility for his release. By now Moro was quite clearly informed of political proceedings, for he referred in this letter to the Communist Party's adherence to the line of rigour, and specifically refuted the implication that he had been coerced or tortured, or that his mind was disturbed. The letter was also a deliberate attempt on Moro's part to weaken the resolve of the party Secretary, on whom he launched a blistering attack: 'I remember my extreme, oft-repeated and deliberate reluctance to assume the role of President which you offered me, and which now has wrenched me away from the family which has great need of me: it's you who are morally in the place where I am materially.' Criticizing the DC's 'brusque decision to terminate any form of discussion with regard to other persons imprisoned as I am', Moro wasted no time in returning to the central issue — an exchange of prisoners. And there was a real note of urgency in his words — 'Time is running out, and unfortunately there isn't enough of it.'

For the first time Moro mentioned his bodyguards, although not in the predicted way: 'If the bodyguards had not been, for administrative reasons, completely inadequate to the situation, perhaps I wouldn't be here.'

Moro tried to justify his plea for a negotiated settlement by reminding Zaccagnini of his own humanitarian views on kidnap cases, as discussed in 1974 with regard to the Sossi case with the then Interior Minister Emilio Taviani, and with Luigi Gui on another occasion. And the ominous threats were repeated: 'If things don't turn out this way it will be your fault, and, I say this without animosity, the inevitable consequences will fall on the party and on individuals.'

The accompanying BR communication gave a form of comment on Moro's letter. The liberation of prisoners was confirmed as being a fundamental aim of the organization, although Moro's comparison of himself with the imprisoned *brigatisti* was described as strictly his own, not their view. The government was warned that the BR would not tolerate 'secret negotiations, mysterious intermediaries, a covering up of facts'. And inevitably, there followed more polemic concerning the validity of the armed struggle in the overthrow of 'counter-revolutionary imperialism'.

The Strategic Resolution was dated February 1978, contained no references to Moro, but provided a resumé of

BR thinking on the current political system in Italy. The 'crisis of imperialism', according to the BR, was destined to end in a war of some kind, either as an inter-empire struggle between East and West over control of the Third World, or else in a 'class war in the imperial homelands'. The BR's aim was to bring about the demise of imperialism in Italy by speeding up the second alternative. Then followed a lengthy discussion of capitalism, of the EEC's co-ordinated attempts to bring about a counter-revolution by the introduction of anti-terrorist agreements, and of the various means used in Italy to 'control and repress' the far left. The PCI and its 'duplicity' in trying to maintain a line both of progress and of repression came in for abundant criticism. The document analyzed the various elements of society which the BR saw as having revolutionary potential, and emphasized the need and urgency to deepen the crisis, to 'dismantle the State until its collapse leads to civil war.' The BR's own history was discussed from its origins in small groups and brief actions called 'bite and run' to prolonged actions such as the kidnaps of Amerio and Sossi. Only by these prolonged actions against the state, it was explained, could they 'exalt and exasperate all its internal contradictions.' The document proceeded to analyze the entire revolutionary movement in Italy, now named as the Proletarian Offensive Resistance Movement (MRPO). The MRPO was described as 'an area of struggle and of partial movements, but nonetheless important and enduring'. Its ultimate destiny was to unite under the combined forces of the 'Fighting Communist Party', whose role was 'to dismantle the machinery of the State and put it out of commission; and at the same time to project itself into the mass movement, provide the politico-military signal to direct, mobilize, guide and organize the MRPO towards the anti-imperialist civil war.' It concluded with the affirmation that such a programme was not solely to be confined to Italy, but was part of a united European strategy to fight 'the monstrous, bloody machine of imperialism.' The revolution, it stressed, was 'necessary and possible.'

By publishing such a long revolutionary analysis at this

precise time, the BR were indicating that, in their minds, a particular phase of the Moro operation was over — the 'demonstrative action' had been executed successfully, the revolutionary initiative had been taken, the provocation given. But to continue the revolutionary spiral, to proceed to the next stage of insurrection, and thence to civil war, they were dependent upon the support of the masses.

The letter to Zaccagnini and selected passages of the Strategic Resolution filled the newspapers of 5th April. The DC's immediate response to Moro's letter was unequivocal: 'morally speaking it is not attributable to him'. Commenting on Moro's references to their earlier discussions about kidnap cases, Emilio Taviani denied that Moro had ever expressed a view in his presence in favour of negotiations with terrorists. His statement was given prominent coverage in the press, although little attention was paid to Luigi Gui, who confirmed Moro's own recollections.

What can be deduced from Moro's letter? Did he really believe in what he was writing? How much did the BR influence what he wrote? The BR would certainly not have allowed Moro to write anything which actively contradicted their own aims or ideology, and if he had written lines of deep sorrow for his murdered companions they would probably have been censored. Did Moro believe he would be killed? The fact that he had begun to stress the time factor more urgently suggests he may have been warned by his captors that if no positive mediation took place, there was only one possible solution. But the letter persists with the author's continuing hope and trust in his colleagues, with the belief, based on a considerable measure of self-importance, that he could not possibly be left to die after all he had done for his party, and because, as he stressed, the responsibility was not his alone but that of the entire party.

Moro's selection of Zaccagnini was quite deliberate — had he wanted to appeal to the highest authority he could have addressed himself to Andreotti or to Cossiga, but 'Zac' was Moro's own man, was of Moro's party faction. He owed his position as party Secretary to Moro and, as a close friend, surely represented the weakest link in the armour of rigour.

In this respect Moro touched a raw nerve. On Tuesday 5th April parliament held a debate on the Moro case. After 16th March this proved to be the one and only time throughout Aldo Moro's imprisonment that parliament debated the consequences of the attack in Via Fani and of the kidnap in full session. Zaccagnini received his letter during the course of the debate and, overcome with emotion, had to be helped out of the Chamber.

Recovering his composure, Zaccagnini hurried to the Moro family house, where his reception was chilly. Exasperated by the DC's intransigence, the family too was inclined to follow Moro's lead in singling him out for special blame. They had also had a letter from Moro that day (not published at the time) in which he asked for assurance about the family's state of health. At this stage the family members began to wonder how and if they could deal autonomously with the BR without involving the politicians, whose resolute refusal to open any form of mediation was, they believed, becoming an increasing threat to Moro's life. In the short term, they could at least respond to his request for news. A letter was composed and sent to the editor of *Il Giorno*, a paper to which Moro had contributed for many years. But before it could appear, another blow was struck against Moro's integrity and lucidity: the *l'Osservatore Romano*, having at first been inclined at least to consider the idea of negotiations, decided in an editorial that Moro was no longer in a position to express his own thoughts in his letters.

Realizing that of all the political leaders Bettino Craxi represented the view closest to their own, the Moro family invited him to come to the Via del Forte Trionfale for discussions. Amintore Fanfani had also made known his cautious approval of some attempt to initiate a dialogue with the BR, and through an intermediary, he was represented around the family table along with Sereno Freato, Moro's close friend and former secretary. Through Freato, another move was made which gave the family some grounds for hope. A Swiss lawyer called Denis Payot was invited to Rome on the strength of his past involvement in negotiations for the West German industrialist Hanns-Martin Schleyer. Although in the end Schleyer had been murdered, Payot had at least succeeded in opening a channel of communication between captors and negotiators. But just as the Pope's initial willingness to become involved had apparently petered out, so the possibility of Payot's intervention faded to nothing.

In both cases, it seems as if the Christian Democratic party acted to discourage any independent or unorthodox moves outside the government's jurisdiction. The party had brought pressure to bear on the Roman Curia, which in turn left the Pope isolated in his wish to mediate. It is also believed that the Swiss authorities were encouraged by the Italian government to create problems for Payot. The DC would later claim that Payot had acted indiscreetly and was something of a publicity seeker, but whatever the truth of the allegations, the lawyer claimed his attempts were being obstructed and after a few days in Rome, he returned to Geneva.

Thursday — Sunday, April 6–9

Noretta Moro's letter to her husband was published in the form of an appeal to the editor of *Il Giorno*, and gave a positive indication to Moro and to his captors that the family and the DC were henceforth to be regarded as separate interlocutors. Pointing to the need to open an alternative line of communication, the letter began, 'in this situation which permits us no contact. . . .', and stressing the family's isolation, continued, 'we have no sign which gives us hope for his return.'

On television that evening Enrico Berlinguer, Benigno Zaccagnini and Bettino Craxi confirmed that whilst every possibility for Moro's release should be evaluated, the state could not give in to blackmail.

On Thursday the inhabitants of a sleepy little village called Gradoli in the Province of Viterbo must have wondered what had hit them, for their rural peace was rudely shattered by the arrival of hundreds of police and carabinieri officials with sniffer dogs and machine guns who kicked down the doors of barns, sheds and chicken coops, and insisted on searching every house. For hours, helicopters circled incessantly overhead. They would have been even more bewildered had they known that the cause of the intrusion was a spiritualist seance held four days earlier in a country house near Bologna, the home of a university professor. The seance had been attended by 12 people, including a number of academics and industrialists, all linked either by friendship or family ties. What had begun as a game took on a more serious tone when the 'spirit' was asked for the whereabouts of Aldo Moro's prison. The resultant name of Gradoli was apparently unknown to all, but on production of a map, proved to be a village near Lake Bolsena. A report was duly made to the Bolognese police, hence the exhaustive but fruitless search. Tina Anselmi, a DC deputy and close family friend, went to the Moro home to inform the family of the seance and of the inconclusive visit to Gradoli. But Signora Moro was convinced there was a street called Gradoli somewhere in Rome, and urged a policeman to look it up. When he was unable to find it she appealed to a senior officer and also to someone in the DC, insisting that the street existed. She was again told it could not be found. In fact, Via Gradoli is on any comprehensive street map of Rome.

Over the 6th and 7th April, police made a number of arrests around the country, in Bolzano, Florence, and in Cosenza where four presumed *Prima Linea* terrorists were arrested. One of these was Fiori Pirri, ex-wife of *Potere Operaio* leader Franco Piperno. However none seemed to be directly implicated in the recent events in Rome.

On the 7th, Felix Schiavetti, President of the Genoa Industrialists' Association, was wounded in an attack for which the Red Brigades claimed responsibility.

On the 8th, Noretta Moro received another letter from her husband. For the first time, Moro seemed conscious of the death threat hanging over him, and used expressions of despair and bitterness. He was obviously well informed now of the parliamentary wrangles on his behalf, and, fully aware of the DC's firmness, complained that only [ex-President] Saragat and the Socialists seemed to be showing 'some slight indication of a humanitarian spirit'. Moro persisted in his attempt to demonstrate the logic and the historical precedents for an exchange of prisoners when necessity dictated: 'These prisoners go abroad and thus a certain relaxation of tension occurs.' The Sossi case loomed large again. Was this an encouragement to a sympathetic state to offer political asylum as Cuba had briefly done four years earlier? Once again Zaccagnini took the brunt of Moro's criticism, in particular for having urged him to accept 'this loathsome office' and thus his enforced separation from his family.

But the real message of this letter was a direct call to Noretta to take matters into her own hands. Having satisfied himself that her state of health permitted it, Moro encouraged her 'to put in motion a humanitarian movement. . . . Now it's up to you to see what you can do with your efforts both in PUBLIC and in private, because if this rigidity does not begin to crumble a bit my life will be over. And that means yours too, my dear ones, and that of the beloved little one. For me it would be a tragedy to die and abandon him. . . . My concern is Luca. I love him and fear for him without me. That will be the greatest loss.'

Who knows if a message was hidden in these words? They certainly show the unique spiritual rapport which existed between elderly man and little boy, and which caused each to exert a powerful influence over the other. Luca was an accident; his parents had not wanted a baby, believing the world they inhabited to be an unfit environment for the bringing up of a child. Before Luca's birth Aldo Moro had decided to give up the hurly-burly of politics and devote more time to his family and to his university teaching. But the extraordinary bond of affection which bound Moro to his first grandchild changed his mind and was the principal motive for his staying on, inspired by the hope that he could contribute to a better world for the boy to grow up in.

Monday — Friday, April 10–14

Spurred on by Moro's direct exhortations, the family began to investigate alternative means to negotiate a bargain with the BR. Giovanni was in contact with his former scout leader Giancarlo Quaranta, who had formed a group called the 'February '74 Movement', a religious cultural organization set up to bridge the gap between young Christians of the PCI and of the DC. Quaranta approached Enrico Berlinguer, who was sympathetic to the family's wishes but could offer no help, believing a categorical refusal to negotiate with terrorists was the only hope for Moro's release. Berlinguer repeated this conviction in a television broadcast on Saturday evening, when he pleaded with all Italians to co-operate in the hunt for Moro and his kidnappers, especially appealing to those who, for reasons of friendship or family ties, might be shielding the terrorists.

On Monday, six days again after their last message, telephone calls to newspapers in Rome, Turin, Milan and Genoa gave details of where the BR's Communication No 5 could be found. In Rome, an extract of Moro's 'interrogation' attached to the BR document, was found in a wastepaper basket in Via Palestro, near the centre of the city. In it Moro was controlled and lucid, but extremely angry, principally with Emilio Taviani for having misrepresented his views on the Sossi kidnapping negotiations. Moro quite specifically recalled the date and place in which their discussion took place, and expressed his amazement that Taviani should have so distorted his views. He accused Taviani of having moulded his political career along the lines of unprincipled opportunism, and speculated as to the close relationship which Taviani had had as Minister of the Interior with the Americans and West Germans, wondering, 'Is there, perhaps, in this hard attitude towards me, some American and German influence?' Taviani had been Interior Minister in 1974, the same year in which, in the course of a visit to the United States, Moro had been warned either to retire from politics or renounce his policies of political conciliation.

Communication No 5 announced that Moro's trial was continuing, and that he was helping to clarify 'the anti-proletarian lines, the bloody terrorist scandals which have extended throughout our country' which Moro had always covered up. Moro had their support in his denunciation of Taviani, 'the thug', who had helped to obstruct the XXII October Group's flight to freedom in 1974. But most of this message was directed to the MRPO: 'ORGANIZE . . . TAKE THE ATTACK TO THE IMPERIALIST STATE OF MULTINATIONALS. EXTEND AND INTENSIFY THE ARMED INITIATIVE AGAINST THE CENTRES AND THE MEN OF THE IMPERIALIST COUNTER-REVOLUTION'.

Setting an example, the BR attacked once more, this time in Turin, where a prison guard, Lorenzo Cotugno, was shot dead. One of the members of the commando team, Cristoforo Piancone, was himself wounded in the assault and was deposited at the gates of a nearby hospital. Had the authorities but known it, they now had the key to one of the mysteries of Via Fani in their hands. For on March 16th Piancone, who had spent many years in France, had exclaimed in French during the ambush of Moro and his bodyguards. But it would take two more years before the testimony of a 'repentant' brigadist would implicate Piancone in the events of that morning.

On the Thursday the DC National Committee met and reinforced its determination not to yield to terrorist blackmail. A government meeting the next day endorsed the decision.

Saturday — Monday, April 15–17

Another Saturday, and Italy almost seemed to have adjusted to the fact that one of its national leaders was in the hands of the Red Brigades. But the BR were soon to provide a forceful reminder — a phone call to the Milanese office of *La Repubblica* described where Communication No 6 could be found — in a wastepaper bin in the Via dell'Annunciata, just north of the city centre. Its message was quite clear — 'The interrogation of the prisoner Aldo Moro is concluded.' It had 'revealed the base complicities of the regime, has indicated with facts and names the true and concealed authors of the bloodiest pages of recent history, has laid bare the intrigues of power, the conspiracies of silence which have covered up state assassinations, has pointed out the link between personal interests, corruption and the favours system which holds together the various figures of the putrid Demo-Christian clan.' Nonetheless, it added, since the DC's corruption was public knowledge anyway, 'there are no clamorous revelations to be made.' And the verdict? The guilt of Aldo Moro and of the DC were identical: 'There is no doubt. ALDO MORO IS GUILTY AND IS THEREFORE CONDEMNED TO DEATH.'

Giulio Andreotti personally took upon himself the duty of conveying this message to the Moro family. The news, made public in the evening, caused uproar. Was the absence of any message from Moro a sign that he had already been killed? The family was at breaking point; 'It's the end, the end', Noretta Moro was heard to say. But self-pity was not in the family's nature. In collaboration with the February '74 Group, an approach to the International Red Cross was being drafted, as was an appeal to Kurt Waldheim, United Nations Secretary General. Whether or not the DC approved, the family was determined to use its own initiative in the search for a solution.

The next day the papers gave maximum coverage to the latest Communication, even giving it precedence over news of a national rail disaster in which over 40 had died.[12] Had Moro really talked, everyone wondered, and if so, what had he said? But on careful study, the document revealed a climb-down on the part of the BR. The fact that there were no 'clamorous revelations' was taken as a sign that, despite the BR bravado, Moro had given nothing of value away, and they were doing their best to compensate for this by stepping up their threats. With the pressure mounting, Giannino Guiso returned to talk once more to Renato Curcio in prison. Curcio told Guiso that Moro would almost certainly be still alive, but that some positive demonstration of a willingness to discuss terms was vital.

To the casual observer it seemed as if the Pope, tired and ill, had given up on Moro, for the Vatican's response to the latest BR threat was resigned: 'There is only one thing left to do — pray.'

After an impassioned conversation between Zaccagnini and the Moro family, the DC at last agreed to encourage an intervention by Amnesty International. Acknowledged as a pure sop to the family, neither the DC nor the PCI approved of the move, fearing that through it the BR would achieve one of their goals — political recognition of the BR's status as an adversary. Nonetheless, two senior government officials left for London's Amnesty headquarters, where they met the Secretary General, Martin Ennals. Amnesty's response to the request was immediate. On the strict understanding that it was acting purely for the well-being of an individual on behalf of his family and those close to it, and not for a government or political party, Amnesty International appealed to the BR to establish contact. There was no reply.

Meanwhile the attacks continued — two cars belonging to prominent DC members were blown up in Genoa and in Trento.

On the Monday the DC committee and the government met again and re-affirmed their intransigent line. It was inconceivable to sacrifice the legal and civil rights of a democracy for the life of one man. But the party was shaken by the announcement of the death sentence. The party newspaper *Il Popolo* brought out a special edition that day devoted to an analysis of the situation, and stressed the need to find some solution. At the base of the party the hard line seemed to be softening fractionally.

The family was especially anxious — the following day, 18th April, was a DC landmark, the 30th anniversary of the party's great electoral victory and the start of its uninterrupted reign of power. The BR had already demonstrated their fondness for symbolic gestures with the kidnap of Judge Sossi exactly four years previously. With Moro in their hands, would they pass up such an obvious opportunity? Noretta Moro telephoned Andreotti but was not consoled by his attempts to reassure her.

Tuesday — Wednesday, April 18–19

It looked as if Noretta Moro was right. In the late morning of the 18th, Communication No 7 was delivered to the Rome office of *Il Messagero*. On the basis of the thirty-year 'dictatorship' of the Christian Democratic party, it announced, 'the execution of DC President Aldo Moro has been carried out. . . . The body of Aldo Moro is submerged in the slimy depths of Lake Duchessa.' Comparing Moro's death to the 'suicides' of the Baader-Meinhof members in Stammheim prison, the BR warned that Moro's was 'only the beginning' and that 'the various Cossigas, Andreottis, Tavianis who uphold the regime should start to tremble.' The document immediately aroused suspicion — its style and tone were different to the previous communications, it had been photocopied rather than hand-duplicated and it had been delivered in only one city. But on being given the news, Giulio Andreotti for one was inclined to believe it, confessing that Moro's death, unfortunately, was 'to be expected'.

Lake Duchessa was some 80 kilometres to the north-east of Rome and lay at an altitude of 1800 metres. Inaccessible by road, it had been frozen over for five months and would require explosives to crack its icy surface. Nonetheless, helicopters, heavy machinery, dynamite, dogs and divers were enlisted for the search. Some 200 specially trained snow specialists from the carabinieri descended on the deserted zone, but to no avail. When the ice, several feet thick, was eventually broken up there was much excitement when a body was actually found, but this faded when it proved to be that of a destitute suicide who had been dead for months. The operation was deemed over, and Communication No 7 pronounced false.

But back in Rome there was some real action: at 9.40 am the inhabitants of an apartment in Via Gradoli watched in dismay as water leaking from the upstairs flat made an ever-widening circle of damp on their kitchen ceiling. Since the couple upstairs had left for the day, the fire brigade was called. Firemen put a ladder up to the balcony of the apartment, forced open a window and quickly turned off the shower head which was causing the flood. Before leaving, the firemen had a brief glance round. Lying on a table were documents stamped with the by now familiar five-pointed star in a circle.

Shortly after 10 am the building was surrounded by men and machines, sirens were wailing and lights flashing. Even the curious crowd of onlookers seemed to know that a Red Brigades hideout had been discovered. All things considered, it was hardly surprising that as Mario Moretti and Barbara Balzerani approached their apartment they changed their minds about entering and slipped away down a side street. There were rich pickings in 96 Via Gradoli: in addition to numerous BR pamphlets there were various types of hand bombs, bullet proof vests, military and police uniforms, false identity papers and false car number plates, including the original belonging to the Fiat 128 used to cause the accident in Via Fani.[13] From one of the windows it was possible to see the top of the houses in Via del Forte Trionfale, a mere three kilometres away. There was no indication that Aldo Moro had been kept in the apartment, but investigations would certainly have proceeded more efficiently had the elementary precaution of taking fingerprints been observed.

It was an odd coincidence that on the same morning police were involved on a massive scale in two separate locations, one inside, the other outside Rome. There has been much debate since on the possibility that attention was deliberately diverted from another action, such as moving Moro from one prison hide-out to another, while the forces of law and order were concentrated elsewhere.

After the failure of the Amnesty International appeal, the Moro family continued to look for an alternative line of contact with the *Brigate Rosse*, convinced that Moro was still alive. Although the line of rigour was still being maintained by all the coalition parties within the government, they were sure that there must exist a solid bedrock of support for some form of mediation within intellectual, cultural and religious circles. A letter was composed which was eventually signed by a cross-section of well known and distinguished figures, including ten bishops and archbishops, the Nobel prize-winner Heinrich Böll and two PCI deputies. The family did not add its name but its collaboration was understood. The letter was an appeal both to the BR to spare Moro's life and to the government to soften its inflexible line. But all efforts to have the letter published in the mainstream press were flatly turned down. Finally, Giovanni approached the editor of *Lotta Continua*, originally the mouthpiece of the far left group of the same name which had been dissolved in 1976 but was now an independent newspaper. In common with most of the New Left press, LC had taken the 'middle road' as far as the BR were concerned, following the line 'neither with the State nor with the BR.' The paper's editorial policy was that the BR had done only harm to the revolutionary cause by the murders in Via Fani and by Moro's kidnap, and now joined in the appeal to both sides for a negotiated settlement. The letter appeared on the 19th, but was given scant publicity by the other papers, with the exception of *l'Unità*, which devoted most of its coverage of the letter to explaining that the two PCI deputies who had signed had done so as private individuals without the knowledge or consent of the party.

Thursday — Saturday, April 20–22

Aldo Moro's imprisonment entered its sixth week.

On the morning of the 20th, three terrorists shot dead Francesco De Cataldo, deputy commander of prison officers at San Vittore prison, Milan. The BR claimed responsibility.

In Rome, Milan, Turin and Genoa the BR announced the distribution of an 'authentic' Communication No 7. In Rome it was attached to a photograph of Moro in which he held a copy of the previous day's *La Repubblica*. Denying any responsibility for the false communication, the BR suggested it was a 'grand spectacle' prepared by Moro's enemies to test public reaction to his death. Pouring scorn over the various 'humanitarian appeals' made to their better consciences, the BR came to their central point: 'The problem to which the DC must respond is political and not humanitarian. . . . The release of Aldo Moro can only be considered in relation to the LIBERATION OF COMMUNIST PRISONERS. . . . The DC must give a clear and definitive answer as to whether it intends to follow this path; it is clear that no other is possible. . . . The DC and its government have 48 hours to do this from 3 p.m. on 20th April — once this has elapsed . . . we will be answerable only to the proletariat and to the Revolutionary Movement, assuming the responsibility for carrying out the sentence pronounced by the People's Tribunal.' The expected ultimatum had arrived — the moment the DC had dreaded from the start. The photograph showed Moro, certainly wearier looking and with a harder expression than he had shown previously, but still apparently in sound health and strength. This was confirmed over the next couple of days by two more letters to the family, a letter to the Pope and a letter to Zaccagnini. Only that to Zaccagnini was published at the time. Attacking him for 'the ease, the indifference, the cynicism . . . in the course of these forty days of my terrible suffering', Moro complained, 'with profound bitterness and amazement I watched as in the space of a few minutes, without any serious humane or political evaluation, an attitude of definitive rigidity was adopted. . . . My poor family has been in some way suffocated, unable desperately to call out its anguish and its need of me. Can you all be in agreement in wanting my death for some reason of State?' The idea of death and dying was repeated obsessively in this letter. The only alternative, according to Moro, was the sending into exile of political prisoners, a solution which, he insisted, would bring about his release without the country's losing face. 'Let not a decision for death take place, I beseech you, as if exile would not satisfy them. . . . Dispel the impression immediately of a party united in a decision for death.'

Moro tried again to break Zaccagnini down: 'You think about this especially, Zaccagnini, the most responsible of all. . . . You have the greatest share of responsibility.' Thoughts of death also dominated Moro's letter to his wife. One by one it seemed to him as if those on whom he was counting to come to his aid were either proving unresponsive or unable to set even the most rudimentary mediation mechanism in motion. The DC was doing nothing and the Vatican too 'is denying its entire humanitarian tradition and today condemns me, tomorrow will condemn women and children to be the victims of those who will not accept blackmail.' But still Moro tried to rouse his wife: 'Try to have the courage to break this fictitious unanimity.'

The proof that Moro was still alive, plus the effect of the ultimatum, heightened the tension to fever pitch. Whilst the politicians debated their course of action, a 'mass of hope' was held in the Church of Jesus, next to DC headquarters.

Bettino Craxi's mind was now made up. Discussions with Guiso and other lawyers with experience of terrorist tactics had finally convinced him that the only way to save Moro was for the DC to display some willingness at least to begin negotiations. After consultations with his party committee, the 'line of rigour' was officially ruptured by the Socialist party's search for a 'line of mediation'. Guiso had advised Craxi that, according to the BR prisoners, Moro himself was the only one able to understand the positions of both sides in any bargaining, and consequently it was essential to 'engage in dialogue' with the hostage himself. No one expected prison doors to be flung open, but if the DC would only respond positively and assume its responsibility as an interlocutor, then a solution might be found.

At a meeting that evening, Craxi deplored the total lack of

success of the criminal investigations, and publicly criticized the DC for its refusal to acknowledge either the weakness of its position or the need to act. 'They only know how to make appeals and prepare Moro's funeral',[14] he exclaimed.

But the press appeared to share the viewpoint of the DC: *La Repubblica* saw the issue as one between 'sacrificing the life of a man or losing the Republic'; the editor of *Il Giornale*, Indro Montanelli, himself a past victim of BR bullets, had harsh words for those who hoped for Moro's release, since it would necessarily involve the state yielding to blackmail: 'If it were true that the DC might try to negotiate at the last minute . . . our anguish, far from being attenuated, would be redoubled. . . . For the DC it would amount to signing its own death warrant at the same time as the contract of barter. And the Honourable Moro alive would become the symbol of its shame. That is why we prefer to think of him as already dead. . . .'[15] For the Liberal party, any kind of negotiations with the BR would imply political recognition and would therefore symbolize 'the end of everything.' The PCI stood firm beside its 'no deals' stance, and attempted to stir up the support of the police and carabinieri to give its arguments more weight.

But Bettino Craxi and the PSI were not entirely without support; Amintore Fanfani was reluctant to add his voice publicly to the 'line of mediation' but gave Craxi discreet encouragement to press on with his initiative, and former Presidents Saragat and Gronchi spoke out in favour of the need to take some positive action.

The government's response to the ultimatum was substantially worked out by Friday evening. It was an attempt to combine a principled stand of absolute loyalty to the state and its institutions with an escape clause which recognized the desperate nature of the situation: the state would not yield, but it would listen. An intermediary was to be offered, in the shape of a charitable organization called *Caritas Internationalis*, through whom the BR could make known their specific demands. *Caritas* had made a telephone line available in Rome for this purpose.

Tina Anselmi, the only DC minister still welcome in the Moro household, went to inform the family of the government's response. It was she who had to bear the brunt of their rage and frustration.

With only hours to go before the ultimatum expired, the Pope read out a letter to the BR over Vatican radio: 'I write to you, men of the Red Brigades: restore the Honourable Aldo Moro to liberty, to his family, to civil life. . . . I beg you on my knees, free the Honourable Aldo Moro, simply, unconditionally. . . .' Trusting that humanitarian feelings would compel them to release their prisoner, he begged, 'Loving you nonetheless, I wait and pray for the proof.'[16] Twice the Pope addressed the terrorist group directly as 'men of the Red Brigades', thus in a sense officially recognizing them as a political force. On the other hand, his use of the phrase *senza condizioni*, 'unconditionally', placed his appeal firmly on a humanitarian basis, and was generally interpreted as a sign of positive support for the DC line of no concessions. The government's reply to the ultimatum was announced shortly afterwards. Predictably, the telephone lines of *Caritas Internationalis* rang throughout the night, both in its headquarters in Switzerland and in its Rome office. None of the calls was from the BR.

Sunday — Monday, April 23–24

A perceptive article appeared in *l'Espresso* magazine written by journalist Mario Scialoja. In it Scialoja attempted an analysis of the course of events from the BR's point of view, based on a reading of the documents and letters of the previous weeks. He came to the conclusion that there was a split in the BR over the outcome of the kidnap; that in effect there was a 'hard' and a 'soft' line, probably due to the respective positions of the Genoa and Rome columns of the organization. The latter would be more in favour of accepting a settlement which would result in Moro's being released, the former might favour the killing of Moro. Scialoja sensed the influence of Rome *Autonomia Operaia* on the soft line, and predicted that some statement would shortly be forthcoming from the Rome far left. In fact, Scialoja was basing his deductions on more than hypothesis.

In his attempt to find a means of communication with the BR, Bettino Craxi had built up a pool of people with specialized knowledge of terrorist matters. Amongst these was Scialoja, whose authoritative articles on the groups of the New Left were well respected. Scialoja was asked by Claudio Signorile, Craxi's deputy, to find a 'way in' to the BR. Thus when Franco Piperno came to *l'Espresso*'s offices with an article for publication, Scialoja asked him if he would agree to a meeting with Signorile. From this followed a series of encounters which, kept secret at the time, represented one of the main strands of the PSI's mediation attempt. Piperno denied that he was in direct communication with the BR, but thought he could probably arrange for messages to be sent. It was he who confirmed the existence of a split between 'hawks and doves' as regards killing Moro. The hawks, whom he believed to be in the majority, did not believe the government would concede anything to the BR, and thought Moro would inevitably have to be killed. Thus, Piperno argued, it was necessary for the DC to show some degree of flexibility in order to strengthen the hand of those in the BR who took the opposite view.

On the Sunday, Craxi took up another strand of his plan. Following Guiso's advice that it was necessary to 'engage in dialogue' with Moro himself, he studied the letters meticulously to look for a possible clue. In a letter to Zaccagnini, Moro had written, 'Some kind of opening, the adoption of some kind of position, some acknowledgement of the enormity of the problem . . . would be extremely important.' Craxi took this to be an indication that if the state were to make even a token dispensation to the BR then Moro's liberty might be obtained. With the aid of a computer, a group of lawyers under the guidance of Giuliano Vassalli (the man saved by papal intervention in 1944) began to research the category of prisoners in Italian jails who came

under the heading of 'political criminals' to see if any of them
could be released into house arrest or into provisional liberty
on the grounds of physical or mental illness without infringing
the law.

Rumours of a Socialist initiative prompted speculation that
some deal was being arranged to exchange Curcio for Moro,
and caused great excitement. The next day gave proof that
Moro had survived the ultimatum. Communication No 8 was
distributed to the usual four cities and in addition, a number
of letters were delivered from Moro to colleagues and family,
from which it was obvious his intellectual powers were
undiminished. But the usual medium for the transmitting of
letters had changed — instead of arriving either at Via Savoia
or being left for Nicola Rana to collect, the intermediary was
now a young priest called Don Mennini, a friend of Moro.

Moro had again written to Zaccagnini, although the letter,
intended for the whole DC leadership, was less personal and
bitter than the previous ones. For Moro, time was of the
essence now: 'We are almost at zero hour: it is more a
question of seconds than minutes. We are at the point of
death.' Humanitarian appeals were a waste of time; the
central issue was the exchange of 'some prisoners of war'.
Bemoaning the state's inertia, Moro called upon it to carry
out a 'simple act of courage'. But again he sensed a sinister
resistance — 'Don't think the DC will solve its problem by
eliminating Moro.' His final instructions were precise — no
state or party authorities were to attend his funeral: 'I ask to
be followed only by those few who have really cared for me
and who are therefore worthy to accompany me with their
prayers and their love.'

Another private (and at the time unpublished) letter
arrived for Zaccagnini which was more brutal, boring away
once more at his personal duty to save Moro — 'The
responsibility is yours, all yours.'

In each of the other letters, written to Moro's press
secretary Guerzoni, to Don Mennini and to Nicola Rana, was
a fervent plea to the recipients to stir up dissent within
journalistic, religious and political circles in order to put

pressure on the government.

With their 8th Communication the BR made their demands crystal clear for the first time: the release of thirteen named 'Communist prisoners' was demanded in exchange for Aldo Moro's liberty. Amongst the thirteen were Renato Curcio, Alberto Franceschini, Roberto Ognibene and even Cristoforo Piancone, one of the commando which had shot dead Lorenzo Cotugno two weeks previously. The list comprised twelve men and one woman, of whom only five were *Brigate Rosse*, the others being a symbolic cross section of the armed revolutionary groups. Only *Prima Linea* was not represented. Collectively, the thirteen had been found guilty of eight murders and were serving a total of three life sentences plus 172 years of prison.[17] The BR demands were published the following day to general public indignation. Panama gave the Italian government the chance to act on the demands by offering the prisoners a safe haven. The offer was declined.

Tuesday — Sunday, April 25–30

For some time, United Nations Secretary General Kurt Waldheim had been in contact with the Moro family and was waiting and hoping that the government would invite him to Rome to intercede for Moro. Craxi had also tried to induce the government to invite him but Andreotti was reluctant, fearing the consequences of a move which might put BR and the state on an equal footing. But Waldheim felt compelled to act. Twice, on 22nd and 25th April, he made appeals for Moro's release. The second and highly controversial appeal was given in English by satellite from the United States. First it reminded the BR of the anguish being experienced by Moro's family. Then Waldheim suggested to the BR that one of their objectives, that of publicity for their cause, had already been achieved in that the whole world was watching and waiting to see what they would do. Their purposes, Waldheim pointed out, would best be served not by Moro's continuing detention but by his release, which would be welcomed by all those who dedicated their lives to the creation of a better and more socially just world. The word 'purposes', translated into Italian as '*causa*', provoked an outrage and the personal accusation to Waldheim that he was not only giving political recognition but even encouragement to the terrorists' aims.

As if to counterbalance the Waldheim appeal, the DC collected the signatures of some 75 'long-time friends' of Moro, who put their names to a letter claiming that he was being manipulated and dehumanized by the BR in an attempt to destroy the DC and the state.

A number of other international contacts came under consideration towards the end of April: on the working hypothesis that the BR might have received assistance from the security services of one of the Eastern bloc countries, Sereno Freato persuaded the government to send an envoy to Yugoslavia to talk to Marshall Tito to persuade him to use his influence, if necessary. Tito promised to sound out his partners but in the end could offer no assistance. Signora Moro received a letter from Colonel Gaddhafi in which he offered his help but no solutions. The February '74 Group put pressure on Andreotti to ask the International Red Cross to intervene.

Another letter from Moro to his family begged them to give reassurances about their state of health.

As Mario Scialoja had predicted, the Rome *Autonomia* became progressively more involved in the debate over Moro's fate. Essentially the New Left pronounced itself against the eventual killing of the hostage, not for any reasons of humanity or compassion, but because the inevitable backlash of repression and political discrimination would be counterproductive for the revolutionary movement. Oreste Scalzone had originally stated his disapproval of the kidnap, declaring that the BR had brought guerrilla warfare 'to a level which the *Movimento* is not able to attain.'[18] But by 5th April he had begun to change his mind: 'We must stop arguing about the Red Brigades, we must think about the consequences of their actions; clearly the state has not emerged stronger since Moro's kidnap but weaker, a fact that opens up new opportunities; we must decide how best to exploit these opportunities, how to accelerate the process of destabilization'.[19] And on the 11th he was beginning to talk about the coincidence of forces necessary for the waging of a successful guerrilla war, in which a number of political and social conditions would permit 'a capacity for synthesizing the different revolutionary variables in a coherent plan.'[20] Scalzone had started to see the possibility of exploiting the Moro kidnap within the context of his own political aspirations. These had evolved since the mid '70's into the so-called 'Metropoli project', a broad-based scheme which extended over the boundaries of legality/illegality and the public/clandestine domain, and involved both peaceful and armed tactics. The legal face of Metropoli was a publication of the same name; its ultimate aim was the unification of all the revolutionary groups of the left into one homogeneous politico/military organization. The co-ordination for this attempt was to be provided through the groups Scalzone had started, principally in Milan and Rome, called Communist Revolutionary Committees (CoCoRi), and the funding predominantly from a systematic series of bank robberies. Amongst those who had been involved with CoCoRi were Luigi Rosati, estranged husband of Adriana Faranda, and Valerio Morucci.

Within the far left an internal bid for supremacy was taking place. Scalzone met BR leaders around this time and promised them a consignment of low-cost arms in exchange for their relinquishment of political control of the kidnap. But the offer was refused. Within the BR the hawks were in command, as determined in their line of rigour as was the Christian Democratic party in its inflexibility.

Towards the end of April the BR Executive Committee sounded out opinions throughout the various columns. It was generally agreed that Moro could not be released without some climb-down on the part of the DC. The members of the Committee came down unanimously on the side of killing

Moro; within the Strategic Directorate (of which Faranda but not Morucci was a member) only Adriana Faranda held out for sparing his life, convinced that Moro was discredited and finished as far as the DC was concerned, and that given the harsh criticisms of his letters, his release would be a greater threat to his party than would his martyrdom to its cause.

The BR's provocative demands for the release of 13 prisoners had undoubtedly made the possibility of serious mediation a less credible alternative to the firm refusal to negotiate. Craxi himself admitted that the BR conditions were 'absurd and unrealistic.' Nonetheless he persisted in his belief that some compromise might be found. On the 26th, with the solid backing of his party, Craxi proposed that the government should undertake an 'autonomous initiative' which in no circumstances could be seen to violate any legal or democratic principle. Professor Vassalli's team of legal experts had decided on two lines of possible approach which might induce the BR to show mercy to their prisoner; one consisted of the easing of restrictions in the country's special, or top security prisons, in which many terrorist prisoners were held, and the other was the granting of liberty to a left-wing prisoner on humanitarian grounds, a simple gesture of compassion to someone who, for reasons of health, could be released without danger to society or to democracy.

On the same day a letter from the Moro family appeared in *Il Giorno*, a response to Moro's request for news of them and their health. It was a simple confirmation of their love and affection.

The violence continued: on the 26th Girolamo Mechelli, a prominent DC member and former President of Lazio Region was wounded; on the 27th a Mirafiori manager in Turin was shot five times. Responsibility was claimed by the BR.

The country began to buzz with rumours about a possible deal along the lines of an 'autonomous initiative.' The DC prevaricated, repeating its 'no deals with terrorists' line; the PSDI came out against any relaxation of conditions in the special prisons but did not rule out the principle of an autonomous initiative completely. The Republican party utterly condemned Craxi's suggestion, believing it would only lead to 'the definitive ruin of Italian democratic institutions', and denounced it as a manoeuvre of pure political opportunism.

On the 28th Craxi gave a concise statement of the position which he and the Socialist party committee had assumed. It was both defensive and aggressive; 'The line of the [party] Committee, decided unanimously, is clear: no to giving in to terrorist blackmail, and no to the prejudiced refusal of any attempt to save Moro.' Trying to dispel fears that he was calling for mercy towards murderers, Craxi expounded his theory more explicitly: 'There are cases of prisoners to whom an act of clemency can be shown, as has happened in the past. . . . Naturally we are talking about cases in which there is an element of humanity. And this obviously excludes those who have blood on their hands, directly or indirectly'.[21] Zaccagnini, he affirmed, was encouraging him in this exploratory path. But as Craxi grew more determined, within the 'party of rigour' resistance was stiffening. The same day Andreotti went on television news and confirmed the government's absolute refusal to negotiate with terrorists.

Despite the massive injection of police manpower, investigations had produced few results. On April 24 arrest warrants were issued for nine presumed *brigatisti* in connection with the Moro murders and kidnap. However the evidence for the warrants was based largely on circumstantial evidence and on the testimonies of eyewitnesses whose names could not be used in a public denunciation for fear of provoking retaliation. The magistrate in charge of the judicial enquiries, Luciano Infelisi, was labouring under the almost impossible task of trying to co-ordinate investigations between three police forces (the civil police, the carabinieri and the finance police), the two intelligence services SISMI and SISDE and the two political and politico-technical crisis committees, as well as having to keep himself informed on day to day progress on the case. Furthermore he had not been relieved of any of his other judicial duties, nor given any extra staff or facilities to cope with the extra work load. Assisted only by a typist, Infelisi laboured in an office which did not have its own telephone, and even his most confidential calls had to be made from a coin-box in the corridor outside. The driving force behind the investigations was not only lacking in human resources but also in sound information. Since the re-organization of the security services in 1977 and the dismantling of the national anti-terrorist squad to make way for a new structure, details of intelligence operations and background material on terrorist practice were completely unavailable. The chief constable of Rome described his forces as 'without eyes and ears', trying to compensate in numbers for what they lacked in direction. According to Infelisi there were no data banks, no experts to give advice, no proper files, no one with any specialized information to advise or guide. During the entire period of the kidnap there was not a single written contribution from either of the security services. On April 29 responsibility for the judicial enquiries was taken from Luciano Infelisi by the Chief Prosecutor, Guido Guasco, and the arrest warrants of April 24 annulled. The reasons officially given were that the evidence to justify them was too flimsy, and that the delicate thread by which Aldo Moro's life was hanging would be further jeopardized by such a move.

In any account of Aldo Moro's imprisonment, Saturday 29th April is referred to as 'letters day.' Moro had been informed of the cross-currents of opinion and of the breakaway of the Socialist party from the line of rigour, and probably sensed that pressure judiciously applied might widen the crack in the government's defences. In all, 12 letters found their way to Noretta Moro, to Craxi, to the president of the Chamber of Deputies Ingrao, to the DC collectively, to individual leaders such as Andreotti, Fanfani, President Leone, and to a number of backbenchers who, Moro hoped, would be sympathetic.

The brief letter to Signora Moro was affectionate but urgent, beseeching her to make 'a protest and a prayer with all the breath in your body', and to disregard the advice being given her by others. Of the political letters the warmest was, not surprisingly, that to Bettino Craxi, the only politician in whom Moro sensed an understanding of his situation: 'Let me urge you to continue, even intensify your important initiative. . . . It must be made clear that it is not a question of making completely useless invitations to others to carry out acts of humanity, but to set in motion with due urgency a serious and reciprocal negotiation for the exchange of prisoners. I have the impression that people either do not understand or do not want to understand this.' Repeatedly Moro stressed that time was running out; matters were 'urgent, with only the slenderest breathing space': Craxi was to act with haste: 'Believe me, there isn't a minute to spare.'

In his letter to the DC, Moro tried his best to cajole, provoke and to reproach the party for its obstinacy, and was at pains to crush the 'unsound of mind' theory which he knew was being used against him. 'Why this support for my non-authenticity? Between me and the *Brigate Rosse* there is not the slightest common ground.' Still pressing home his prospects for salvation, he remonstrated, 'How can one deduce that the state will go to ruin if, every now and again, an innocent person survives and in return someone else goes into exile instead of to prison? It all depends on this.'

For the first time Moro mentioned an exchange of prisoners in terms of a single exchange, with the emphasis, 'it all depends on this'. In his letter to Craxi he had talked of 'a reciprocal negotiation.' Was this a way of saying that the release of one prisoner would suffice to meet BR requirements?

Reminding the government of an earlier exchange of prisoners in 1973, when Palestinian terrorists were released (after an agreement whereby no further atrocities would be committed on Italian soil), Moro persisted with his plea. In that particular case, he pointed out, 'the necessity for making an exception to the rule of law was recognized.'

Moro pulled out one last card: using his authority as President of the party, he called a full party meeting to discuss his case, at which he hoped the grass roots might rally to his support. But his concluding sentences returned to a tone of bullish pessimism: 'This blood bath will not turn out well for Zaccagnini, for Andreotti, for the DC or for the country. Each will have his responsibility to bear. . . . Let no one hide behind an assumed position of duty.'

The idea of a 'one for one' exchange gave encouragement to Bettino Craxi and his advisers. Giannino Guiso consulted the BR prisoners in Turin who thought it might be the absolute minimum the organization would accept.

On the evening of Sunday 30th, the telephone rang in the Via del Forte Trionfale. When Signora Moro answered, the voice on the other end of the line mistook her for one of the daughters, and announced himself as 'one of those who have something to do with your father.' The call, said the voice, was being made as a matter of conscience, as it was felt that the family was being misled by bad advice. There was only one chance left to save Moro's life, and that was a clear and unequivocal statement from Zaccagnini as to the DC's willingness to open up mediation. If this did not occur within the following few hours, the *Brigate Rosse* would have no option but to carry out the sentence of death. And even the BR, said the caller, did not take such decisions lightly.

Contacted immediately, Zaccagnini tried desperately to placate the family and defuse the situation, without in reality doing anything at all. But the Moro family had reached breaking point. They made one last attempt to unblock the line of rigour, making an appeal which was read to the press outside their apartment. It urged the party to summon a national meeting as requested by Moro, and castigated the overwhelming majority of politicians and the so-called 'friends of Moro' for their united assumption that he was 'effectively mad'.

Monday — Saturday, May 1–6

Labour Day. Demonstrations 'on behalf of democracy' were held throughout Italy. The family's appeal to the DC went unanswered, and their official severance from the party was made known. Out of 147 potentially suitable prisoners, Professor Vassalli's group put forward one as a possible candidate for release. Paola Besuschio was the one woman on the list of 13 named by the BR. There was no charge of wounding or of murder against her name, and she was ill. Giannino Guiso's reaction was tentative but encouraging. That day Craxi presented an outline of his proposal to Enrico Berlinguer in an effort to break down the PCI's unyielding stance, but Berlinguer would hear no talk of 'autonomous initiatives' or of political recognition, which to him were one and the same thing. If the DC were to agree, he warned, the PCI would pull out of the majority and cause the government to fall.

Five weeks after the anonymous telephone call giving the names of 5 people 'who should be watched', police enquiries had finally led to a small printing works in Via Foà run by Enrico Triaca. One of the suspects, Teodoro Spadaccini, had been tailed for some time and been seen getting into a car subsequently traced to Triaca. A report was duly made of the information collected thus far, and a request made to tap Triaca's private and business telephones. After this had been granted, a further request was made for a warrant to search the premises. Permission was given on 9th May, but the building was not searched until the 17th.

On 2nd May a PSI deputation confronted the DC leadership with the conclusions of Vassalli's legal team. In the course of a four-hour meeting, Craxi explained the methodology of the approach, and argued for a move which, he insisted, remained within the confines of legal and democratic boundaries. 'We cannot talk about negotiations, but rather about a humanitarian challenge, an act unilaterally and autonomously undertaken by the Republic.'

Within the DC committee some appreciation of Craxi's efforts was shown, but it was unanimously agreed that the party could not accept sole responsibility for such an act, and would have to consult the other majority parties. A decision was postponed, with promises to study the matter in greater depth. To allow time for this, the committee announced the postponement of its next meeting from Friday May 5th to Tuesday the 9th. Craxi reputedly became very angry.

The following day Andreotti presided over a meeting of the Interministerial Committee (CIS) which decided to investigate the question of the 'autonomous initiative' more thoroughly, on the understanding that no violation of the legal code was to take place.

But from various quarters within the Socialist party the tide of approval was beginning to turn against Craxi, as his party's political isolation deepened. Sandro Pertini was the first to break the PSI united front by declaring himself openly hostile to any concession to the terrorists. *La Repubblica* was in agreement; disputing the idea that an act of clemency was a realistic alternative to negotiation or non-negotiation, it proclaimed, 'the pretence of a third way is a lie behind which negotiation is being concealed.' The anti-Craxi feeling was deepened by a rumour that one of the widows of the bodyguards in Via Fani had telephoned DC headquarters, threatening that if a single 'assassin' was released she would set fire to herself in front of her children. The origins of this rumour were never established, and it proved to be entirely without substance. Signora Ricci, one of the two widows, even telephoned Noretta Moro to assure her that neither would dream of making such a provocative statement and that despite the loss of their own menfolk, they were in favour of a move that could restore Moro to his family. Nonetheless the story was widely believed.

In Milan and Genoa two managers of the companies Sit Siemens and Italsider were knee-capped.

At last, after 11 days of silence, the BR issued their 9th Communication. It was addressed to 'Fighting Communist Organizations, to the *revolutionary movement, TO ALL PROLETARIANS.* Companions, the battle begun on 16th March with the capture of Aldo Moro has reached its conclusion.' Indicating the DC's refusal to negotiate and its history of 'brutality and corruption', the document boasted of victory over 'the men of the imperialist counter-revolution' who had been unsuccessful in preventing further attacks or in finding Moro's prison. Harsh criticisms were passed both of the DC's stubbornness and of the superficial approach of the Socialist party, which, the BR claimed, 'ignored the real issue' of an exchange of prisoners. Then the communication came to its final message: 'We therefore conclude the battle begun on 16th March by carrying out the sentence to which Aldo Moro has been condemned.'

The only ray of hope in the entire message was the word '*eseguendo*', 'carrying out' from which it was assumed, Moro was still alive, at least at the time of writing.

On Saturday the last desperate efforts to save Aldo Moro were put in motion. Fanfani and Craxi went to Via del Forte Trionfale to confer with Noretta Moro. It transpired that after studying the Besuschio case, Justice Minister Bonifacio had decided that her release was impossible, as a further charge against her was still pending. However, another name on Vassalli's list was that of Alberto Buonoconto. Although not one of the 13, Buonoconto was a former member of NAP, had no record of violence to persons, he was due to be released within a short time from Trani prison, and he was very ill.

In the early days of May the secret discussions between Socialist deputy Claudio Signorile and Franco Piperno were continuing. They met for the third time around 6th May, this time in the presence of Lanfranco Pace. Piperno and Pace warned Signorile that matters were moving rapidly to their conclusion and that, according to their 'soundings', the DC had to act immediately to save Moro. The BR rumblings had ceased, and this could mean only one thing, namely that the final decisions were being taken. Signorile went to Fanfani and passed on the warning.

On the Saturday a large meeting of *Autonomia Operaia* was held in Rome university, attended by Oreste Scalzone, Toni Negri and Franco Piperno. The mood was predominently against the killing of Moro, envisaged in Scalzone's words as 'a political error of great proportions.' At Novara a prison doctor was shot in the legs.

Sunday, May 7

Alberto Buonoconto was moved from Trani prison to
hospital in Naples. The Moro family contacted Giuliano
Vassalli who in turn went to President Leone. Leone assured
the family that, in principle, he was ready to sign a release
order for Buonoconto if all the necessary legal checks showed
it would not be in violation of the law.

The Pope made his Sunday address from St Peters without
mentioning Aldo Moro's name.

In the evening Craxi had a meeting with PSI Senator
Landolfi and with Lanfranco Pace, who was a friend of
Landolfi. Pace told Craxi of his feeling that a personal
intervention by Fanfani might be decisive. Craxi's response
was confident — 'We have his word on it.'[22]

Bartolomeo, a close colleague of Fanfani, made a speech in
Tuscany in which a number of ambiguous allusions to Moro
were intended to show some movement on the part of the
DC; however, these were lost on the press who gave the
speech no exceptional coverage. Neither Craxi nor the Moro
family were reassured. That evening, Fanfani promised to do
more.

Monday, May 8

From his home town of Arezzo, Fanfani made a convoluted
speech in which he made a veiled criticism both of the
government and of Andreotti, and suggested that Moro's life
could be saved without infringing the legal code. But as he did
not explain whether he was supporting the PSI initiative or
was proposing an alternative solution, Fanfani's line
remained obscure. He promised, however, to clarify his
position in the course of the DC National Committee meeting
the following day.

A request for provisional liberty was presented to the
President of the Naples court on behalf of Alberto
Buonoconto.

Tuesday, May 9

The Socialist paper *Avanti* supported Fanfani's attack on the government. *L'Unità* criticized the speech vehemently.

The President of the Naples court studied the release request for Alberto Buonoconto. He decided to postpone any decision on the matter until he had a fuller report on the prisoner's state of health.

At 12.10 the telephone rang in the house of Professor Franco Trittò, Moro's university colleague and friend. The caller introduced himself as 'Dr Nicolai', then as an emissary of the *Brigate Rosse*. 'We are carrying out the last wishes of the President in communicating to the family where they can find the body of the Honourable Aldo Moro. . . . You should tell the family that they will find the Honourable Aldo Moro's body in Via Caetani, the second street on the left after Via delle Botteghe Oscure.'[23] Now in tears, Trittò listened as the caller described the Renault 4 in which Moro's body was concealed.

The news broke just as Amintore Fanfani had risen to make his speech to the DC Committee in the party's headquarters, a mere 100 yards from Via Caetani. The mud-spattered car was parked in the spot described. Fearing that it might be booby-trapped, police cut away the tail section of the car with saws. A crowd of hundreds hung out of windows, climbed lamp-posts and fought to have a better look as Moro's crumpled, lifeless body was revealed at last, partially covered by an orange blanket. Underneath it, paper handkerchiefs had been used to staunch the flow of blood. The face had two days' beard growth.

At 17:30 the family gave out its own last communication. Out of respect for Moro's wishes, as stated clearly in his letters, it requested that no public mourning and no state funeral should take place. It concluded: 'The family surrounds itself with silence and asks for silence.'

The post-mortem gave conclusive proof that Moro had been neither maltreated nor drugged during the course of his imprisonment. He had been shot ten times by a Skorpion automatic fitted with a silencer and once with a 9 calibre Browning without a silencer. Bullets lodged in the car bodywork showed that he had climbed into the car and had then been shot.

Strenuous efforts by the DC to persuade the family to allow a public funeral ended in the hasty, secretive transferral of his body for a private ceremony to Torrita Tiburina, the coastal resort where the Moros had a country cottage. Nevertheless, a state memorial service went ahead on May 13th in the church of San Giovanni in Laterano at which the Pope, now weakened even more by grief and illness, held mass. Signora Moro thanked him publicly but none of the family attended. Neither did Francesco Cossiga, whose resignation as Minister of the Interior had been tendered and accepted.

On the 11th the BR Turin trial resumed. Renato Curcio announced that murder could be 'the highest gesture of proletarian justice in a class-ridden society.'[24]

On the 15th, administrative elections gave the Christian Democrats a resounding victory and 40% of all votes cast. The Socialists advanced from just under 10 to almost 15%, and the PCI vote dropped by one third.

Alberto Buonoconto returned to Trani prison. He was released in 1979 on medical grounds but committed suicide in his home one year later.

President Leone resigned on 15th June when accusations of involvement with the Lockheed scandal made his position untenable.

Pope Paul died on 6th August.

References

1. *Commissione Parlamentare d'Inchiesta sulla Strage di Via Fani, sul sequestro e l'assassinio di Aldo Moro e sul terrorismo in*

   Italia, Vol. I, pp. 51.
2. *I Giorni dell'Ira,* Robert Katz, Adn Kronos, Rome, 1982, pp. 16.
3. Il Giornale, 18/3/1978.
4. *Il Tempo*, special edition, 16/3/1978.
5. *Visti da Vicino*, Giulio Andreotti, Terza serie, Rizzoli, Milano 1985, pp. 42.
6. *Comm. Parlamentare*, Vol. I., pp. 152.
7. *Frammenti . . . di lotta armata e utopia revoluzionaria*, Quaderno No. 4 di CONTROinformazione, Milan 1985, pp. 72.
8. The 9 Communications appear in full in the following text: *Moro, Una Tragedia Italiana, a cura di Giorgio Bocca*, Tascabili Bompiani, Milano, 1978.
9. Aldo Moro's letters from his 'people's prison' have been widely reprinted. The originals (with a few exceptions) are in the custody of the Fondazione Aldo Moro and are reprinted in Aldo Moro, *L'Intelligenza e gli avvenimenti*, Garzanti, Milano 1979.
10. '*L'Espresso 1955–1985, 30 anni di Terrorismo*', a cura di Enzo Forcella, Roma, 1985, pp. 48.
11. Brigate Rosse-Stato, Alessandro Silj, Vallecchi, Firenze, 1978, pp. 163.
12. ibidem, pp. 63.
13. Robert Katz, op. cit., pp. 123.
14. *La Repubblica*, 21/4/1978.
15. Alessandro Silj, op. cit., pp. 140.
16. Moro, Una Tragedia Italiana, pp. 129–130.
17. Robert Katz, op. cit., pp. 160.
18. *L'Espresso*, 26/3/1978.
19. *Comm. Parlamentare*, Vol. I, pp. 114.
20. *L'Espresso*, 16/4/1978.
21. *La Repubblica*, 28/4/1978.
22. *L'Espresso 1955–1985*, pp. 61.
23. *L'Affaire Moro*, Leonardo Sciascia, Sellerio Editore, Palermo 1978, pp. 124.
24. Quoted in Robert Katz, op. cit., pp. 232.

7
GUERRILLA WARFARE
TOWARDS DEFEAT
JUNE 1978–JANUARY 1982

Italy and the Italians were different after 9th May, both
publicly and privately. Outside the immediate grief-stricken,
embittered circle of the Moro family and friends, cynicism
was the most prevalent national emotion. Once the
excitement was over realism set in, and no-one was exempt
from criticism: the DC politicians were blamed for prevaricat-
ing and for having seemed unwilling even to talk, the
Socialists for being political opportunists, the Communists
for using the situation to gain political respectability, and the
forces of law and order for being inefficient. But most of all
there was horror at the BR's merciless treatment of their
hostage and at the indignity of Moro's death. The discovery
of his body in a dusty car down a Rome side street was
somehow shocking and unexpected.

One of the first repercussions of the Moro affair was a
widespread withdrawal from political commitment: turnout
at local elections was low, political meetings and rallies were
poorly attended. Politics at every level was tainted with
danger, indifference and inhumanity. The variegated groups
of the *Movimento* whose greatest expression of solidarity and

revolt had been the street demonstrations of 1977 went into fragments as fear and political persecution caused many to abandon revolutionary idealism in favour of safer pursuits. For those who remained on the side of the armed struggle there were two important changes after Moro: firstly, the battle between state and terrorists intensified, and secondly the Moro affair became the issue over which the entire revolutionary movement began to split and eventually decline. For example, from the spring of 1978 onwards the 'Walter Alasia' column in Milan under its leaders Vittorio Alfieri and Pasqua Aurora Betti began to operate semi-independently, in competition with and opposition to official policy.

In the northern cities, and in Milan in particular, new organizations emerged which tried to reduce the level of conflict to more social issues such as housing, unemployment and the increasing proliferation of hard drugs.

The Rome column had revealed its cracks during the kidnap with the opposition of Adriana Faranda and Valerio Morucci to Moro's killing. The couple remained for some months within the organization but their continuing obstructiveness and dissent from the BR tactics of cold-blooded murder led to incessant arguments, and violent threats were directed against them. In February 1979 Morucci, Faranda and five others left the BR, taking with them money and weapons for the formation of a new group in which murder, if not violence, was deemed unnecessary.

Inevitably, major changes took place within the police forces and in the judiciary. The fear of becoming terrorist targets drove some away and those who stayed became tougher. With Moro beyond redemption, police operations to trace his kidnappers were no longer obliged to tread such a delicate path. On May 17 the raid on the printing works in Via Foà finally took place (postponed from 9th May in the tumultuous events of that day). Inspection of the premises led to the immediate arrest of Enrico Triaca, Teodoro Spadaccini and three other members of the *brigata universitaria*. However the compartmentalization principle on which the

BR structure was based meant that their knowledge of the operation's organizers stopped at identification of Mario Moretti as the 'Maurizio' from whom they were accustomed to receive their instructions. This link was further reinforced by the matching of documents printed in Via Foà with those found in the Via Gradoli apartment occupied by Moretti and Barbara Balzerani. The Via Foà operation would have been more successful had a watch been kept on the premises after the police raid: a man later identified as Moretti turned up some days afterwards, but finding the building abandoned and its shutters down, he quickly departed.

When in June the BR murdered a prison marshal in Udine and the police commissioner of Genoa, newly-appointed Interior Minister Rognoni turned in desperation to the one man who had the necessary experience and intelligence to tackle the spiralling crescendo of violence. General Carlo Alberto Dalla Chiesa was appointed on September 1st on a one-year mandate (subsequently renewed for a second year) to revive the anti-terrorist force which had been disbanded during the reorganization of the security services in 1977. Dalla Chiesa's brief gave him the freedom to act virtually independently of the traditional structures of the judiciary, police and carabinieri, and made him responsible only to the Minister of the Interior. The results were immediate: Corrado Alunni, an early BR member and suspected (later cleared) of participation in the Via Fani attack, was arrested in mid-September.

On October 1st a raid on a BR Milan base in Via Montenevoso brought spectacular results — the arrest of 9 *brigatisti*, including Executive Committee members Franco Bonisoli and Lauro Azzolini, and the discovery of a wealth of documentary and archive material. Of most interest were outlines of letters written by Moro during his captivity, some of which were never delivered, others of which had been modified before being sent, with inclusions or exclusions obviously dictated by his captors: also a transcript of Moro's 'interrogation' which the BR were preparing to publish.

The topics upon which Moro had been questioned ranged

widely, and included the DC's political decision-making over the previous thirty years, the neo-fascist atrocities of Piazza Fontana and Brescia, corruption in the security services and the divorce referendum. The BR had also interrogated him thoroughly on his own political choices and his justifications for making them. From the style and language of the responses, the document is considered authentic.

For the DC the most humiliating aspect of the 'memorial' document was Moro's judgements on his colleagues, and on Andreotti in particular, on whom he spared no mercy. Admitting to an 'innate, unconquerable, forty-year distrust of this man', the description continued: 'a cold, inscrutable operator without doubts, without emotions, without a single ounce of human compassion . . . Andreotti, of whose orders the others have all been obedient executors . . . who will last a bit more or a bit less, but will disappear without trace.'

Benigno Zaccagnini was another target of Moro's bitterness: '. . . the pale shadow of Zac, sorrowful without sorrow, preoccupied without preoccupations, impassioned without passion; without doubt the worst secretary the DC has ever had.' Amidst speculation more damaging to its reputation than the merely embarrassing truth, the government allowed the transcript to be published.

Undeterred by the Milan arrests, the BR continued their campaign of violence, committing four murders and eight woundings between September and December. Most prominent amongst the murder victims was Gerolamo Tartaglione, Cassation Court judge and senior official at the Ministry of Justice. The wounded were industrialists and DC officials.

In October police investigations culminated in a raid on the apartment at 8 Via Montalcini, but its occupants, the 'Altobellis', alias Anna Laura Braghetti and Prospero Gallinari, had vanished. The latter had reputedly gone to Turkey in June 'for professional reasons' whilst his partner had removed furniture and belongings to an unknown destination just a few days previously.

In January the BR struck in Genoa, murdering Communist party and union member Guido Rossa, a labourer in the

Ansaldo plant, in retaliation for his denunciation of a fellow worker seen distributing BR leaflets in the factory. This occurred at a time when the PCI had issued thousands of questionnaires asking the public if they would inform police about suspicious persons or behaviour. The response had been poor. Nonetheless it nourished BR contempt for a party which it now considered beyond recuperation. In their eyes Rossa was a traitor and a spy. But the murder backfired: Genoa was a city with a proud working-class tradition and fierce loyalty to the Communist party. In condemning a worker to the same fate as their capitalist victims, the BR simultaneously killed off any remaining support in the ranks of party and union membership.

The BR's miscalculated murder of Rossa was paralleled five days later by the murder of Milan judge Emilio Alessandrini at the hands of *Prima Linea*. Despite Alessandrini's position within the state judicial system, he had won the respect of many on the far left for his investigations into the Piazza Fontana bomb attack, which he had doggedly maintained was of neo-fascist inspiration. It is believed Alessandrini had opened a major enquiry into the activities of *Prima Linea* members, and that this was the reason for his murder. Undoubtedly as an intelligent, 'reforming' judge, Alessandrini was bringing too much respect to a profession whose enemy status required continual justification in terrorist eyes.

Under the auspices of the Padua judiciary a major anti-terrorist initiative resulted in the arrest on April 7th of some 70 members of the extra-parliamentary left *Autonomia Operaia* including Toni Negri, Franco Piperno and Oreste Scalzone. According to judge Calogero these three were held to be the instigators or 'bad masters' of the entire terrorist movement, and according to the 'Calogero theorem' had deliberately piloted the dissolution of *Potere Operaio* in 1973 in order to reconstitute a new, clandestine organization with undiluted terrorist aims. A series of charges subsequently brought by Rome judges included detention of arms, armed insurrection and, in some cases, complicity in kidnap and murder. Negri was accused of being a leading member of the Red Brigades and of involvement in the Moro kidnap — his voice was identified (mistakenly) as that of the caller who had telephoned the Moro house on 30th April to urge the immediate intervention of Zaccagnini.

The aim of the '7th April arrests' was to prove continuity between the public pronouncements of revolutionary ideologues such as Negri and the clandestine terrorism of the Red Brigades. If there was some truth in the allegations of incitement to violence, the blanket accusations which enveloped *Autonomia* were the result of near-paranoia, ignorance and misplaced revenge. Albeit a prophet and preacher of revolution for years, Negri had repeatedly criticized the use of violence by a clandestine minority such as the BR, emphasizing instead the need for the masses to act spontaneously and together. In his words, the BR 'shoot, but have not the least idea of a revolutionary project which is realizable by the masses.'[1] The *Movimento* had been surprised and appalled at the gratuitous bloodshed of the Moro operation, and had 'underestimated the effect of a crazy variable — the BR — in the workers' struggle against the state . . . proletarian victory and your very liberation can only be the result of mass action.'

The difference between the revolutionary activity favoured by Negri and the ruthless, military actions of an armed vanguard was exemplified by the BR attack on May 3rd 1979 on the DC's Rome headquarters in Piazza Nicosia. The building was raided, documents seized, and in the gun battle that ensued as the commando team made its escape, two police and one carabinieri officer were shot dead. Dalla Chiesa took his revenge in a purge of the BR in Genoa, where he made 18 arrests and virtually wiped out the column. On May 29th there was more rejoicing as Valerio Morucci and Adriana Faranda were arrested in Rome. On September 24th Prospero Gallinari, Moro custodian and presumed material executioner, was captured.

Conditions in the factories had worsened during the year; crime of all kinds was rampant, from petty thieving and industrial sabotage to the intimidation, wounding and even murder of department heads, such as that of Fiat Executive Ghiglieno in September. In an atmosphere of suspicion and outright fear, morale reached its lowest ebb. As one Fiat employee remarked, 'Inside Fiat no one is in charge any more while outside the guns are firing.'[2]

With the exception of a hard-core minority, general indifference to terrorism had turned to disgust, but despite the arrests, the denunciations and the weariness, the violence went on. On October 2nd the Fiat management tried to restore order by dismissing 61 workers accused of 'indiscipline, intimidation and violence in the factory'. There were protests and the factory was occupied. But the unions were nervous, promising to provide legal defence only if the sacked workers signed a statement deploring the use of violence under any circumstances. Eight of them refused to sign. A number were taken back to work immediately, but comprehensively the tactic worked and was emulated by a number of other companies.

On two successive days in November the BR killed two carabinieri in Genoa and a marshal of the civil police in Rome. In December a Fiat manager was shot in the legs in retaliation for the sackings. On December 11th *Prima Linea* raided the Turin School of Industrial Management, took 190 students and lecturers hostage of whom they selected five of each, and proceeded to shoot them in the legs — a warning to the would-be captains of industry and their masters of the iniquities of their chosen trade. Four of the five lecturers were Fiat managers. This action marked the end of *Prima Linea*'s period of dramatic gestures. Beginning to fear exposure and arrest in a climate of increasing repression, the organization fragmented and many of its militants fled to France, where a network of Italian 'refugees' was already in existence.

By the end of 1979, the far left was coming under extreme pressure, with the implementation of several crucial changes in the law: the maximum period of pre-trial detention was extended by a third for terrorist crimes; the police could arrest on suspicion, and could hold a suspect for up to 48 hours without informing the judiciary (in practice, the period was often longer); and a suspect could be questioned by police in the absence of a defence lawyer.

Many laws such as these, passed during the most intense years of terrorism, were in fact revivals from the fascist era, introduced by a government with its back to the wall and facing up to its worst ever year for terrorist attacks — 2,513, or almost seven per day.

On January 8th the BR shot dead three police officers in Milan. Trying to rally the morale of the forces of law and order, President Pertini urged an intensification of the anti-terrorist struggle. The response was immediate — on February 12th Vittorio Bachelet, Vice-President of the Superior Judicial Council was murdered by the BR in Rome University. Between 16th and 19th March judges Giacumbi in Salerno, Minervini in Rome and Galli in Milan were also shot dead, the first two by the BR, Galli by PL.

But the tide had begun to turn. BR members Patrizio Peci and Rocco Micaletto were arrested on February 19th in Turin. Almost immediately Peci decided to 'talk'. His decision to turn state's evidence initiated the phenomenon of 'pentitismo' enshrined by law in 1982, whereby those who confessed their own crimes and collaborated actively in the prevention of further acts of terrorism were given significant reductions in their prison sentences. Despite its connotations, 'pentitismo' was assessed not by evidence of remorse or the sincere desire to atone for past crimes, criteria quite extraneous to the word's legal interpretation, but principally on the contribution made by the 'pentiti' to the arrest of former companions.

Peci's evidence would lead to the arrest of 85 BR members, as well as to the discovery of arms stores, documentary material and bases. After Dalla Chiesa's round-up the previous year there was little left of the Genoa column, but Peci helped to eliminate it completely by directing police to a base in Via Fracchia which was raided at dawn on March 28th. The four BR members inside put up token resistance, but the carabinieri took no chances and killed them all.

Prima Linea leader Roberto Sandalo, captured on April 29th, would follow Peci's example, although his revelations extended beyond the incrimination of his former companions. A few days before Sandalo's arrest, his close friend and fellow PL militant Marco Donat-Cattin had escaped to France. Sandalo informed the authorities that Donat-Cattin's father, who was Deputy Secretary of the Christian Democratic party, had warned his son on Prime Minister Cossiga's advice to leave the country. The implications for Donat-Cattin and Cossiga were extremely damaging — Donat-Cattin resigned from party office and the allegations against Cossiga were examined by a committee of enquiry to ascertain whether they justified the bringing of legal proceedings. Cossiga escaped the law courts but resigned as Prime Minister in September to be replaced by his DC colleague Arnaldo Forlani. Donat-Cattin junior returned to the Italian border, gave himself up and — together with Sandalo — was granted a light sentence in exchange for turning state's evidence.

Throughout May 1980 attacks continued, with the BR murders of an anti-terrorist squad inspector in Mestre (near Venice) and of a DC regional councillor in Naples. Meanwhile in Milan a new formation arose whose name, 'March 28th Brigade', commemorated the four BR killed in Genoa. It was composed of six well-heeled young Milanese, barely out of school, who hoped to demonstrate to the BR that they were grown-up militants capable of serious actions such as wounding and murder, and therefore worthy to become members of the organization. The leader of the group, Marco Barbone, had first come under the ideological influence of Tini Negri before progressing to active militancy in the *Formazioni Comuniste Combattenti* with Corrado Alunni.

The members of the March 28th Brigade moved freely through the upper echelons of journalism and publishing thanks to parental connections, and exploited the facility to collect data on targets in the media. Early in the morning of May 7th *La Repubblica* journalist Guido Passalacqua opened the door to callers claiming to be the police. He was tied up by his assailants (one of whom he recognized) and as one held a pistol in his mouth, another shot him in the legs. But Passalacqua was lucky, the next victim of the group, *Corriere della Sera* journalist Walter Tobagi was murdered on May 28th. Tobagi was a well-known and respected figure both on the paper and in his capacity as President of the Lombardy Journalists' Association. He had been warned that his name was on a hit list of 46 journalists, judges and lawyers discovered in January 1979, but beyond a few elementary precautions he had done little to remove himself from danger. The members of the March 28th Brigade were arrested in October on charges unconnected to Tobagi, but Barbone and his accomplice Paolo Morandini quickly confessed to their crimes and turned *pentiti*. Acting on their evidence, police made many arrests.

After a series of court trials in the mid '70's revealing the 'strategy of tension' proposed by the neo-fascists and the involvement of corrupt members of the security services, the far right threat had been deemed to be effectively over. In the absence of sympathetic regimes in Spain, Portugal and Greece to provide either refuge or active support, it was assumed that the neo-fascists had given up their hopes of bringing about a military dictatorship through the '*stragismo*' or slaughter tactics, which had characterized the period 1969–1974. In fact, although the years 1975–1980 were dominated by left-wing terrorism, statistics show that of the 8,400 terrorist attacks in the period, just over 35% were attributed to the far right, clearly far from dormant.[3] But the tactics, if not the ideology, had changed. The main neo-fascist groups of the late '70's, *Terza Posizione* (Third Position) and *Nuclei Armati Rivoluzionari* (Armed Revolutionary Nuclei) had taken to emulating left-wing tactics by attacking individuals and other symbols of the democracy they wished to destroy.

But *stragismo* returned on August 2nd 1980, to gruesome and tragic effect: a bomb exploded in the 2nd class waiting room of Bologna station, killing 85 and wounding 177. A document found afterwards would dispel any illusion that the neo-fascists had renounced their former aims: 'We must reach a point where not only aeroplanes but boats, trains and roads are unsafe. We have to restore terror and paralysis to the movement of traffic. . . . Let us give an unmistakable sign of our presence . . . we need to cause an explosion from which only ghosts will emerge.'[4]

In the factories, shrewd industrial management finally brought its reward. A dismissal announcement had led to the occupation of the Fiat factory in late September, but when Fiat offered to lay off workers on 90% of pay for up to 3 years, opposition crumbled. On the 35th day of the occupation 40,000 marched through the streets of Turin demanding the reopening of the factory and the right to work.

In Milan the 'Walter Alasia' column claimed to be the last line of resistance to the restructuring of industry. Its membership, 100–150 strong and almost entirely factory-based, aimed to reinstate the factory worker as the central figure in the revolutionary process. Although their BR membership was not revealed, the column members made no secret of their politics and, initially at least, enjoyed the confidence of their fellow workers, who in many cases elected them on to factory councils and committees, fully aware of the implications of their vote. Had their tactics remained at the level of early BR actions they might have retained that support. However, in November the 'Walter Alasia' murdered Renato Briano, personnel manager at the Magneti Marelli factory and Manfredo Mazzanti, technical director of Falck. In February 1981 they attempted to extend their field of concern to the poorly-paid grades of hospital ancillary staff, murdering Milan Policlinico director Luigi Marangoni. Judging these actions to be undisciplined and misguided, the BR Executive Committee expelled the 'Walter Alasia' from the organization.

The original BR leadership also disapproved, and passed

judgement on the renegade column in a document written in prison the following October, criticizing the 'Walter Alasia' for giving too narrow a definition to the armed struggle, and of concentrating on the factory worker to the exclusion of the non-producers, the unemployed and the prison population. The Milan group was accused of bringing 'outdated interpretation and fossilized ideology'[5] to contemporary issues and of seeing the state as an ensemble of static 'things' rather than as a dynamic force concentrated on the continual maintenance of the class system.

By the end of 1980, the Red Brigades were the only armed revolutionary organization still capable of challenging the state and its institutions, its isolation and tightly-knit military structure partly shielding its membership from the revelations made by the *pentiti*. Nevertheless, some 3,000 left-wing militants were now detained in Italy's prisons. The BR focus of attack changed accordingly: 'the heart' which kept the state alive was no longer represented by DC politicians, but by those who controlled and pumped life through the arteries of the prison system.

In 1977, General Dalla Chiesa had been given overall responsibility for prison security, and had immediately inaugurated a series of 'special' or top security prisons in which those considered particularly dangerous or likely to escape were detained, including many prominent BR and PL members. The huge influx of prisoners from 1980 onwards meant that already deteriorating conditions were aggravated by overcrowding, drug problems and the tension and suspicion caused by the declarations of 'penitent' prisoners.

Now under the control of Giovanni Senzani, the Rome column of the BR murdered the health inspector of Regina Coeli prison on December 1, 1980 and on the 12th, kidnapped Judge Giovanni D'Urso, senior official in the Ministry of Justice, and responsible for the allocation of prisoners to the special prisons. Senzani was a criminologist whose researches had given him first-hand knowledge of the penal system and its structures. He had worked in the Ministry of Justice for some years and had been a colleague of judge Giuseppe   De

Gennaro, kidnapped briefly by NAP in 1975. In the late '70's Senzani founded a group called the Tuscan Revolutionary Committee which had provided considerable aid to the Rome column during the planning and execution of the Moro kidnap operation. Senzani was ambitious both for himself and for the BR, whose leadership he hoped to wrest from the dedicated militarist Mario Moretti. His own programme for the future centred on two specific areas: the expansion of the *Fronte delle Carceri* (Prison Front) in a concerted attack on the prison system from without and from within; and the encouragement of the revolutionary potential within the proletarian masses of southern Italy through a 'guerrilla party of the metropolitan proletariat.' But first, he put his professional experience to work in Rome.

The kidnap of judge D'Urso was carried out to fulfil objectives of which, in typical BR style, some were symbolic, others practical. As with previous kidnaps, the BR made their aims known through the issue of written communications whose whereabouts were given in telephone calls to newspapers or press agencies. The first demand was the closing of the special island prison of Asinara, off Sardinia. With surprising alacrity, the Forlani coalition government conceded the request, and an order to close the prison was given on December 24th. Under attack for the apparent show of weakness, DC Justice Minister Sarti protested that the closure had already been envisaged. Even President Pertini tried to prevent it but could do nothing. On the 28th a riot broke out at Trani prison during which 70 prisoners took 18 guards hostage. The revolt was forcefully crushed. Three days later the BR murdered the official responsible for security in the special prisons, General Enrico Galvaligi. The chances given for D'Urso's own survival were estimated to be around 50%.

During the first few days of the kidnap, approximately half of the press and media declared a voluntary blackout on the affair, but its very partial nature rendered this largely ineffectual. Those who chose could buy the 'non-blacked-out' papers or watch the television news programme controlled by the Socialist party rather than the DC-run channel which had opted for silence. As the kidnap progressed, the ambiguity of the situation was exploited and manipulated by the BR. As part of their bid to focus public attention on prison conditions, the kidnappers insisted on the publication of certain documents written by those in Trani and Palmi special prisons who had formed 'Action Committees of Prisoners Accused of Terrorism.' In Trani these included BR members Piccioni and Seghetti; in Palmi Renato Curcio, Alberto Franceschini and Corrado Alunni. The written material was entrusted to a delegation of Radical party deputies who visited the prisons to see conditions for themselves and to attempt some form of mediation.

The D'Urso family devoted most of the first week of January 1981 trying to persuade newspaper editors to print the documents, even offering money in exchange, as D'Urso himself had suggested in one of his letters from 'prison.' On January 4th the BR announced that D'Urso's 'trial' was over, his guilt had been established and his death sentence pronounced — a sequence of events parallel to the Sossi and Moro kidnaps. But this time power of life and death was not closely guarded by a handful on the Executive Committee, it was delegated by the kidnappers to the Action Committees in Trani and Palmi. On the 10th the ultimatum was issued — the 'major organs' of the mass media were to transmit the text prepared by the Committees within 48 hours or D'Urso would be killed. The Action Committees were to decide whether or not they were satisfied with the response.

Before the debate over publication began, *L'Espresso* journalist Mario Scialoja and a colleague were approached by a BR 'representative' and invited to submit a number of written questions to D'Urso's captors. Not only did Scialoja receive replies to these and to questions made up by the BR, but also an extract of the judge's 'interrogation', a photograph of D'Urso sitting under a BR banner and a copy of the latest BR communication. These were published in full (with the exclusion of one or two names) on January 11th. Senzani was clearly an astute and persistent questioner, alternating between asking probing questions on the organization of the special prisons, the rationale behind prisoner allocation and the hierarchy of responsibility for discipline and supervision, and accusing D'Urso of gross incompetence, cruelty and negligence. Replies were given to Scialoja's questions on the Moro kidnap, current BR strategy and on the specific reasons for seizing D'Urso. The BR had taken a new direction and wanted this known.

The overall aim of the operation was firstly, 'to deal a blow to the stragegy of proletarian annihilation and to indicate those responsible for it',[6] and secondly, 'to open up a political space for those in prison to express themselves.' As a representative of the state prison system which the BR hoped to destroy, D'Urso embodied 'the fundamental tool of the preventive counter-revolution.' Nonetheless, he was 'collaborating with proletarian justice' and had 'implicated all his colleagues near and far'.

Senzani also used the columns of L'Espresso to give the BR standpoint on other matters. The spate of pentitismo, he warned, would bring revenge on those collaborating with the authorities, who could consider themselves 'walking corpses.' When asked to defend the murder of bodyguards such as Moro's, who were frequently members of the proletariat, Senzani came back with a scornful reply reminiscent of that made by the BR defendants in Turin after the triple murder of Coco and his guards in 1976. The principle was the same, they were 'mercenaries in uniform', had 'sold their class identity to the bourgeoisie and its interests, betrayed their origins and have transformed themselves into ferocious assassins of the proletariat.' But before copies of L'Espresso went on sale at the news stands, Mario Scialoja and his colleague were in prison, arrested on the charges of 'reticence and complicity with terrorism'. (They were subsequently acquitted).

Despite impassioned pleas by the D'Urso family, most national newspapers defied the ultimatum and refused to print the terrorist tracts. A number of papers did publish the documents, including the official Socialist party paper

Avanti. The parties of the governing coalition declared a 'non-negotiation' stance with regard to the terrorists, but took no official part in the press debate.

Most involved in the whole affair was the Radical party: not only did Radical Radio transmit the entire text of the Trani and Palmi documents, but on January 11th, the party put its television time on the programme *Tribuna Politica* at the disposal of the D'Urso family, during which D'Urso's 14 year-old daughter read a passage from the BR document calling her father 'that pig D'Urso who deserves to be condemned'.

The incarcerated terrorists pronounced themselves satisfied with the result of their propaganda campaign and D'Urso's captors released him on January 15th. From the BR point of view the action had been hugely successful; it had resulted in the closing of Asinara, the mass diffusion of propaganda and the humiliation of a senior representative of the state. Furthermore it had soldered the interests and sympathies of those inside prison to the strategy and objectives of the external organization, exactly as Giovanni Senzani had planned.

D'Urso's kidnap represented the first direct terrorist challenge to the state since Moro, and as such the changes on both sides were illuminating. One major difference between 1978 and 1981 was the absence from the government coalition of the PCI, which meant the party's resistance to any form of terrorist negotiations was unable to influence the course of events directly. Secondly, as one of Italy's post-war architects, Moro was a symbol of the state itself; although D'Urso also represented the state he was merely a government official performing his official functions. For the state to have given ground in 1978 would have implied yielding up a part of itself as well as part of its sovereignty — the same could not be said in 1981. However, the biggest factor of all was the besieged condition of the judiciary: Giovanni D'Urso was kidnapped at the end of a year in which five judges had died at terrorist hands. The good will and support of those who administered the government's laws had to be safeguarded and recompensed with adequate protection.

Following his successful handling of the D'Urso kidnap, Giovanni Senzani's position in the BR was further consolidated in April when a tip-off from a police informer in Milan led police to the arrest of the hitherto elusive Mario Moretti, putting an end to Moretti's 11 years of clandestinity and his six-year leadership of the organization. Some optimists predicted that the BR were finished, but between April and July 1981 the organization undertook four kidnaps simultaneously in different parts of the country.

The kidnapping of DC regional councillor Ciro Cirillo in Naples on April 27th put the second phase of Senzani's project into motion — the attempt to unify and politicize the urban masses of the south in a 'guerrilla party of the metropolitan proletariat.' Cirillo was seized from his car after both his driver and bodyguard were killed. The BR's initial demands centred on the requisition of houses for earthquake victims in Irpinia and distribution of benefits to those on the unemployment register in the area. Senzani also hoped to prove that Cirillo was involved in building speculation, financial corruption and mismanagement of the earthquake funds.

The second kidnap took place on May 20th at the other end of the country in the industrial centre of Porto Marghera, and was carried out by the Veneto column under the leadership of Antonio Savasta (who had run the *brigata universitaria* at the time of the Moro kidnap). The victim was Giuseppe Taliercio, director of the Montedison petrochemical plant, considered responsible for restructuring and therefore for a series of redundancies in the factory. The third hostage was another industrialist, engineer Renzo Sandrucci, manager of the Alfa Romeo factory in Milan and kidnapped by the 'Walter Alasia' column. Sandrucci was in charge of the organization of work within the factory, and thus in the BR's eyes responsible for the maintenance of maximum productivity at the expense of an exploited workforce. He was kidnapped on June 2nd as part of a bid to prevent Alfa from implementing the 500 redundancies which had been announced.

The fourth kidnap was an undisguised act of revenge, as had been promised by Senzani in his *L'Espresso* interview. Roberto Peci, younger brother of the *pentito* Patrizio, was seized on June 11th; the main motive being to use Roberto to stem the tide of *pentiti* such as Patrizio, showing what reprisals would be taken against those who collaborated and betrayed. Under pressure from his captors, Peci wrote letters pleading with his brother to renege on his evidence and to admit to being a police informer prior to his 'official' arrest in February 1980. When no such response was forthcoming, the BR tied Peci up in a disused shed on a stretch of waste land near Rome on August 3rd and shot him 11 times. The assassination was filmed and the video sent to the authorities.

Negotiations between the Veneto column and the management of Montedison failed to produce positive results for the terrorists, and Taliercio's body was dumped in a car on 6th July.

Within the spectrum of 1980's terrorism, the Sandrucci kidnap was unique in that it aroused little disapproval from the Alfa employees, who demonstrated in their thousands during his captivity to call for the revocation of the redundancy announcement. From the outset the 'Walter Alasia' column had decided that neither Sandrucci nor his accompanying bodyguard was to be physically harmed, and devoted much of the 51 days of his kidnap to interrogating him at length on the objectives and strategies of the company. When on July 23 the redundancy orders were rescinded, Sandrucci was immediately released.

In the case of Cirillo the BR won not only humanitarian but also substantial financial concessions: it seems that the ransom sum of 4½ billion lire (approx £2,250,000 or $4 million) was the result of co-operation between the Christian Democratic party, the Camorra, the Red Brigades and a section of the Italian military security service, SISMI. Only a third of this sum is believed to have found its way to the kidnappers themselves, the Red Brigades, the destination of the rest is unknown. The negotiations included discussions in the prison of Ascoli Piceno between imprisoned Camorra boss Raffaele Cutolo, a representative of the BR prisoners from Palmi prison, SISMI General Pietro Musumeci and his deputy Belmonte, and Francesco Pazienza, who enjoyed a privileged relationship both with SISMI and with the then DC Secretary, Flaminio Piccoli, whose confidant he was.

It is believed the ransom money was raised from security services funds, from the family's own efforts amongst DC business men in Naples and from Roberto Calvi's Banco Ambrosiano. However investigations have been hindered by the disappearance of prison records listing visits to Ascoli Piceno for the period, by the absence of security service files on the matter, and doubtless by the fact that Musumeci and Belmonte are themselves in prison with convictions for corruption, embezzlement and for having deflected enquiries into the bomb explosion at Bologna station.

If the Christian Democratic party could participate in such an operation, or at least stand by as convicted criminals directed the paying of ransom sums to companions who would undoubtedly continue to shoot, steal and extort, then this was an astonishing evolution from the 'days of rigour' enforced in 1978. Not only was the deal struck in the immediate aftermath of three murders (of Taliercio, Cirillo's driver and his bodyguard) but during the captivity of two other hostages, Peci and Sandrucci, for whose fate the negotiations could have had unpredictable consequences. But the era of *pentitismo* had begun, and with it a period in which practical expediency would triumph over abstract ideals of morality and justice.

In the autumn of 1981 most of the leaders of the 'Walter Alasia' column were arrested, leaving the Veneto column the most active group within the Red Brigades. Hoping to regain the ground lost by defections, political isolation and *penititismo*, and to benefit from the rapid growth of the peace and anti-nuclear movements, the brigadists decided to internationalize their challenge to the state with the kidnap of General James Lee Dozier, commander of the NATO land-based forces in southern Europe. The action may even go back to an arms deal made three years earlier in Paris, where using a Red Army Faction intermediary, Mario Moretti met a member of the Palestinian Liberation Organization. Impressed by the BR proficiency during the Moro kidnap, the PLO was keen to use the BR to store arms and to commit anti-Israeli actions on its behalf in Europe. In the summer of 1979 Moretti and two others went by boat to Cyprus where they collected a large consignment of heavy and light arms. The light arms (predominently Sterling sub machine guns) remained in Italy, the heavy weapons were passed on to the IRA and ETA. The BR committed no anti-Israeli actions but the choice of an 'imperialist' target such as Dozier may have been a gesture of solidarity with the Palestinian cause and a recognition of past or hoped-for future help.

In the absence of any knowledge of NATO rankings on the part of the BR, identification of the most suitable victim was a major problem, finally solved by the purchase of a box of lead soldiers in a Verona toy shop which contained full instructions as to how to paint on the soldiers' ranks correctly. After a number of reconnaissance trips, Dozier was singled out as most senior officer at the NATO base. His kidnap was a relatively simple matter as he travelled unescorted and his apartment was unguarded. He was seized from his home on December 17th, 1981.

The choice of victim naturally aroused world interest, not least on the part of the Eastern bloc, whose attempt to influence the course of the kidnap has been affirmed. On the grounds that the forthcoming installation of Cruise missiles on Sicily would make Italy the 'diamond point' of NATO, it is believed the Bulgarian security services offered the BR arms and money in exchange for political control of the kidnap, although discussions apparently foundered at an early stage. Dozier was liberated in Padua on January 28th, 1982, by a special assault group of the police force. The driver of the

kidnap escape vehicle, arrested during a visit to his girlfriend
whose house was under surveillance, was persuaded to lead
police to the hideout where the hostage was found unharmed
and his captors surrendered without a struggle. Subsequent
allegations of torture of the BR prisoners by four members of
the special police unit were upheld by a Padua court but were
quashed two years later on appeal in Venice.

With the dismantling of the Veneto column after the arrest
and 'penitence' of the Dozier kidnappers, followed by the
capture in Rome in January of Giovanni Senzani, the Red
Brigades dynasty was decimated. Only in Naples did
Senzani's leaderless column continue with its 'spring
campaign' of four murders (carried out, it is thought, with the
collaboration of the Camorra) before its members headed for
Turin where they too were captured.

References

1. Reproduced from *Rosso* magazine in *Il Caso 7 Aprile*, Giorgio
   Bocca, Feltrinelli Editore Milan, 1980, pp. 142.
2. '*La Repubblica*,' 11/10/79.
3. '*Rapporto sul Terrorismo 1969–1980*', a cura di Mauro Galleni,
   Saggi Rizzoli, Milano 1981.
4. Quoted in '*La Destra Eversiva*' by Franco Ferraresi in
   '*Terrorismi in Italia*', a cura di Donatella della Porta, Società
   Editrice Il Mulino, Bologna 1984, pp. 287.
5. '*Frammenti . . . di lotta armata e utopia rivoluzionaria*,'
   CONTROinformazione, Milan 1984, pp. 112.
6. '*L'Espresso*' 11/1/81.

8
PENITENCE, DISSOCIATION, FORGIVENESS AND SILENCE

A study of the penal system and the way it is administered within a democracy generally provides an accurate reflection of the country's political and public attitudes towards crime. Italy is no exception.

The Reale Law of 1975, the first expressly introduced to deal with the problem of terrorism, was largely the result of the 'strategy of tension' and the public outcry which followed the neo-fascist atrocities of 1969–1974. Emergency provisions added to this law in the immediate aftermath of the Moro kidnap were ratified by national referendum in the summer of 1978. Further anti-terrorist measures taken in 1979 were enshrined in the so-called 'Cossiga law' of 1980. However, the government's determination to act firmly against terrorism during the 'years of lead' has been considerably relaxed in recent years by two other laws whose aim has been not to subdue the wave of violence by legal repression but to encourage voluntary collaboration and the renunciation of terrorist aims and methods. These are the penitence law of May 1982 and the dissociation law of March 1987.

In order to benefit from the penitence law, which ran for one year, there were two basic requirements: firstly the *pentito* had to make a full confession of all crimes committed, and secondly he/she had to make an active contribution towards the prevention of further acts of terrorism. It was then up to the court of law to decide on the relevance of the evidence provided, how much a prison sentence could be reduced. Those intending to avail themselves of the dissociation law had to make their intentions known within one month of the law appearing on the statute book, and fulfil three requirements: the confession of all their terrorist activities, the formal abjuration of violence as a means of political struggle, and the demonstration in prison of behaviour corresponding to a renunciation of the beliefs and principles of the armed struggle. In return, with the exception of convictions for '*strage*' or massacre, sentences were reduced from 'life' to 30 years; crimes of bloodshed involving direct responsibility by a quarter; for associative crimes by half and all other crimes by a third.

Both laws have given rise to prolonged controversy at both a moral and a judicial level, but in practical terms represent a cornerstone of the Italian state's fight against terrorism. Many are in favour of one law but not another, some deplore both, and others (a minority) are in favour of an amnesty for all politically-inspired crimes not involving bloodshed in a gesture of conciliation such as the amnesty of 1946.

Application of these two laws has profoundly altered the balance of justice in Italy: they have radically transformed the work of those whose responsibility it is to wield the law and have shaken the foundations of the organizations on whom they have been exercized, no longer shielded by '*omertà*' or the protective silence of fellow combatants.

Let us look more closely at their origins and effects. Although Patrizio Peci is considered the inaugurator of *pentitismo*, the first member of the armed struggle to benefit from turning state's evidence was Carlo Fioroni, known as '*il professorino*' (the little professor) who was a member of the intellectual leadership of *Autonomia Operaia*. Fioroni was arrested in 1975 in connection with the kidnap and sub-sequent (accidental) murder by suffocation of the engineer

Carlo Saronio, for which he was sentenced to 27 years. He provided a substantial part of the evidence for the '7th April arrests' and, after 7 years' imprisonment, was discreetly released. When the '7th April' trial first came to court in 1983 Fioroni was officially 'untraceable' and did not reaffirm his accusations in open court, although it now seems as if his new identity, his address and work in the town of Lille were known to both the French and Italian authorities. Under French judicial protection, Fioroni returned as a witness in the Appeal trial in March 1987 where his evidence was cast in doubt.

The process which led to Patrizio Peci's 'penitence' in 1980 is recounted with disconcerting frankness in his book '*Io, L'Infame*' (literally, 'I, the Vile One') in which he lists a number of reasons for his decision, none of which initially involved remorse for the eight murders for which he was responsible. The first and most dramatic experience after his arrest was the realization of his own utter helplessness confronted with the might of the state. The myth of the invisible, ever-elusive crusader was abruptly and rudely shattered by his cursory handling by police, the isolation of a prison cell and the interminable hours spent in contemplation of the years of prison ahead. According to Peci, reality began to dawn when he learned of the maximum sentence for the first and lightest of his charges — illegal possession of a gun — for which he stood to serve three years and four months. His resolution to remain a 'political prisoner' began to waver as the years mounted up in his mind of all the occasions on which he had used it. Another milestone was reached when he heard that BR member Alberto Franceschini's reaction to his arrest had been one of joy — Franceschini apparently believed that with another prominent *brigatista* behind bars, those still at liberty would intensify their efforts to find a way of escape for their imprisoned comrades. Unwilling to end up nurturing the delusions of Franceschini, Peci looked around for a more pragmatic approach to his prison sentence. Before beginning his outpouring of evidence, however, he prepared his ground carefully, seeking assurances as to a reduction in sentence, his personal security and the possibility of starting a new life abroad.

If the original rationale was a direct result of the demythologizing of his own image, the second process was one of intellectual resignation on a collective level which Peci summarizes in three stages: firstly he decided that the BR did not enjoy the consensus of the masses, secondly that their actions were restricting the space available for peaceful protest, and finally that the armed struggle was actively damaging the interests of the working classes. 'All in all', he concludes, 'we were beaten, militarily and politically'.[1]

Peci's psychological shift from a position of resolute militancy through gradual disaffection to hatred for and wish to destroy the organization is an understandable one. It was encouraged at a crucial stage by two men with whom he built up a relationship of trust — General Carlo Alberto Dalla Chiesa and Turin judge Giancarlo Caselli, by whose combined efforts the penitence law received its initial momentum.

In fact Peci's awareness of the consequences of his collaboration is much more complex and difficult to understand. One of the least convincing aspects of his book is his superficial justification for giving the evidence which would implicate his former companions. Within days of his arrest Peci was working together with men whom he would previously have murdered gladly, betraying those who had helped him, saved his life, given him food, money and friendship. Although confessing to some qualms of guilt, Peci claims that he was really doing his friends a favour, since they would be arrested in due course anyway, and he was only saving them from further crimes and possibly injury or even death in a gun battle with police. With the benefit of hindsight, he also affirms that his collaboration was one way of repaying his debt to the families whose lives he had wrecked. The pain, he admits, came much later. Of those who suffered as a result, he admits to anguish over the deaths of the four BR murdered in Genoa (two of whom were close friends) and of his brother Roberto. Yet for all the suffering given and received, the pages of '*Io, L'Infame*' are remarkably free of sentiment or grief. The distinguished journalist Enzo Biagi, who conducted an interview with Peci in 1983, had this to say of his interviewee: 'When they arrested him he was already "in crisis" but even when he confesses some remorse his face is inscrutable, and his words unhesitating. . . . I never once found him lost for words and only once, for a single moment, embarrassed: when I asked him how they killed my friend, Casalegno. But then out came a bureaucratic, precise, detailed analysis, quite without emotion.'[2] Patrizio Peci, who has admitted to being 'a defeated terrorist not a repentant terrorist', is now a free man.

The collaboration of most of the *pentiti* who followed Peci's example, an estimated 350 from left-wing terrorism, seems like his to have been prompted by the recognition of defeat and a desire to salvage youth and freedom as far as possible, rather than by any altruistic concerns. BR member Antonio Savasta would justify his 'penitence' in these terms: 'The necessity and the inevitability of the armed struggle represented our bet with history. Well, we lost that bet, and our isolation and defeat are the price we paid for having defined reality by abstract theories which oversimplified it, for having concentrated the social reasons for change in an instrument unable to express it, for having diminished our own force and capacity for change and isolated them in an absurd and futile project.'[3]

In his evidence to the Parliamentary Commission studying the Moro case, Savasta elaborated further, talking of the 'real incapacity to construct a political programme commensurate with the level of knowledge and organization of the proletarian masses . . . and fully realizing this defeat, why it happened, I understood that along this path, from this direction, we were getting absolutely nowhere.'[4] Having convinced himself that the weaknesses of the BR were innate and insuperable, Savasta concluded that the sooner the organization was destroyed, the sooner the proletariat could begin to reorganize and develop its own plans for change.

Those who 'repent' in the legal sense do, it seems, eventually experience genuine remorse for their actions as time passes, or at least profess to do so. On the fifth anniversary of the death of Giuseppe Taliercio, Savasta, who had shot him 17 times despite being implored by the dying man to spare his life, wrote to Taliercio's widow, 'In those days your husband was . . . calm, devout in his faith; unable to hate us and extremely dignified. . . . Even in those moments your husband showed great love, it was so powerful that despite my efforts against it I could not eradicate its force within me. Believe me, I am in your debt for this and other things. I only hope to fill this vacuum by restoring and teaching to others what you have given and taught me. If it were not for you I would still be lost in the desert.'[5] Taliercio's widow has forgiven his murderers.

Similarly, Marco Barbone would say at his trial for the murder of Walter Tobagi, 'I can tell you that my future life will be spent in search of true expiation in an awareness of guilt which I will not be able to silence.'[6]

Despite general support for the penitence law, it has also been sharply criticized: many feel that the legal code no longer represents a moral concept of justice but has become a flexible instrument to be bartered over, one which operates on a sliding scale of values without a fixed point of reference. Former President Sandro Pertini is one who opposed the law through every stage of its parliamentary progress. Lawyer Edoardo Di Giovanni has commented that the judge can no longer be an impartial administrator of justice, but has been forced to become a *giudice di lotta*,[7] has had to enter the legal ring as protagonist in order to 'do battle' with the law.

In some cases open hostility has arisen between those who pass the laws and those who administer them. The politicians, who are largely in favour of any measure with a beneficial effect on public order and therefore on political stability, have been accused of neglecting the predicament of the judiciary, who are obliged to turn the 'penitent' defendant into a prosecution witness. The summing up in the Tobagi murder trial was savage in its indictment: 'The politicians have shown little respect for the judge by imposing not only the "maieutic" of getting information, which ought to be a police responsibility, but also the administration of premiums to informers. In this way the magistrate has been stripped of his most precious gift — his impartiality. . . . The vocation and the interest of this hotch-potch of terrorists in turning state's evidence is a widespread and unstoppable phenomenon . . . in keeping with the principle of the end which justifies any means. A principle which, in common with the use of the lie, is dear to anyone who engages in politics.'[8]

Defending the law on behalf of the politicians, former Minister of Justice Mino Martinazzoli describes it as 'useful and necessary', but is forced to admit that with it 'Italian law reached its lowest point.'[9]

Peci is free. Barbone is free. As are *Prima Linea* members Roberto Sandalo after three murders and Michele Viscardi after eight, including those of judges Alessandrini and Galli. Yet the colleagues of these murdered judges have been compelled to recognize the valuable contribution of the *pentiti* by awarding premiums in exchange for their information. How do they cope with this role?

Armando Spataro, public prosecutor in the Barbone/Tobagi case and a staunch believer in the value of the *pentiti*, acknowledges the problem of overcoming personal sentiment in the face of professional duty, as occurred when he shook hands with Viscardi, assassin of his close friend and colleague Guido Galli. In this case, he admits, he was greatly helped by one factor, namely, 'the absolute certainty that both Alessandrini and Galli, especially Galli, whom I knew much better, in my place would have done exactly the same'.

Taking refuge in his 'professionalism and sense of duty', he insists first and foremost, 'We must rid ourselves of any inclination to pass moral judgement on *pentitismo*', and defends the impartiality of the magistrate, which he believes can be guaranteed by 'verifying the truth of what has been confessed and assessing its relevance in open court.'[10]

He has not, he stresses, been required to play God or father confessor, nor to gauge feelings of genuine repentance should these coincide with the collaboration. But he believes this does occur, as in the case of Barbone, who confessed to the Tobagi murder before any evidence connected him to it. Barbone's lawyer concurs, and points to the risks run by those who give evidence against their former companions: 'It is not an irresponsible step, it is a responsible and a risky one, verified by judges in public debate.' He also points to the need to 'win back' or rehabilitate those who have realized their errors and wish to make amends: 'Tobagi himself taught us that these young people are not monsters but victims of bad masters, of a deviant culture, of degenerate ideals.'[11]

Despite the moral discomfort felt by some, all would agree that the contribution made by the *pentiti* has undoubtedly been great, not only to the dismantling of terrorist structures throughout the country, but also to the understanding of motivation and operational methods. It was Peci, for example, who first revealed the divisions in the BR of fronts and columns and the hierarchy of authority running down from executive committee to column leaders. The information given by Peci and Savasta in the Moro trial would cause public prosecutor De Gregorio to comment, 'The *pentiti* are the first real stroke of fortune this country has had.'[12]

A law which favours those who make an 'exceptional contribution' to the defeat of terrorism is clearly one which favours the terrorist leaders, who in all probability are answerable for more crimes than those less prominent in their organizations. But what of those who would have liked to make an 'exceptional contribution' but lacked the information to do so, such as an irregular member of the BR? Instructing judge Rosario Priore shrugs off as a fact of life the observation that those most implicated have most to tell, and sees the problem in other terms: 'Is it preferable for the state to keep a terrorist in prison for 30 years and allow the cycle of killings to continue? Does society suffer more or less by giving reduced prison sentences when by doing so a hundred fewer deaths occur?'[13] The logic and realism behind Priore's comments are undeniable, yet the problem remains. As the writer Leonardo Sciascia has pointed out, the law on *pentitismo* has 'created a confusion between immediate utility and the ideal of justice.'[14]

The law on dissociation has also raised matters of morality and judicial discretion, but of a different nature, given that the *dissociato*'s revelations only involve the personal assumption of responsibility. For the former terrorist, the critical issue of dissociation is the renunciation of his past, the admission that it has been aberrant and misjudged. For those who genuinely arrive at such conclusions the road to dissociation is a slow and painful one, as in the case of Alberto Franceschini, founder member of the Red Brigades. Franceschini's early commitment to the Communist party was gradually transferred to armed militancy in the BR by the apparent failure of the PCI to follow the founding premises of Marxist/Leninist theory. He and the other members of the 'historic nucleus' believed that they were the true disciples of revolutionary thought and action. They saw themselves as the torch bearers of the '*filone rosso*', the 'red tradition' which had been temporarily lost amidst the disappointed ambitions of the 'betrayed resistance', but which would surge up again within the revolutionary consciousness of the proletarian masses. Today Franceschini looks on these myths from which he constructed his hopes and his militancy as his 'bad masters'. With their gradual collapse came his dissociation from the armed struggle. Captured in 1974, Franceschini did not become a *dissociato* until 10 years later. He describes the process as beginning in 1980 with the layoff of 23,000 Fiat workers and the march of the 40,000 through Turin. Two aspects of this period struck him particularly: the first was that instead of reacting violently against the management proposals, the Fiat workers accepted their compensation meekly and set about opening shops and small businesses, thereby becoming small-scale capitalists themselves. The myth that the world would one day be populated only with the proletariat was slowly replaced by the realization that it was becoming entirely populated by capitalists. The second was a remark made by one angry Fiat worker who had reportedly exclaimed, 'If the BR were here this would never have happened.' Franceschini suddenly began to feel that the BR had been 'used' by the workers to fight battles in which they did not dare to engage, a bitter and humiliating experience.

Franceschini considers the concomitance of *pentitismo* with the changes taking place in the factories and in the trade unions to be no coincidence, and comments, 'We soon realized that the point at issue was not the weakness of a few individuals but our whole world which was crumbling.'[15]

Franceschini's 14 years in prison, and in particular his revolutionary commitment, drawn from the anti-fascist, working-class communism of the immediate post-war generation of Reggio Emilia, have undoubtedly made his dissociation a different experience from that of younger, middle-class militants. Many of today's *dissociati* entered the armed struggle in the wild, insurrectional days of 1977 when Piazza Fontana was a myth rather than a personal memory. For them defeat was perhaps a less bitter pill to swallow, since their commitment was more immediate, more rooted in the present than the nostalgic idealism of the 'historic leaders'. For them it has been easier to renounce violence, reconcile the past with the present and accept defeat not as the collapse of a universe but as the end of a dangerous and exciting game, accepted and recognized almost with relief.

At a conference held in Bergamo prison in March 1986, dissociated and repentant terrorists, judges, politicians and journalists contributed to an evaluation of the armed struggle. In a document produced at this debate by a group of prisoners the changes which occurred as the battle between state and terrorists intensified were described as 'a tendency towards war', 'an onward movement that was sacrificial because we were incapable of finding a way out'.[15] The first, instinctive reaction was one of greater determination; but this too gave way to the gradual realization that 'terrorism neither transforms society nor liberates man.'

Dissociazione, unlike *pentitismo*, did involve an assessment on the part of magistrates and prison staff of a genuine change of heart. Such a transformation had to be studied over a number of years before prisoners could officially benefit from application of the law, which only referred to crimes committed before 1983. The renunciation of violence is the point over which the greatest public controversy exists. Some consider it a mere trick of no substance, easily adopted by those who wish to feign a repentance they do not feel, and with no lasting value or guarantee. The fact that the *dissociato* was not required to assist in any active way towards the cessation of violence is a fact which certainly makes life more difficult for the authorities.

The ambiguity of the *dissociato* has led judge Spataro to believe that 'the overwhelming majority of *dissociati* are not repentant at all, but manipulate the fact of being dissociated to obtain better treatment.' Nonetheless he has supported the law, firstly in the interests of rehabilitating those who have genuinely broken with their past, and secondly because of the unlikelihood of any of the *dissociati* returning to the ranks of the armed struggle after fully confessing to all their past crimes.

Almost all the left wing terrorists in Italian prisons (approximately 450) can be described as *pentiti, dissociati* or as *irriducibili* (those who remain committed to the terrorist struggle). However, these three categories exclude a small group generally referred to as the '4th position', which includes such figures as Mario Moretti and Renato Curcio. Curcio elaborated on his position in an interview in January 1987, explaining why he would not join the *dissociati* despite not wishing to take up the armed struggle once more: 'The *dissociato* denies his past experience without being able to go beyond it. . . . He reduces the social and political complexity of the revolutionary experience to a judicial fact and talks of the '70's with the language of a cavilling lawyer . . . the *dissociate* is in fact an "associate" in the sense that he associates himself with a precise political line founded on abjuration and the exorcism of history.'[16]

In early 1987 Curcio, Moretti, Piero Bertolazzi and Maurizio Iannelli wrote an open letter to former companions. In defining their own position *vis à vis* the other categories of 'political prisoner', the authors criticize the legal and political solutions by which, they believe, society has shelved the problem of trying to understand and learn from the years of conflict.

Talking of a 'cycle which has run its course but which will only be properly concluded when those who gave it its impetus are out of prison', the authors propose the creation of a 'political and social opening.' They discriminate between 'going beyond' (*oltrepassare*) and what they call, 'the regressive terrain of dissociation, the sacrificial denial of one's own history and of one's own identity in the process of legitimizing the alleged victor. To go beyond means to realize the unrepeatable nature of one's past experiences . . . recognize a discontinuity between that experience and our present. To cling obstinately to a vision of the present as an immutable repetition of the past is nothing but a symptom of metaphysical paralysis, preoccupying for those who do not intend to give up fighting for the transformation of present forms of social relations, for Communism. . . . The danger is that an experience as rich and complex as ours . . . may finish up lost in silence or without any awareness of the present.'

Curcio and companions see the premium laws as an attempt by society to oversimplify and even ignore reality: 'petty cowardice on the part of those who want penitence, dissociation and self-criticism only to breathe life into their own ghosts and to avoid looking at what really happened. . . . What did happen was that an archaic, rigid, sterile political system, constructed from fascist origins which it never abandoned, unable to face up to the innovating drive of students, workers, youth and feminists movements, tried to bar their way by every means, having recourse alternately to terrorism or to pacts of national solidarity in order to avoid having to change. . . . At this stage it is too easy to separate "the good" from "the bad", calling us by the latter name. Calling us terrorists for example. And then dividing us again into "good" and "bad" — those who have not committed "acts of bloodshed" from those who have. As if we hadn't said a thousand times that responsibilities are political and collective. . . . The point is that for everyone we represent a challenge; the challenge to interrogate oneself before interrogating others. And in so doing, to unblock the situation, creating the conditions for an effective reopening of a dialogue. Political conditions, naturally. This means arriving at a liberation of the 70's by liberating prisoners without demanding abjuration or promises, without discriminating between "good" and "bad", reopening the frontiers to the exiles, dismantling the infinity of traps which threaten the tens of thousands of companions at every turn.'

Curcio has obstinately refused to give evidence in any court trial, believing that an assessment of the past can only be undertaken in conditions of physical and political freedom, unencumbered by judicial pressures. He argues that the law has been twisted to operate a negative bias against those who remain silent, thereby violating one of the fundamental rights of prisoners throughout history. There are many who respect this view. One of these is Indro Montanelli, newspaper editor and victim of a BR shooting in 1977: 'I don't like the *pentiti*, but I respect Renato Curcio. . . . He has never betrayed his companions and has never murdered anyone. I don't understand why he is still inside.'[17] In March 1987 Montanelli publicly shook the hands of the two BR who shot him, Lauro Azzolini and Franco Bonisoli, both now dissociated. His justification? 'They command respect because they are paying for all the wrong they have done through justly awarded prison sentences. They are paying for it but they have not betrayed their companions. . . . They were clever, they shot four bullets at me without killing or laming me and it's not easy. Still, if they had shot my father or my son I wouldn't be here'.

Indro Montanelli has on several occasions made critical references to the forgiveness extended by some victims' families towards terrorist aggressors such as that demonstrated by Aldo Moro's widow and daughter. In October 1984 Moro's daughter Maria Fida made the first of many visits to offer the family's forgiveness to Valerio Morucci and Adriana Faranda. She explained her reasons thus: 'The first is that I am a follower of Jesus Christ and for Christians, to pardon is a necessity rather than a duty. The second is that in my place my father would certainly have done what, apart from anything else, is an errand of mercy. The third is that from the human point of view it was intended to be an important experience, and it has been.'[18] Believing simply that 'we will be forgiven only in the measure that we forgive', Maria Fida has found it in her heart to pardon all those responsible for her father's death, although Morucci and Faranda have been the conspicuous beneficiaries of her charity. In them she has found a unique source of understanding, comfort and shared suffering which she believes will continue in all three of them for a lifetime. She has even attempted to take her son Luca to visit them, but this move has so far been vetoed by the prison authorities. To the 12-year old Luca she has explained that Valerio and Adriana were amongst those who took Grandfather away, but when they realized it was wrong they tried to save him. The inability to share such generosity of spirit is no justification for condemning it, nor should one criticize a mother for teaching her son to love rather than to hate. Nonetheless, Maria Fida Moro received a torrent of condemnatory letters for her action, as has Indro Montanelli for his. For some it re-opens personal wounds on which the blood is barely dry. Ileana Leonardi, widowed by the ambush in Via Fani, finds the public reconciliation with terrorists unbecoming and insulting to the families of other victims, and commented, 'that lady is free to do as she likes. But please let her do it in privacy and in silence. It would be more dignified.'[19]

The church has frequently led the way in demonstrations of Christian forgiveness. Pope John Paul II is the third pope to visit the country's prisons but, typically, made his visit in December 1983 part of a personal crusade, in this case on behalf of greater respect for human rights and dignity within the prison regime. On his tour of Rome's Rebibbia prison he not only talked and shook hands with many terrorist prisoners but even embraced his own would-be assassin Ali Agca. The Archbishop of Milan, Cardinal Martini has also been active in encouraging a return of prodigal sons to the fold. After an appeal made to those contemplating the use of violence to renounce their aims he was rewarded when a consignment of arms was deposited at his door.

Others such as Carole Tarantelli, widowed only in 1985, have found comfort not through the consolation of religious faith but by trying to understand and help former exponents of the *lotta armata*. Her frequent visits to *dissociati* in prison have helped her to cope with her loss, but she has a word of warning for those who believe they can forgive: 'Those who aspire to pardon put themselves above the human, play a dangerously omnipotent game; cancel out that part of themselves which inevitably hates the assassin.'[20]

Despite all the criticisms of penitence and dissociation, these laws represent the positive recognition that the Italian state wishes to make peace with the former enemy within, has opted for reconciliation and rehabilitation rather than eternal punishment. This principle should not be judged or abandoned in the light of any renewed terrorist activities. Indeed, to do so would be to fall headlong into the trap laid by the 'new BR', one of whose avowed aims is to jeopardize the rehabilitation of former militants, considered to be contemptible for their 'surrender'. That Italy has decided to call an end to the period of emergency has been further demonstrated by the Gossini law of 1986 which allows many ordinary and terrorist prisoners to work outside during the day and grants up to 45 days' holiday a year. Prisoners may return to their families for Christmas and New Year, and have been allowed to present art exhibitions and to stage plays in public venues.

Legal measures can do nothing to alleviate suffering or

bring the dead back to life, but for those who have genuinely turned their backs on violence, recent legislation has offered some hope for the future, and perhaps a chance to make some reparation for the past. One of the most optimistic signs that Italy is winning back the values shaken by the 'years of lead' came from the country's Director of Prisons, Nicolò Amato, who closed the conference in Bergamo with the following remarks: 'I consider terrorism politically finished. . . . I believe it is right to reflect on the causes of malaise and malfunction which we have been dragging behind us for years, and I cannot help wondering if there has not been more incomprehension on the part of society than there should have been. I believe it right to continue along this path, not to find justifications for senseless violence, but because I believe such reflections are useful if we wish to understand a story which incontestably belongs to each and every one of us.'[21]

References

1. '*Io, l'Infame*', Patrizio Peci, a cura di Giordano Bruno Guerri, Arnaldo Mondadori Editore, Milan 1983, pp. 194.
2. '*La Repubblica*', 27/4/83.
3. Quoted in '*Missione Antiterrorismo*', Rino Genova, Sugarco Edizioni, Milan, 1985, pp. 150.
4. Commissione Parlamentare d'Inchiesta sulla strage di Via Fani, sul sequestro e l'assassinio di Aldo Moro e sul terrorismo in Italia, Vol. IX, pp. 387.
5. '*La Repubblica*', 7/7/86.
6. '*La Repubblica*', 29/9/85.
7. '*L'Espresso*', 25/1/87.
8. '*L'Espresso*', 8/1/84.
9. Interview conducted by the author, Brescia, 24/11/86.
10. Interviews conducted by the author, Milan, 15/4/86 and 2/4/87.
11. '*La Repubblica*', 20/9/85.
12. '*Il Giorno*', 19/2/85.
13. Interview conducted by the author, Rome, 7/5/86.

14. Quoted in '*Rapporto sul Terrorismo 1969–1980*', a cura di Mauro Galleni, Saggi Rizzoli, Milan, 1981.
15. '*Una premessa d'obbligo*', Casa circondariale di Bergamo, dated 18/2/86.
16. '*L'Espresso*', 18/1/87.
17. '*La Repubblica*', 20/3/87.
18. '*Il Mattino*', 20/10/84.
19. '*L'Espresso*', 19/1/86.
20. '*Antigone*', No. 3/4, summer/autumn 1985.
21. Speech given by Nicolò Amato, Direttore Generale degli istituti di prevenzione e pena, casa circondariale di Bergamo, 15/3/86.

9
EPILOGUE AND CONCLUSION

I

The cumulative effects of the anti-terrorist laws of 1979–1982, and in particular the destructive power both materially and spiritually of *pentitismo*, drove most of the surviving exponents of the armed struggle either abroad or into hiding in Italy. On 24th January 1983 the first trial for the kidnap and murder of Aldo Moro and his five bodyguards concluded in Rome with the passing of 32 life sentences. It was also the month in which the BR came back to life, with the murder of a wardress at Rebibbia prison. In May they struck again, this time wounding Senator Gino Giugni, consultant to the government on labour law. This second attack coincided with the run-up to a general election, called because of continuing disagreements between the Socialists and the Christian Democrats. The attempt to exploit political tension recalled previous BR attacks before the divorce referendum in 1974 and the election of 1976.

On February 15th 1984 Leamon Hunt, American director-general of the peace-keeping force in Sinai, was shot through the windows of his bullet-proof car. Responsibility for the murder was first claimed by the Lebanese Armed Revolutionary Factions (LARF) in Beirut, then by the BR in Paris and Rome on February 17th and 18th respectively. It was subsequently discovered that two prominent members of LARF, arrested later in the year, had left Rome on the morning of the attack. It is now believed that LARF, which had at least 2 bases in Italy at the time, commissioned the attack and provided the powerful weapons.

On March 23rd a robbery occurred at the Brinks Securmark depot in Rome from which 35 billion lire (approx £17½ million or $32 million) was stolen. It was carried out by a group of common criminals with the complicity of two employees and the forcing at gun-point of one of the three key holders to the depot. The robbery was staged to appear as the work of the BR: left in the depot were BR leaflets dating from 1978, a responsibility claim from the organization for the theft, a banner with the BR logo and a handful of 6.72 bullets. A few days later the BR 'evidence' was discarded as a deliberate falsification.

Nonetheless, the leader of the group, Antonio Chicchiarelli, tried to rekindle the affair, delivering to a Rome newspaper some more 6.72 bullets and original BR files on Roman judge Gallucci, PCI politician Ingrao and journalist Mino Pecorelli, against whose name the word 'eliminate' was written.

Yet copies of these same files had been found by two American tourists in a Rome taxi on 14th April 1979, a few days after Pecorelli had indeed been murdered. In the leather bag found in the taxi there were eleven 7.65 calibre bullets and a .9 calibre cartridge case the same type as used to kill Aldo Moro; an IBM typewriter golf ball head, 2 polaroid flash cubes, and other items which identified whoever had placed them there not only as being connected to the Moro affair, but also as having a thorough familiarity with the codes and procedures of the Italian security services. Both Pecorelli and Chicchiarelli were known to have contacts in the security services, and Pecorelli had been a P2 member. Chicchiarelli is now believed to have been the driver of the taxi in which the bag was found in 1979, and to have been responsible for the false communication No 7 which led police on a wild goose chase to look for Aldo Moro's body in the frozen Lake Duchessa in April 1978. Chicchiarelli himself was murdered on September 28th 1984.

Since 1985, left-wing terrorism has resurfaced in a series of direct attacks against the state. The offensive is the result of a meeting in Paris in September 1984, at which a strategy for renewing the armed struggle was evolved. Effectively the Red Brigades split into two groups, generally known as 'militarist' and 'movementist'. The first group, as the name suggests, retained a tight clandestine structure aimed at waging a 'war of long duration' through a selected number of carefully planned actions against targets representative of international imperialism and domestic reformism. The second group, rejecting the elitism of the military vanguard, opted for a commitment to more immediate, generalized and diffused actions with a broader level of participation at local rather than national level, concentrating on the problems of socially and economically disadvantaged sections of the population. Whereas the former were advocates of the Moretti line, the latter were more aligned to Senzani principles. The militarist majority won the day.

On March 27, 1985 the 'new BR' illustrated their intentions explicitly with the murder of economist and trade union consultant Enzo Tarantelli, shot in the courtyard of Rome university. Responsibility was claimed by the BR's 'Strategic Resolution No 20', which linked his murder to the 'anti-imperialist struggles' being waged by the French group *Action Directe* and the West German *Rote Armee Fraktion* (who had themselves issued a joint declaration of solidarity in January). Tarantelli, the document claimed, was targeted to 'hit the brains behind the restructuring of industry and of trade union relations'[1] and to recruit support from amongst the workers, particularly from the 30–40,000 laid off from the factories, whose wages were being eroded by inflation.

The BR carried out no more major actions in 1985,

probably due to a series of crippling arrests: in April, Vittorio Antonini, Dozier kidnapper and also wanted for a succession of murders and robberies, was captured with four others in a base full of arms and documents in the outskirts of Rome; in June Barbara Balzerani was finally run to ground in a base in Ostia, near Rome, where she was arrested with fellow militant Gianni Pelosi.

After Balzerani's capture the group of *irriducibili* or unrepentant terrorists of which she was the mouthpiece provided persistent warnings of present and future BR strategy in the course of the court trials up and down the country in which they appeared. At the Taliercio murder trial in July 1985 she warned that with the Tarantelli attack the BR were relaunching their strategy against 'one of the cardinal points of the Craxi/Carniti*–Confindustria** coalition.'[2] It was admitted that after 1982 there had been 'the necessity for a general reflection on the reasons for our defeats, which determined the choice of strategic withdrawal, without putting in doubt the strategic plan of the armed struggle or the fundamental rationale of the BR.' At the conclusion of the trial Balzerani announced, 'We are not witnesses to a past experience but are still militants, still active in every respect within the Fighting Communist Party.'

In November a Milan courtroom would hear her again; the BR had carried out a self-examination and 'have reconstructed the thematic unity between attack on the heart of the state and practical anti-imperialist struggle.'[3] Such dissent as had existed over the issues of 'armed domestic warfare' and 'European anti-imperialist struggle' had been resolved. In February 1986 they attacked twice, with the murder in Florence of former mayor Lando Conti, and the wounding in Rome of Antonio Da Empoli, economic adviser to PM Bettino Craxi.

* Carniti — Secretary of CISL, the trade union organization to which Tarantelli was consultant.
** Confindustria — Italian employers' association.

Beside Conti's body was found a copy of Resolution No 20, identical to that left on the scene of Tarantelli's murder; the bullets which killed him came from an identical Skorpion machine gun. The responsibility claim which followed, from BR — *Partito Comunista Combattente* (Red Brigades Fighting Communist Party) pointed to Conti's shareholding in a company producing electronic equipment for the aerospace industry (also reputedly contemplating participation in the American SDI 'Star Wars' project) and to Conti's friendship with fellow Republican Giovanni Spadolini, Italy's Defence Minister, considered pro-US and pro-Israel, and described as Italy's 'Minister of War'. The claim exalted the struggles of Libyans and Palestinians (now with the explicit exclusion of the PLO, considered a 'liquidator of the Palestinian interests') and concluded, 'War on War, War on NATO, Unity of International Communists'![4]

Antonio Da Empoli might have met the same fate as Conti had it not been for the lightning reactions of his driver, who shot dead one of the firing group of four, 28 year-old Wilma Monaco. The others escaped. This attack showed the BR had split again, no longer divided into 'militarists' and 'movementists', but into BR '1st position' and '2nd position'. Whilst the Conti murder was claimed by BR — PCC, or 1st position, the Da Empoli action was the work of 2nd position or *Unione dei Comunisti Combattenti* (Union of Fighting Communists, UCC) whose foundation manifesto was found on Monaco's body. The document criticized the old BR for 'endlessly mixing up Marxist–Leninism with petty bourgeois anti-materialist ideology' and for its 'underestimation of the specifically political role of the Communist vanguard'.[5] In contrast to the international aspirations of 1st position, UCC put the anti-imperialist struggle low on the list of areas of specific attention, professing to be, 'the conscious vanguard of the working class, linked to the proletariat but at the same time an attacking division within the strategy of armed insurrection.'

On the evening of January 22nd 1987, a group of terrorists

opened fire on police who tried to approach them in a busy central Rome street. Three were arrested, a fourth member escaped. Police believe a Transit van discovered nearby was parked in readiness for a kidnap attempt.

On February 14th an eight-strong BR commando team ambushed a post office van carrying cash to offices in southern Rome and fired on the occupants of the accompanying police escort vehicle, killing two and seriously injuring a third. The terrorists escaped with 1.15 million lire (approx £600,000). Responsibility was claimed by BR–PCC (1st position) on February 17th in two documents, one left by the BR near the offices of *L'Espresso* magazine and a second, which was produced within a few hours of the first, prepared by Barbara Balzerani and nine other *irriducibili* in a Rome courtroom. This claimed, 'the proletarian expropriation . . . is not an isolated action but an offensive linked to other actions of fighting European organizations for a united international front against NATO and United States imperialism'.[6] But their statement contained a crucial admission of international strategy: 'The policy of alliances in our name is at the centre of the broader anti-imperialist strategy practised by us; an alliance which must relate to revolutionary forces whose criteria and aims may be other than the conquest of power for the proletariat, whose political unity is provided by the struggle against a common enemy and its realization in the levels of unity and co-operation already achieved.'

This is, I believe, the first time that the BR have ever publicly owned up to solidarity with organizations 'whose criteria and aims may be other than the conquest of power for the proletariat.' What would have been unthinkable to the founding members of the BR has become a last desperate tactic for the later generation of militants. It is an admission of defeat but also a declaration of war.

And the war certainly goes on. On March 20th 1987, 62-year old General Licio Giorgieri was assassinated in Rome by two assailants on a motorcycle, who shot him through the window of his car as he was being driven home from work. Giorgieri was Director General of Costarm Aereo, a technical-administrative subdivision of the Ministry of Defence, whose specific responsibilities included the assessment and recommendation of all the weapons systems used by the Italian Air Force. The responsibility claim which arrived three days later was on behalf of UCC (2nd position) and gave four reasons for the action: firstly, Giorgieri was killed 'exclusively for the responsibilities he exercized relative to the Italian adhesion to the Star Wars project'. (In fact this accusation is inaccurate, since neither the Italian government nor the armed forces are involved in the SDI programme, although individual firms may participate if they wish.) Secondly, the attack aimed to hit 'Giovanni Spadolini and his "clique" because they have given life to the most reactionary and chauvinistic sections of the Italian bourgeoisie.' The third aim was to stir the masses out of their apathy towards Italian defence and nuclear policies, to create a 'mass mobilization' to pull Italy out of NATO, and in particular to point out the Communist party's non-aggressive stance in this regard. The PCI, the document claimed, 'lives in ambiguity and offers no guarantee of efficient struggle against militarization.' The BR aim was therefore to 'fill the vacuum.' Finally, the timing of the action was a deliberate attempt, in the long-practised BR tradition, to exploit political uncertainty, caused in this case by the collapse of the five-party governmental coalition, 'to construct a new unity from below', and to put on trial 'the political parties which have had governmental responsibilities and which have brought about the reactionary swing'.[7]

The Giorgieri attack caused consternation in Italy, not only because it gave further proof of the Red Brigades' operational capacity, but also because it raised the alarming possibility of terrorist co-operation on a European scale: Giorgieri's position in Italy was similar to those held in France by Réné Audran and in Germany by Ernst Zimmermann, assassinated in 1985 by the left wing organizations *Action Directe* and the *Rote Armee Fraktion* respectively; documents found in an AD base only a month before had proved that contacts existed with the Italians. Despite its previous claims, it seemed as though UCC had decided to adopt the 'international' struggle in open competition with the rival BR faction. In fact this was the last action to date by BR–UCC; thanks to highly efficient intelligence work and in particular to increased European collaboration, almost 100 members of UCC were arrested in the course of 1987 in Italy, France and Spain. But if one half of the terrorist equation was destroyed, the other half, BR–PCC was far from finished.

In April 1988, amidst the numerous events recalling the 10th anniversary of Aldo Moro's death, and days before the installation of a new DC-led government, the Red Brigades were almost bound to commemorate the occasion. Posing as postmen with a parcel to deliver for DC Senator Roberto Ruffilli, two members of BR–PCC entered his appartment in Forlì and shot him dead at close range. Ruffilli was a minor figure compared to Moro and had never considered himself a terrorist target, but his position as adviser on institutional reform to the new De Mita government satisfied the linear logic of the brigadists: a logic by which any apparent attempts to reform and modernize are merely a means by which the consolidation of state power is masked by a pretence of democratization.

Ironically, it seems as though the last generation of Red Brigadists may have been halted in its tracks by a contact with the first: some years ago one of the 'historic leadership' received a letter in prison from two young Milanese asking how to go about joining the organization. With understandable scepticism, the BR leader ignored the letter, but more arrived, of which one fell into the hands of a magistrate. In 1986 a long, laborious period of observation began, involving not only the two authors of the letters but all their movements and contacts. The arrest in January 1988 of a BR-PCC militant with a Rome-Milan rail ticket in his pocket reinforced police belief that the northern industrial cities, and Milan in particular, was the new terrorist growth area. During April and May BR documents were found outside 6 Milan factories and also in Naples. The police operation culminated

on June 17th with the arrests of 9 BR–PCC members and the
discovery of a fully operational base on the outskirts of Milan,
in which were found 2 Sterling machine guns, 3 pistols, the
Skorpion sub-machine gun used to assassinate Tarantelli,
Conti and Ruffilli, and a vast store of BR documentation.
Discovery of another five bases and 21 arrests followed in
Rome in September.

But as those around him patted each other on the back and
announced the final demise of the Red Brigades, Milan judge
Armando Spataro refused to share the general complacency,
and warned, 'Let's get this clear once and for all: in Italy
terrorism is pretty well endemic; we're no longer at the level
of the "years of lead" but deep down, the fires are still
burning.'[8]

II

We saw what kind of an impact the Moro affair had within
Italy and on the continuation of the 'armed struggle.' By way
of a conclusion, it is perhaps relevant to make a critical
assessment of the Moro case to see what went wrong in the
spring of 1978, and to see what mysteries still remain. Could
the kidnap have been prevented? Could Moro have been
saved?

To the question, 'Could the kidnap have been prevented?',
the answer is 'yes, almost certainly.' It is all too easy to use the
benefit of hindsight to criticize what seem glaringly obvious
facts, but Moro and his entourage had had warning signs in
profusion. The BR had often threatened and attacked DC
targets. Moro himself was a controversial public figure with
unconventional political ideas which were viewed with alarm
in many quarters both at home and abroad. Signora Moro
admitted, 'He was a nuisance to an awful lot of people', and
reports that on the eve of his kidnap and of the presentation to
Parliament of the 'government of national unity,' Moro had
commented, 'Today at least I certainly have a hundred more
enemies.'[9]

Moro had taken some precautions, such as insisting on bodyguards for his family and on the installation of reinforced glass in his office. He had also asked for a bullet-proof car which never materialized. But in general the security measures adopted for his protection were insufficient and perfunctory. At the very least, greater efforts should have been made to alter his routes and timings to work each day. The escort car always followed directly behind the official Fiat 130, which meant that both cars were inevitably caught up in any attack. On March 16th this was aggravated by the fact that the Alfetta's brakes were faulty and its radio was out of order. The wife of protection squad leader Oreste Leonardi testified that her husband had complained to her about the ill-preparedness of the civil police members of the team, but there is no record of his having made an official protest. All members of such squads were supposed to have weekly target practice but this recommendation had not been followed by Moro's guards.

The gap of about twenty seconds which must have elapsed before the BR commando opened fire should have given a well-trained team sufficient time to respond. Yet four out of the five had their revolvers in their holsters with the safety catch on. The one weapon the BR seized, a machine gun, was so badly rusted that, according to Patrizio Peci, it was unusable and thrown away. The fact that only Raffaele Iozzino drew his gun and fired a shot was not so much indicative of the BR's military brilliance, but rather of the general level of inattentiveness of men who do a routine job with only routine care.

Regretfully, the only conclusion one can reach is that the measures taken to protect Aldo Moro fell far short of those required for a man facing a constant threat to his life, and that inadequate attention was paid to keeping men and equipment at a suitable level of operational efficiency. Had better protection existed, the BR might have turned their attention to a different target.

In the immediate aftermath of the kidnap there were too many people doing the same job, not enough people doing others, some people trying to do too many jobs and in some cases no one doing the obvious. Moro's Fiat 130 was towed to Rome Police Headquarters where it stood in a courtyard for five days before anyone thought to examine it. Between March 16 and 19, the BR managed to park three of the vehicles used in the getaway in the same street close to the scene of the ambush without anyone noticing. It took 45 minutes for a road block around Rome to be functional, and even then only the major routes were covered; had the BR wished to make an escape with their prisoner they could have certainly done so by using a minor road or by leaving swiftly which, with most of the morning traffic heading for the city centre, they could have done. Despite the hordes of police in and around the apartment in Via Gradoli, finger prints were not taken.

Two crisis committees were set up, but as they were formed by the most senior politicians and representatives of the military and security services who were already committed to pre-existing responsibilities and were fully involved in the crisis, there was a complete lack of an unbiased, objective approach to possible negotiations for Moro's release. A single crisis committee comprising a good spread of experience and expertise and with continuously open channels of communication to the government would have avoided or overcome some of the prejudices and political bickering which at times blurred the crucial issues.

Many of the investigative problems could have been attenuated by information from the security services, whose reorganization in the autumn of 1977 had virtually dismantled its anti-terrorist department and dispersed the competent manpower. It is generally agreed that the peak of terrorist achievement coincided with the nadir of security service operational capabilities, which were described as being 'in a state of vacation.'

The police were doubtless unlucky in that despite the thirteen thousand men employed daily on the manhunt and the 6½ million people stopped and questioned during the 55 days no one led them to Moro. The blanket approach gave an impressive public image of efficiency which ignored the finer aspects of investigative technique.

These errors and omissions are today viewed with due humility by the authorities. Instructing judge Rosario Priore admits the level of knowledge of the BR was 'minimal', and points out that the activities of the '77 Movement' had caused confusion between extremism and terrorism which was not resolved until much later. There was a general feeling that many of the members of the dissolved *Potere Operaio* had entered the BR, but even this, he says, proved to be only partially true. Nonetheless, on the very day of the ambush in Via Fani, eight out of the twenty suspected terrorists on the 'wanted' list were indeed terrorists, four had been in Via Fani and two others were full-time members of the BR. Adriana Faranda and Valerio Morucci were identified at the end of March. There was information, but it was simply not used correctly.

The biggest question mark that hangs over the whole Moro affair is whether the omissions and errors which occurred were the result of genuine inefficiency or, even partially, of deliberate policy. There are still many unresolved mysteries which prevent a full reconstruction of the 55 days and an army of conspiracy theorists willing to expound complex intrigues of power and politics. The theory which has had most credence has centred on the possible involvement of the P2 masonic lodge. During the planning and duration of the kidnap the three individuals at the head of the security services SISMI, SISDE and of the co-ordinating committee CESIS were all P2 members. A specialist advisory committee was set up by Francesco Cossiga two days after the kidnap to analyze Moro's letters and the BR communications. Of the deliberations of this committee, comprised almost entirely of P2 members, there is no written record. Many politicians have urged a serious investigation into the lodge's role in the Moro affair, encouraged by Tina Anselmi, President of the Parliamentary Commission of Enquiry into P2's activities, who stated, 'that the P2 had a political programme has been proved. And that it undoubtedly had amongst its objectives that of "getting rid of" the DC of Zaccagnini and Moro is another certain fact, as can be textually proved.'[10]

But former Justice Minister Mino Martinazzoli is sceptical of any direct involvement by P2. Admitting that the BR action made space for 'parallel games' to be played, he believes the lodge had no cause to interfere with terrorist activities, and that 'for the P2 it was enough that the BR existed.'[11] There are some, including Moro family lawyer Saverio Fortuna, who are convinced that the security services knew of the whereabouts of Moro's prison but prevented the police from raiding it. If so, there could be two explanations — either that they were afraid of provoking a bloodbath and the death of Moro himself, or simply that someone did not want him released. One of the original investigating magistrates, Ferdinando Imposimato, demonstrated that Via Montalcini, the presumed hiding place, had come under suspicion whilst it was still occupied by terrorists. Only at his insistence and after lengthy searches did an undated and unsigned report reveal that the tenants of the building had been questioned about their neighbours, the 'Altobellis'. And there may have been a third, still unidentified, Moro custodian.

Some accuse the DC of having impeded the autonomous attempts to mediate with the kidnappers, such as those of the Swiss lawyer Payot and of the Pope. But, once again, there is space for two interpretations — that a possible rescue attempt was deliberately sabotaged, or simply that the government was determined that the debate with the BR be kept within the political domain rather than slip into private and secret negotiations over which it had no control.

Some questions have received no answer at all. Just after the Via Fani ambush a passer-by with a camera happened to photograph the crowd clustering around the murdered bodyguards. The photograph and its negative were handed over to the authorities but subsequently disappeared. A tapped telephone conversation between Sereno Freato and a Calabrian deputy, in which Freato is asked for a copy of the photograph because 'Calabrian friends' were 'interested' in it is mysteriously indistinct and scarcely audible. Some have suggested a Mafia or n'Drangheta connection here. Other tapes of tapped telephone conversations have disappeared, such as one between the priest Don Mennini and a BR 'postman' which an eavesdropping police officer suddenly broke in on, as if to give warning that the conversation was being overheard. At about 8.15 am on March 16th the left-wing radio station Radio Città Futura broadcast a warning of an impending attack by the BR on a DC politician, and the name of Aldo Moro was mentioned. The station director Renzo Rossellini admits to having given the message, but asserts that he was only repeating rumours already circulating within the far left at that time. But, strangely, neither the radio station nor the security service SISDE, which customarily taped all private radio stations considered subversive, has any record of the broadcast.

Speculation still turns on the exact composition of the firing group in Via Fani, and whether it numbered nine or eleven. Valerio Morucci has repeatedly denied that a motorcycle was one of the vehicles used, yet several witnesses saw it and shots were fired from it. Some believe that the presence of two unknown participants in the ambush could be the clue to the manipulation of the BR from an outside source. Or did someone in the organization know something? All the BR have consistently denied the possibility of infiltration but Mario Moretti fuelled the theory by remarking at the start of the Moro Appeal trial, 'There is someone who won't be pleased if I talk. That's the reason I'm in here.'[12]

The discovery of Moro's body raised other perplexing issues: beside his body in the boot of the Renault were found a number of personal effects such as his watch, keys and various documents, as well as the blood pressure meter which he habitually carried with him. These items were originally in the two bags taken from Moro's car at the time of the kidnap but which, if Signora Moro is correct, could not have been taken until after the blood of the bodyguards had had time to flow around them. No one saw the bags being taken, but some, if not all of the contents ended up in BR hands. In the dead man's pockets were coins amounting to approximately 2,000 lire (£1). But his family insists that Moro was fastidious about personal hygiene to the point of obsession and never carried grubby coins loose in his pockets. One possibility is that he was told he was to be freed, and given change to make a telephone call. Yet his last letter shows an unequivocal resignation to death. Together with the still unproven certainty of who pulled the trigger to kill him, the doubts remain.

As the years pass, more information has gradually filtered out about Moro's imprisonment and the BR's own position during the 55 days, although little is known about the personal relationship that must have developed between captors and captive. The little that has emerged has been an admission that Moro was courageous and dignified through-out and that, on a personal level, the decision to kill him was regretted.

After his arrest in 1981 Mario Moretti's public pronounce-ments were few, hence the interest of a long interview given to Giorgio Bocca and published in *L'Espresso* magazine in December 1984. Challenged by Bocca to admit Moro's life had been doomed from the start, Moretti responded, 'Moro's life could have been saved right up until the last moment.' Stressing that the BR were not pressing for political recognition but merely mediation, he pointed to the telephone call to the Moro house of April 30, 'Well, that phone call means that at the beginning of May we were still ready to negotiate.' As to the exchange of prisoners, he commented, 'We knew that the battle would be hard, very hard, but even though we made demands that were obviously impossible, we still wanted to reach a first breakthrough, a first opening. If that had happened, the conclusion of the Moro affair could have been different.'[13]

Renato Curcio also believed there was bargaining space, and says, 'Moro could have been saved. It was obvious from reading the explicitly clear messages from the BR. Reading them in prison, I was in no doubt about the existence of ample room for manoeuvre offered by the Red Brigades. The thing is, there is none so deaf as him that will not hear, and the problem of Moro's life must be seen in the context of the deaf men of the time and of the exorcists of today.'[14]

Valerio Morucci explains that Moro was killed on 9th May to pre-empt any gesture from the DC Committee meeting that might have put the BR in difficulties. Had the result been a public recognition of the organization, such as an appeal, he claims the decision to kill Moro would at least have been delayed. Adriana Faranda thinks one of two factors might have led to Moro's release — either the liberation of Paola Besuschio or revelations by Moro of hitherto undiscovered DC corruption. She is dubious whether Buonoconto's liberation would have had the desired effect, since his state of health was so perilous that discharging him from prison into medical care was 'an act of justice, not of clemency',[15] and thus without any political significance for the BR.

One former terrorist admits that, from the state's point of view, the decision not to deal was the correct one; any concessions made would have increased the BR's popularity, prestige and recruitment, and would have been exploited for propaganda purposes. This is the precise reason that the judiciary in general was opposed to negotiations. Rosario Priore agrees that a 'one for one' exchange might have led to Moro's release, but believes that, rather than quietly accepting the mediation as could happen with common criminals or with foreign terrorists expelled or exchanged, the BR would have made maximum capital out of the bargain and would have lost no opportunity in depicting the state as the humiliated loser. The BR had everything to gain and nothing to lose by doing so. But could the state not have done anything more for Moro? 'It could have done, but not without jeopardizing democracy',[16] was his response.

Those close to the Moro family are understandably convinced that he could have been saved by the release of one prisoner without deleterious effect on public or democratic order. Signora Moro's attitude to the attempts to save her husband can be summarized in the prayer written by her for a private memorial service on May 16th 1978. The prayer begged mercy for 'all those who, out of fear, cowardice and jealousy allowed the crime to be committed.'[17] And when asked by the Parliamentary Commission for her views on the efforts made by the government her reply was equally succinct: 'They did nothing!'[18]

Bettino Craxi still believes that the release of Paola Besuschio would have neither rocked the foundations of democracy nor unleashed a wave of terrorist violence in exuberant emulation. But Mino Martinazzoli regards the Socialist initiative as an opportunist move to gain the support of the church and of the extra-parliamentary left, and staunchly upholds the validity of the DC decision. He believes that the BR were convinced the government would never yield, and were set on a course of murder from the start. He justifies the DC's line of rigour on the grounds that to do otherwise would have been to substitute personal for political considerations and might have necessitated the dissolution of the DC as a political party.

The Moro family members continue to live out their private tragedy in a state of siege, trying valiantly to defend Moro's reputation against sporadic accusations of wrongdoing or misjudgement, and fending off the threats and warnings which have never ceased to arrive by post or telephone.

Periodically, the case officially resurfaces when terrorists suddenly decide to 'talk' in the course of a court hearing, victims' lawyers speak out, or when politicians voice dissatisfaction over the lack of efforts to find solutions to the remaining mysteries. The creation in 1988 of a new Parliamentary Commission of Enquiry into terrorism is an admission not only of the total failure to understand the phenomenon of 'stragismo', but also an acknowledgement that court records and criminal responsibilities for left wing terrorism may not tell the whole story of the Red Brigades' success.

III

In one sense Italy's political problem is an endemic one — for the last 40 years its leaders have been engaged in the task of trying to reconcile fundamentally irreconcilable elements, to achieve a synthesis of 'opposing extremes' which can never materialize. The failure of the private citizen to identify with public government, the lack of coincidence between individual interest and common good and the Catholic/ Marxist clash have never been overcome, despite the efforts of those such as Aldo Moro to 'make the parallels converge.' The private citizen, if he ever cared, has given up worrying about such matters, but it is the politician's lot to keep on trying. Some cynics have suggested that the period of Aldo Moro's kidnap was a rare moment when personal expediency and 'reasons of state' were indistinguishable. It is certainly the case that a balancing act of great finesse was played out around the Moro tragedy, as each political force tried desperately to retain authority and advance itself, whilst simultaneously exercizing the utmost restraint and discretion. It is also true that although Moro died, democracy was saved and so were the Christian Democrats.

If there is one lesson that Italy (and all democracies) should have learned from defending itself against terrorism it is that in a democratic country democratic rules must not only apply in theory, they must be seen to operate in practice. It is the dictum proclaimed in every Italian courtroom; 'The law is equal for all.' And this means *all*, making no exceptions for corrupt administrators, rich financiers, devious politicans, for those who wound and kill, nor for those who encourage others to do so from the security of their university studies.

And the future? Renato Curcio, Mario Moretti and others candidly admit that the phase of violent confrontation with the state is 'historically finished . . . but not concluded' and can only be concluded 'by creating the cultural and political means by which it can be transcended.' In isolating themselves ideologically from the 'new BR' they have arbitrarily closed the circle of armed struggle around themselves, and now claim the right to political dialogue within conditions of intellectual liberty — indispensible, in their view, for the relevance of their actions to be given their due place in history.

This prompts the obvious question — if the armed struggle is finished, why do some continue to fight? Those with warrants out for their arrest obviously cannot lead a normal life in Italy, thus are obliged either to flee abroad or go underground. Others, released from prison before being tried, at the expiry of the maximum pre-trial detention period have fled rather than face trial and further imprisonment. But many of those arrested in 1987 and 88 had no criminal record, yet still chose armed confrontation in preference to peaceful political methods. The internationa- lization of the conflict in recent years may be an indication that they recognize the political, if not the military battle to be lost at home. Alternatively, it may be that they refuse to accept defeat at any level, and are hoping to turn Italy into an international battleground between 'imperialist' and 'anti- imperialist' forces on to which the proletarian masses will emerge in due course, having decided that the state's attempts to reform itself are a mere cover for gaining greater powers of control and repression.

In contrast, Renato Curcio and Mario Moretti have admitted defeat, have come to accept that an armed minority will not gain political recognition or popular support in the foreseeable future in Italy. Once, they really did believe their commitment and dedication to a proletarian revolution might set in motion a movement that would be understood and followed. But, as Alberto Franceschini points out, the fatal mistake the BR made was to identify themselves with the dawn of a new era, when in fact they were the vestiges of an old one. In the days of Piazza Fontana and the 'strategy of tension' perhaps they had their last chance, encouraged by the militancy of students and factory workers and with proof

of corruption, cheating and conspiracy within the organs of
the state. But a lot has changed since then. All but a tiny
proportion of the population has job protection, a minimum
wage is guaranteed by law and an acceptable standard of
living is enjoyed by most. It's not that there is nothing left to
fight for, rather that hunger and anger no longer gnaw the
way they did.

The way in which most of the '70's militants have come to
terms with this, whether in or out of prison, is simply to
redraw the parameters of the word 'revolution' along more
personal lines. Instead of shooting industrialists or judges and
trying to overthrow the state, a 'revolutionary action' can
constitute almost anything which involves taking over greater
control of one's own life to the exclusion of economic
subservience to a *padrone*; forming a co-operative to produce
jewellery, to farm a piece of land or to print a newspaper. In
other words, you can be a non-violent revolutionary.

This, I believe, is the message of pacification, the 'battle for
liberty' in which former terrorists are keen to engage. What it
amounts to is, 'We're getting on for 40 now and we want to
live in peace with society but also with ourselves, which is why
we refuse to deny our past, say we were wrong and opt for
penitence or dissociation. Let us get on with our own lives and
we won't give you any more trouble. But beware of passing
judgement on us before having a critical look at yourselves.'

The message is probably sincere, but most Italians
understandably find its arrogance hard to swallow, especially
with murder still being practised in the name of the Red
Brigades.

Still, slowly and with some reluctance, Italy *is* beginning to
feel the need for a reappraisal of the 1970's, abandoning the
notion that what happened was simply a generation conflict
between trigger-happy revolutionaries and the status quo.
Many Italians now realize that it represented a reaction,
albeit extreme, to the profound social crisis of an immature
democracy unable to cope with the transformations going on
within it, and to the political crisis of the Italian left,
struggling to find a new identity.

In the end the mass rejection of terrorism by the Italians unified and strengthened Italy, and may have vaccinated future generations against the belief that violence can be an effective weapon for change in a democratic society. But the costs on all sides have been high. Quite apart from the injuries and loss of life the material cost has been high — Italy spent two hundred thousand billion lire that is, 30.4 billion lire, or roughly £13,000 per day, on defending itself against terrorism between December 1969 and January 1988.[19] And in the process intolerance cast long shadows over Italian daily life.

There is no doubt that the impact of political violence went far beyond the numerical strength of those who used it. The shooting and kidnapping of prominent public figures prevented them from achieving greater influence and prestige. Terrorism altered the way thousands of Italians lived. Its importance was undoubtedly dramatized by the mass media, increasingly drawn into an almost symbiotic relationship with the terrorists in the pursuit of action, truth, or simply a good story. Nonetheless, indiscriminate censorship would have been a more perilous trap to fall into than over-exposure, since to have imposed it would have been to prove the terrorists' point.

Nowadays, interviews given to the media by former terrorists are having quite the opposite effect — the debunking of the myth. Seeing the rather tired, haggard-looking faces of the 'historic leaders' on their television screens, the Italians' reaction has been one of em-barrassment, almost shame — 'to think how frightened we were of *them*! Just imagine — they seem so banal, yet they had us all running.'

A curious friend asked recently, 'Well, why *did* they do it then?' In one way it's what this book is about, but in another, there is no answer; or rather — there are as many answers as there were terrorists. Of course there was a common denominator: the acceptance of violence as a valid means of political struggle. But long before that, every individual's route to militancy developed through an infinitesimal number of haphazard circumstances in ways too distinctly personal to be open to generalized explanation. Undoubtedly some were looking for danger and adventure, others enjoyed the phallic fantasy of the P.38, while many more simply wanted to escape from a stifling home atmosphere. It has been suggested that some male terrorists who lacked discipline as children went to find it in the enforced rigidity of an armed clandestine organization. None or all of these may be relevant, and many people have experienced the same desires without ever having picked up a gun. But I do believe that in every case what gave an ideological coherence to individual choice was the construction of a mythological framework which permitted the reconciliation of the egoistic with the altruistic. They wanted to change the world, make it a better place, but they also had a desperate need to find an identity, avoid irrelevance, to achieve self-realization through action. Once I was told, 'Everything we did was for fantasy.' At first I was surprised at such an ingenuous admission. It was naive, but not as frivolous as it first sounded. The world of the Italian armed struggle begins and ends with myth, is maintained and justified in the imaginations of those who practise it until the moment when reality intrudes on myth and gradually destroys it.

References

1. *La Repubblica*, 29/3/85.
2. *La Repubblica*, 18/7/85.
3. *La Repubblica*, 20/11/85.
4. *La Repubblica*, 15/2/86.
5. *La Repubblica*, 22/2/86.
6. *La Repubblica*, 18/2/87.
7. *Il Messagero*, 24/3/87.
8. *La Repubblica*, 18/6/88.

9. *Commissione Parlamentare d'Inchiesta sulla strage di Via Fani sul sequestro e l'assissinio di Aldo Moro e sul Terrorismo in Italia*, Vol. V, pp. 33–34.
10. *Panorama*, 6/6/83.
11. Interview conducted by the author, Brescia, 24/11/86.
12. *La Repubblica*, 21/1/85.
13. *L'Espresso*, 2/12/84.
14. *L'Espresso*, 18/1/87.
15. Interview with the author, Paliano prison, 26/2/87.
16. Interview with the author, Rome, 7/5/86.
17. *Panorama*, 24/10/78.
18. Comm. Parl. Vol. V, pp. 56.
19. *Corriere della Serra*, 5/4/88. The figure refers to direct and indirect costs.

APPENDICES

THE ARMED DREAM
by Mario Massardi

Biographical note

Mario Massardi is 40 and was active in groups of the revolutionary left from the mid 1960's onwards, alternating between work as a labourer and that of 'professional revolutionary'. He was arrested for the first time in 1980 after almost a year of being on the run. The charge against him was that of involvement in a bank robbery. He was acquitted, but was arrested again in early 1983, accused of belonging to Comitati Comunisti Rivoluzionari *(Revolutionary Communism Committees). He was released again at the end of 1985 and, after a period of supervised liberty, has lived and earned a living moving between Milan and Southern Tuscany, working periodically as lorry driver and farm labourer.*

In the past he has collaborated on numerous publications produced by the revolutionary left.

1. The Great Ghetto

I am nearly forty and my doubts certainly outnumber my
years, but luckily I have a daughter who, perhaps to console
me, assures me with an air of worldly wisdom that doubts and
crises are common to everyone, and are not the exclusive
property of someone like me who was twenty in 1968 and
thirty when they kidnapped Moro. Still, the doubts go back a
long time, perhaps to before she was born, to the mid '70's
when the experience of the New Left was virtually over. It
was a time when the organizations created in the wake of '68
were becoming weaker as, one by one, the certainties that
had inspired them began to fade.

The crisis was not just one of organizational structure but of
the entire cultural framework which had sustained and
nourished it for years; it affected all the organizations,
created in the mould of pre-existing models and principles
which were now considered obsolete. All were fighting for
survival, trying to re-establish the purity which had been
betrayed by the bureaucratic and revisionist tendencies
inflicted by Stalinism and the working-class parties associated
with it.

The crisis spared no one, not even *Lotta Continua*, the
'newest' and undoubtedly the most original of the Italian
groups, where for years workers, Leninists, militants of
catholic origin and semi-anarchic elements had co-existed. It
was dissolved around 1975. One factor which contributed to
the disintegration of the New Left was the emergence in Italy,
somewhat later than in other countries, of the feminist
movement, which had hitherto been restricted to a few
groups and to a few publications of very limited circulation.
The left in general (and the New Left was no exception) had
paid scant attention to the ideology of women's liberation,
entrusting the task of resolving all the contradictions and evils
generated by the society of profit to the cathartic flames of
revolutionary fire. But women, and especially those within
revolutionary groups who were the most politicized, rejected

the tradition which united them with the proletariat in the struggle for common emancipation in a common cause against a common enemy, and claimed the right to their own individuality as women with their own needs, ways of life and of behaviour which were frequently incompatible with those of men, proletarian or not. You could compile entire volumes of letters written to 'our newspapers' in which former militants-turned-feminists accused their partners of 'domestic fascism', or protested about the tedium of the work they were obliged to do in back offices amidst ink and paper — 'angels of the photocopier' just as their mothers had been 'angels of the fireside'.

In one way or another, the shuffling of the cards brought about a total realignment of the positions held during previous years. Some people even emerged from the confusion with a set of values quite opposite to that held by their erstwhile companions. Realizing that the attempt had failed, many began to return to the ranks of the traditional left: PCI, PSI and trade unions; or simply abandoned revolutionary aspirations altogether and returned home to a wife in shawl and long flowery skirt who no longer wanted to cook or look after children; or, after years of professional revolutionary activity, began the anxious quest for a well-paid job in a country already grievously afflicted by unemployment.

But things changed even for those who did not wish to withdraw from the political scene. The remnants of AO, PdUP, MLS* and others which had somehow survived the crisis despite a substantial modification of their founding premises, began to set in motion a process of reaggregation which, decidedly reformist in nature, would eventually lead to the formation of *Democrazia Proletaria* (Proletarian Democracy) a small, vociferous party somewhat reminiscent of the PCI of the 1950's, which nowadays has an insignificant parliamentary representation equivalent to just under 2%. The route was more tortuous for the others, who

* *Avanguardia Operaia; Partito di Unitá Proletaria per il Comunismo; Movimento dei Lavatori per il Socialismo*

were obliged to use an assessment of their more radical experiences of the past and their relationship to armed violence as principal guidelines for the future.

Until at least 1974–75 there was an unwritten but essentially unanimously accepted rule for all the New Left and for certain sectors of the PCI with regard to violence: it was generally assumed that the revolution would be armed if it happened at all, and that violence, strictly limited to self-defence or retaliation, was justifiable, for example in resisting the evacuation of occupied houses by the police, in the defence of street demonstrators or of strike pickets. After fascist acts of aggression it was also justifiable to retaliate by attacking offices or activists. In this connection existed the great fear or perhaps for some the great hope of an attempted *coup d'état* by the right wing — Fascists and Christian Democrats — to overturn the democratic order and abolish left-wing organizations. Had this happened, popular resistance to the *coup* would have provided the most legitimate and shortest path to the revolutionary seizure of power. But in reality there has been no serious threat of a *coup d'état* in Italy since the founding of the Republic, with the possible exception of the Sifar/De Lorenzo plot of 1964.

In 1975 the only proponents of the armed struggle as an immediate and urgent course of action were small groups from *Potere Operaio*, *Lotta Continua* and from smaller organizations who maintained a precarious balance between legality and illegality. To these must of course be added the Red Brigades, who were going through a particularly difficult period after a spate of arrests and the loss of some important bases, and would only regain their combative efficiency during the course of the following year, when they were deemed to be definitively wiped out. Nonetheless their allure was great, enormously enhanced by their choice of clandestinity and of guerrilla warfare as a political strategy *tout court*. The failure of the groups which opted principally for legal means of action confirms the correctness of their decision, even if the BR were criticized for their aloofness, their separateness from the rest of the revolutionary movement and from social struggles, and concentrated instead on waging their own private war against the state machine. But the outcome of that debate and of the whole course of events would have been quite different and certainly less explosive had it not been for the emergence and subsequent expansion of the youth movement, whose continuously aggressive impact would be felt from 1977 until the end of 1980.

The *Movimento* took everyone by surprise, not only the mass media and the sociologists who always understood things before everyone else, but even us. It was no small thing suddenly to find the streets invaded by young people eulogizing the armed struggle, rejecting every invitation offered by the traditional left to return to normality, and who were not only not averse to confrontation with the police but often went looking for it. From the point of view of us 'old hands' there was curiosity and interest, but also a certain distrust of this strange movement which rejected the old organizational forms and used the street slogan more like a war cry, as an affirmation of their own desires rather than as a careful exemplification of a political programme such as Lenin used to advise. Those like me (and there were many of us) who were accustomed to interpreting things according to Marxist/Leninist criteria and, it must be admitted, in a fairly stereotyped way, despite our pretence of bringing significant innovation to a traditional framework, found ourselves stumbling into a sequence of ever stranger and more frenetic events. It was like going into your usual bookshop where everything is always well ordered by author and by subject matter, and unexpectedly finding a collection of Circassian fables on the same shelf as the first volume of *Das Kapital* and a book on nutrition.

Until then there had been a certain uniformity, if not within the minds then at least within the language and literature adopted by the militants: Marx, Lenin and Gramsci were good for all occasions, or almost; although of course there were variations according to the ideological preferences of any particular group which could range from Stalin to Trotsky

to Mao. But now it was like being on a beach the morning
after a shipwreck when the tide throws up everything: you
need the patience to collect and catalogue carefully and then,
once all the material has been collected, you can ask yourself
finally just what kind of cargo the shipwrecked vessel had on
board. For my part, I am still trying to work it out; there's no
point in saying that it's with some uncertainty, but at least I
have my daughter to explain it all to me.

The printed word and the rest

I wouldn't like to give the impression of being one of those
gloomy, sullen people who, ever since the Spanish Inquisi-
tion, have banned, censored and (until recently) made
bonfires of printed paper: God forbid, I'm even a tiny bit
Jewish. Still, books and more generally, the image and the
imagination have had a great part to play in the birth of
guerrilla warfare in Italy. Mark Twain used to say that the
American Civil War was the start of the exceptional
popularity of Walter Scott amongst the southern landlords. I
don't know if he was right, but sometimes reading Faulkner, a
writer of whom I am particularly fond, I can almost believe it.

At that time Cooper and Laing, and *The Anti-Oedipus* by
Deleuze and Guattari were all being translated into Italian;
Nietzsche went the rounds even within the left. Marxism was
printed in thousands of editions, in paperback, in complete
works or else in selected form, in addition to the endless
stream of essays and critical studies. Fiction made a return
appearance, although at first no one dared to mention it —
Hermann Hesse, the Beat Generation (again!), and Robbins
(Tom Robbins, of the Camel cigarette packet, obviously).
We only got to the really great writers later, in prison, when
we had enough free time to venture into the boundless plains
of *War and Peace*, the intrigues of *La Comédie Humaine* and
many others.

But as often happens, one's cultural input is controlled
either by a particular school of thought, by the most
influential groups of the day or by political circles which

behave as if they alone were the sole repositories of one truth or another. Rarely does a movement go right back to original sources, and in this the Italian *Movimento* of the 70's was no exception. We got to know Lenin (as do others elsewhere, I imagine) bit by bit, via the interpretation that Stalin and the parties affiliated to the Third International gave him, and on up to the most recent theoreticians of the New Left. The most up-to-date version in the bookshops was '*La fabbrica della strategia*' ('The factory of strategy: 33 lessons on Lenin'). Its author, of whom much would be heard in successive years, was Toni Negri. His was a Lenin who seemed to come straight out of the pages ready to intervene in the mass movement of that particular moment. But poor old Vladimir Ilyich, I think even he would have had difficulty in understanding what was going on, just as we did, and we were certainly no Lenins.

Despite what is often said abroad and especially within our national boundaries, Italy is an industrialized and democratic country which has partially resolved some of its historic problems; it's true that we have serious unemployment but there is also a family-based economy and a black economy which together permit you to take home a salary at the end of the month and live more or less decently, even if you don't have the benefit of a trade union behind you. It is a country where other problems remain or have been added, such as corruption within public administration, arrogance in the police forces, an inefficient judicial system, a cost of living which is continually rising and the progressive emargination of entire social sectors. But as far as I know these are not just our problems: Europe and the capitalist West are only too familiar with them. To use an old Marxist expression, the primary needs of the population have been satisfied. And on to this scene erupted the *Movimento*, claiming the desire and the right to consume society's wealth and to enjoy total liberty, clearly rejecting out of hand any policies of denial or sacrifice.

'We want everything' was not a slogan born in 1977. It goes back much further: amongst other things it is the title of a good novel by Nanni Balestrini, constructed around the memories of a Fiat worker, but at that particular time it took on a new significance. It was a period when you heard the obsessive repetition of the formula 'here and now', or put slightly more poetically,

'If not now, when?
If not me, then who?'

The *Movimento* lived above all from its desires, not the least of which was to live as protagonists, political subjects. One could turn to academic schools of thought to discover the exact cultural roots of this behaviour, but what really counted were the interpretations provided by its leaders and its publications such as *Rosso*, *'Senza Tregua'*, *'A/Traverso'*, *'Primo Maggio'* etc., which in many different ways provided the currents of opinion and the steady flow of ideas which surged within them.

Although it took us years to accept the actions of the BR, and then only critically, and before that to accept them as part of the revolutionary left, armed violence became the accepted norm for the *Movimento*. The myth of guerrilla warfare, even in its terrorist form, exercized a tremendous fascination on the collective imagination: all the extremist texts were devoured eagerly as were books on ETA, the IRA and the Red Army Faction. The first book published by Feltrinelli on the BR, which some said was almost a work of praise, went out of print immediately. We read the biographies of political bandits such as Bonnot, Kamo, Sabate etc and in particular the memoirs of partisan commander Giovanni Pesce, because in addition to being an autobiographical account of the Resistance, it is also an excellent handbook for armed bands.

With Vietnam over, and disillusioned by post-Maoist China, we were obliged to create new poles of reference; the cult of what I would call 'our America' was born: America as a country where you could solve any social conflict simply by picking up your Winchester. Any bibliography for this category would be very long indeed and as well as including books, films and songs, would go from Industrial Workers of the World to the black ghettos and in some instances to the truck drivers of Jimmy Hoffa and others. I remember people who on the eve of an action would go to see Sam Peckinpah's 'The Wild Bunch' if it were on in some part of the city. One lad confessed to me in prison that he had seen it 22 times; I never asked him how many charges he was standing trial for: it seemed totally irrelevant.

Thus a number of widely varying influences all flowed under the common denominator of the armed struggle. In reality it was a very slippery and ambiguous terrain and one in which you could find everyone, both young and old, and everything — revolutionary programmes, unsatisfied appetites, the desire for liberation and aspirations towards active protagonism.

The link up

'Do you remember our bars, all the tables divided by groups? Everyone was there — there was a PL table. At another, faces that might have been BR, in a far corner the lesbians who looked as if they had an iron grill between their legs, and the inevitable kids on their first action, pacing up and down and making a metallic noise as if they were walking hardware shops.'

I remember, and how, my friend.

I remember the bars, the leather jackets and the trench coats, and certain faces who you weren't sure if they were police or clandestine militants. It was from this heterogeneous population that the armed groups were formed, mostly workers, students who had given up studying and lived from one irregular job after another, and young Sicilians or Calabrians now living in the outer suburbs. There were few intellectuals in the traditional sense, and the working class predominated, even if the factory worker was no longer in the majority, as once had been the case. And there were the women, a small component of the feminist movement who had chosen violent conflict as a way to free themselves from bourgeois male oppression. It was a noisy and impatient collection of people who marched in demonstrations, often armed; who went to occupy houses and to shop in supermarkets, sufficiently numerous that they couldn't be forced to pay at the checkout counter. There was nothing institutionalized about them, even though one or other armed formation might have been particularly active in a given sector, district or factory, thus making it relatively easy to guess who had been responsible for certain actions. It was all highly fluid, so that a good organizer could begin to recruit from within a pool of people considered the most trustworthy, initiating them by degrees into the practise of combat.

There is a certain symbiosis between the *Movimento* and armed groups; within the *Movimento* you could argue for or against the validity of any particular action but the correctness of 'criticism with arms' was never doubted for a moment. One proof of this amongst the many I could cite was the anti-fascist demonstration which took place almost spontaneously after the murder of the MSI councillor Pedenovi in Milan in 1976, in retaliation for an attack which had caused the death of a young revolutionary.

It was the existence of this aspect of *Movimento* which ensured the continual flow of people into the armed organizations; although in reality, rather than being proper organizations, some were merely clusters of people which formed and then dissolved again in an *ad hoc* manner within the *Movimento* itself, existing just long enough to perform a specific action or reach a specific objective. The breakup of the dialectic *Movimento*/armed groups was in fact the real reason for the end, temporary or definitive (I don't know) of the armed struggle in Italy. In any case, a combination of intrinsic weaknesses and state repression made it obvious from the end of 1980 onwards that we were heading for defeat. Now that the armed organizations have been decimated and the *Movimento* has run its course, guerrilla warfare has been reduced to virtually nothing, a volcano which occasionally sends up a menacing puff of smoke. But there is no doubt that the fire, even if invisible, continues to burn.

The Instruments

I returned to Milan recently, a bit emotional as we all are when we go back to our home town after a long absence. Don't worry, I'm not going to enumerate all the changes I saw, which were many and obvious. Instead I'll be content with describing a road junction in a suburban street, where I noticed a small and unimportant difference that made me smile. The traffic lights were intact, a bit discoloured by the sun and by weather damage, but intact: minus the holes you used to see there at the end of the '70's. At that time there wasn't one minor road junction in the city suburbs where the traffic lights weren't riddled with bullet holes. If a decent ballistics expert had looked carefully at the holes, he could have made a good guess as to the proficiency of whoever had shot.

When I think back now to what the newspapers printed during those years, I wonder what routes the journalists took every morning to get to their newspaper offices and then home again in the evening; undoubtedly different ones from the streets we used. Otherwise they would never have dreamt up training camps in Lebanon or Syria or some other exotic place. They would have found them close to home, or else in the same shooting ranges to which many of them, seized by the fear of terrorism, went to train in the use of arms. For indeed public shooting ranges, all properly affiliated to the Italian Olympic Committee, were another training ground, certainly much more convenient than crossroads, although they did have the disadvantage of obligatory enrolment. If today you were to have a look through the membership lists for those years you would find many names of militants who either ended up in prison or were sought by the police to face charges of membership of an armed band.

And if you were careful you could go home in credit, by using up only part of the bullets issued by the management and putting the rest in your pocket. They were usually 38 or 7.65 calibre bullets, those most common in civil use. Unfortunately they were only made of soft lead and didn't have a metal casing. Who knows if the directors of the Olympic Committee realize that a public institution was amongst the principal suppliers of ammunition, albeit of low quality, to the urban guerrilla war.

This then, was the very rustic or, as we say, 'homemade' beginning to the armed struggle. And what goes for training is also true of weapons, despite the fact that towards the end, the AK-47, Sterling and Belgian FAL light machine guns began to make a sporadic appearance. But the early stages and almost all of its subsequent development were founded on a much more modest type of weapon of a lower firing capacity. Short guns were more common than long: either automatic pistols or revolvers which were relatively easy to buy on the black market, at least in the days before the introduction of the emergency laws (later it became common practice to steal from armouries, or private gun collectors, or else to disarm security guards, policemen or night watchmen.) On the whole, court records give a reasonably faithful account of the type of armaments used. The greatest proportion is accounted for by pistols, but hunting guns with sawn-off barrel and butt appear regularly; at the very least those with a smooth bore were shortened so that they could be more easily concealed under clothing. Loaded with large bullets and used over a short distance, these could be used to devastating effect. In Italy this is the traditional weapon of the Mafia and of southern crime organizations in general, or at least so crime reporters, always careful to point out the ritualistic aspect of every crime, would have us believe. You could also find quite a number of Stens Mark II and III, and it's worth having a look at these.

Just as the sawn-off shot gun is *the* Mafia weapon, the Sten is the equally mythical weapon of the Italian Resistance, even today alternately praised and derided for its virtues and faults by all old partisans after the first half-litre of wine. After 1943, the British aid to Italy came as manna from Heaven and in considerable quantity, because many were still circulating within the ranks of the urban guerrillas, passed on from hand to hand or from revolutionary faction to revolutionary faction.

According to Giorgio Galli's *History of the Armed Party* one or more Stens were used in the Moro kidnap. But I don't know if Galli is talking from conviction, from personal experience or out of awe for the British armaments industry when he praises the precision and efficiency of the Sten, because Giorgio Bocca, another historian of terrorism, who in his youth was a partisan commander and as such certainly had more than one opportunity to use it, is of the opposite view and describes the Sten as about as precise and efficient as a stove pipe.

But the Sten was not the only residue of the Second World War — the Tocarev Nagant, Walther P.38, Colt 45 and Luger were also used, and you could even come across single action revolvers. And to broaden the scope between the rustic and the domestic there were also machine guns, which I have mentioned, and which I'll come back to later on.

Short and long guns

Having provided a description of the type of weapons used, I'd like now to attempt a brief military background. Revolutionary war is deployed war with an army, rear zones and zones liberated from the enemy; guerrilla war is important in the sense that it is the initial phase of a progression towards a larger, open conflict. With some differences, all revolutionary theorists who have also been military leaders, such as Mao, Giap and Che Guevara are agreed on this. Even if guerrilla war never manages to get beyond this initial phase, it can survive as an endemic phenomenon, as is still the case in Latin America, or else it can ebb and flow sporadically as seems to be happening nowadays in Italy, but without hope of success.

The call that the armed clandestine groups made every now and again to the mass of their sympathizers was to construct a revolutionary army or some analagous formation; a call which obviously met with scant success. It is a fact that guerrilla warfare in Italy has always remained at the level of short arms, of the little nuclei conducting little actions, which at the most elementary level were known as 'bite and run'.

When he was writing *Guerrilla Warfare* Che recommended the Garand (M1) as the ideal weapon for fighting formations, since apart from being one of the best guns of the time, replenishment of its ammunition in Latin America was relatively easy. He was obviously addressing himself to men who could move freely through the countryside with a long gun over their shoulder, a rather more unlikely spectacle in Milan or Rome, even during the period of maximum offensive capability which followed the Moro kidnap.

I know little about ETA or the IRA except what one can read in books and newspapers, but judging by the actions they have conducted and by the weapons they had or may still have at their disposal, they certainly were or are more of an 'army' than the Red Brigades or *Prima Linea* ever were.

To become an army signifies having a rear ground of popular support or, if you like, an area of broad complicity for your actions. It also implies the carrying and use in daylight of a heavy duty military weapon; the only kind which permits you to hold your own against the forces of state repression and to win the battle. The overwhelming prevalence of small arms, only good for low level attacks in cities (and the Moro kidnap falls into this category) is the most obvious proof, along with other factors of course, of the weakness of an armed movement.

However, both *Prima Linea*, together with other minor groups variously linked to it, and the BR attempted a qualitative leap in terms of arms in 1978 and the summer of 1979. The judicial records for these operations talk of 150 Sterling machine guns for the BR (the number seems excessive to me) and of around 15 AK 47s, plus a few Belgian FALs and perhaps two Soviet-made missile launchers for *Prima Linea*.

Both consignments came from Lebanon and were collected by boat from Italy; it is not true that the arms were a present from a foreign power as part of an attempt to destabilize Italy, but were instead the result of normal, albeit illegal, business deals. The operation must have cost *Prima Linea* approximately 100 million lire and was funded by an incredible number of bank robberies. But the AK-47s with the suitable ammunition arrived almost totally oxidized and unusable due to saline deposits and to the general conditions in which they had been transported. The BR were smarter, at least in their choice of arms. The Sterling is both more practical to use and is an easier weapon to find ammunition for in the West than the AK-47. I don't know what they cost, but I believe the money to buy them came from the ransom of the shipowner Costa, kidnapped in Genoa in January 1977.

The most significant aspect of this is that of all these weapons, which would have permitted the firing capacity of the armed groups to increase considerably, hardly any were ever used, and most were discovered in the course of the following few years, either buried underground or hidden in cellars.

Thinking about all this reminds me very much of an old friend of mine who had a passion for powerful cars and saved for years to buy a BMW which he neither knew how to handle nor could ever use. He lived in an old quarter of the city full of tiny narrow streets and little courtyards full of rubbish, where to manoeuvre properly would have involved knocking down at least half the houses in the district in order to widen the streets. In this sense, even when it was technically possible, guerrilla warfare in Italy never even reached BMW level.

Explosives

To paraphrase from memory, Walter Laqueur (with apologies in advance to a historian of his seriousness and documentary precision) defines terrorism in *The Age of Terrorism* as a category unto itself, independent of the social and political groups which practise it. Laqueur dedicates a large section of the book to the bomb, its philosophy, its use, its high priests and one in particular, J. Most, to whom he devotes an entire chapter of the book. In my opinion he is right, the bomb represents indiscriminate terror and death, as do fire and flood. At the end of the last century, in Carrara, still the sacred city of Italian anarchy, the marble quarriers used to sing, 'the redeeming call: dynamite!', even if for them dynamite was and is a dangerous work mate with whom they must co-exist, as well as an instrument of struggle and liberation.

It's a fact that the bomb-dynamiting-anarchist-left-wing-extremist equation has almost always existed in the imagination of the man-in-the-street, such that sectors of the security services in collusion with fascist groups have tried more than once to plant bombs which incriminate the left (the burning of the Reichstag could serve as the best example of this.) This only really ceased to function after the massacre of Piazza Fontana, although it took years of struggle for the anarchist Pietro Valpreda, initially accused of the massacre, to be acquitted. I don't mean to infer from all this that plastic, TNT, cheddite and other explosives have never been used by the guerrilla left, rather that terrorist use of them has never been made against people. As I recall, the only fatalities have been militants themselves who on one occasion were mixing the components for a bomb in Vicenza, and two others who died in the same way in Naples. The only extraneous fatality was an old age pensioner who died in the explosion which followed the dynamiting of a perimeter wall of Rovigo female prison in a successful operation in January 1982 to free a number of companions.

Before that, left-wing bombs had gone off in offices of government parties, of employers' associations, on prison construction sites and in bars frequented by drug pushers during campaigns to prevent hard drugs from entering working-class districts. The most important action carried out with explosives that I can remember took place in Milan in March 1977. A government decree had abolished a number of public holidays, six or seven as far as I remember, feast days of saints or madonnas, officially rewarded by demonstrations of faith, and designated compulsory in all work contracts (such are the small advantages of catholicism.) Nowadays it is hard to imagine a clandestine group with a meagre following calling a strike as if it were a legally recognized trade union, nonetheless *Prima Linea* opted for an extremely spectacular act of sabotage: during the night when traffic was suspended, the lines of the underground trains were blown up, as were a number of electric cables. Years later in prison, I happened to hear a lad saying that during the days prior to the action he had read the whole of *The Seven Pillars of Wisdom* to learn how to mine a railway line. Still, it must be said that people did get to work all the same, albeit on foot and very tardily. The attempt to revive the legendary memory of similar acts of sabotage, carried out during the Resistance in March 1944 under Nazi occupation, in order to extend the strike which had broken out in a few Milanese factories, drew laughter and derision rather than set a new heroic precedent from which inspiration could be taken.

Specialization and money

The professionalism and the resources which the armed struggle had at its disposal have been mythologized a great deal by those who either do not understand or do not wish to understand that terrorism is a job to be learned like any other. To learn to shoot is not difficult. If conflict always occurs over a short distance then you don't even have to be an excellent shot. It's far more important to have the determination to do so; after all, a man is never just a 10 lire coin. What counts in this job is to know how to drive, and better still how to steal cars — or at least that was the opinion of a bank robber who shared my cell for a while, but I think it would be endorsed by many if not all the militants of the armed struggle.

Every action, like every robbery, requires one or more vehicles, if possible fast and inconspicuous, to get to and from the scene in a hurry. Cars are central to the first order of problems: where to hide them, how to fake numberplates, log books etc. I have taken cars as an example, but I could have used others to demonstrate how guerrilla, or if you prefer, terrorist professionalism is formed. The need for means of transport creates the good car thief and the forger whose vital task is to furnish the wanted militant with false identity papers, etc. The number of needs, and therefore of specialities, tends to increase as guerrilla activities grow: houses in which to keep printing machines for clandestine publications, and money, always money (if you are on the run you can't just go to the employment office and ask for a job or for unemployment benefit because the fridge is empty and the children are crying).

The first and only ones to tackle all these problems of logistics thoroughly and right from the beginning were the Red Brigades, in whose autonomous, self-sufficient column structure can be found an echo of Che's *The Construction of the Guerrilla Front*. Whilst for the BR secrecy was initially a choice, for other, smaller groups it was determined by the overall expansion of the conflict; a factor which caused greater organizational fragility.

In general terms, improvization was the name of the game. If you could, you resolved problems as they occurred and went looking for money when the coffers were about to run dry. Money is almost certainly the greatest problem of all for clandestine groups. In a country where political parties and the press are financed out of public money the clandestine parties are the only ones not to benefit from state aid. As far as I know the BR were extremely rigid about money. Each month the central committee asked for a detailed statement of all outgoings, and according to an old Leninist principle gave each professional militant a monthly wage which corresponded to that of a middle-ranking factory worker. In other groups administration was rather more light-hearted: a new leather jacket or dinner in a good restaurant could quite well be the conclusion of a day which had begun with a self-financing robbery.

I should say that the era of large bands of bank robbers which started to operate in Italy in the aftermath of the Second World War ended quite some time ago; not that they have disappeared altogether, but nowadays the criminal underworld has taken up more lucrative business — drugs, financial rackets, etc. In reality, such activities were only filling a gap left empty by others. I think the police and judiciary took a good while to realize this, but nowadays it seems as if they have gone to the other extreme. Every time a robbery occurs now they assume it's the work of the *brigatisti*. Too generous of them! Nonetheless it's true that as at least the minor groups began to disband at the end of the '70's, a number of them, having once learned the art of bank robbery, took up the job on a full time basis.

This relatively minor phenomenon recalls very different, but in some ways analagous, situations which affect disbanded troops at the end of any war or any political experience of particular ferocity. It happened in 1945 with thieves and robbers, half of whom were partisans and half Fascists. It happened in America after the Civil War when the soldiers of the dissolved federal army invented the bank robbery. On the other hand, once a profession has been learned, it is difficult to unlearn it and learn another, especially if you're no longer at the age of apprenticeship.

The word of an 'infame' and that of another

When all's said and done the metropolitan guerrilla is a new anthropological species in this country. He has at his disposal a number of practical organizational abilities usually united to a cultural level and a knowledge of politics which are above the average. Even if he lives in secrecy he moves amongst people to whom he does not necessarily feel hostile, although he may not find them especially sympathetic. He may on the other hand live a normal life, be a good husband and father, linked in a thousand ways to the social life which goes on around him, carrying out clandestine actions rather than living a clandestine life. So, no 'samurai warriers' then, but simply men and women at war, rightly or wrongly, with an order of things which they consider inimical. Let's face it, in any society there can exist whole sections or even just groups of individuals who are quite normal in their own way, but who reject all public and private regulations, and who in order to defy them are prepared to take up arms. This is difficult to accept, especially, perhaps, in a democratic regime. It explains why the phenomenon has always been demonized, why people have always looked for external causes and agents; such as the Arab countries, the USSR, Mafia intrigues etc. And yet the truth has even been confirmed by the depositions of the *pentiti*. Patrizio Peci, the BR's biggest *pentito*, says in his book that there was no one hero, no one militant with particular fighting qualities, but only rough factory workers who left Fiat or Alfa Romeo dirty after a day's work; or else women like any others — a bit too fat or a bit too thin, but with all the problems that women always have. Terrible to admit it, but ordinary people. I think the subversive value of this statement is obvious. I don't know how much Peci realized it, but his editor must have had some doubts, because despite the book's considerable success, '*Io, L'Infame*' has never been reprinted.

It's curious how, from a totally different approach, the word of an *infame* coincides with that of *compagno* Mario Moretti, historic leader of the BR and organizer of the Moro kidnap: 'You'll never accept that those who had you running for years were nothing but a little band of workers dying of hunger.'

2. Changes

I entered prison at the beginning of 1982 and waited almost four years for freedom. It wasn't the first time, so I was accustomed to loneliness, to hunger, to forced cohabitation and to the expectation of pain, both that of the soul and that experienced in the body. I believe I behaved correctly, that is in accordance with the things and ideas by which I tried to regulate my life for those four years.

I was one of the many — one of almost 4,000. No one has ever come up with an exact figure, neither the organizations which fought repression and tended to exaggerate the numbers, nor the state institutions, intent on minimizing the presence of so many revolutionary militants in prison.

I was arrested when the last fires of guerrilla warfare, though much diminished, were still burning, and I returned to freedom in a country apparently pacified. When I left prison I said goodbye to companions who were no longer the same as those with whom I had shared an important part of my life. They, like me, had changed.

Within the existential patterns of a revolutionary, prison ought to have its own normality, an obligatory but transitory stage. Or at least so we thought during the many years of the *Movimento*. But by 1982 the number of imprisoned militants was already very high; *pentitismo* and the spate of arrests which followed were predictable phenomena. And for many of us, the possibility that imprisonment could be very long or even final began to harden into painful certainty.

Until then a kind of solidarity had bound companions inside to those outside, as demonstrated by campaigns to liberate a particular militant, actions to organize escapes or else reprisals against prison warders. The most notorious of these was the murder of the commander of the prison guards at Milan's San Vittore prison in the summer of 1981, followed during the night of September 22nd by one of the most ferocious bloodbaths in recent prison history. Warders sent in from other other prisons beat up hundreds of prisoners, both political and ordinary. When I arrived at San Vittore months afterwards, the signs of that night were still to be seen; dried blood on the walls, cells smashed up with pickaxes in order that those who had taken refuge from the butchery by barricading themselves in could be reached and dragged into the corridors.

To a movement born young — so young that in the beginning it was often defined as youth contestation — the idea of growing old in prison, abandoned by everyone, was quite inconceivable. In reality very few had absorbed the normality of prison into their ideas of revolutionary life. As it gradually became clear to everyone that the state would never concede political recognition, for many, the renunciation of their own past seemed the only practical route to a shortened sentence, even though dissociation was only talked of explicitly in the course of the following year.

The Community

We lived separately from the other prisoners. This wasn't the case everywhere. It was a rule only in the main prisons. The constant fear was that the encounter of revolutionary militants with ordinary criminals was a potentially explosive mixture, hence the institutional preference for relegating political prisoners to special sections. Conditions ranged then as now from those in the maximum security prisons where isolation is total, where conversations with relatives take place behind glass and by intercom, and where you are allowed nothing from outside, to those where controls are less rigid. Allocation is determined by criteria of danger, although there is also a certain element of chance in being assigned to a particular prison or to a particular section. The grouping together for reasons of affinity in a particular cell is something which happens spontaneously, and is usually encouraged by the prison authorities in the interests of avoiding internal friction. This goes for both political and ordinary prisoners.

Tradition has it that prison is a school for revolution, that the arrested militant educates his fellow prisoners and transforms the burglar or bank robber into a conscious proletarian. In reality this only happened by chance and only at the beginning when the prestige of the urban guerrilla was still high, unaffected by *pentitismo* and dissociation. Usually, any attempts to politicize ordinary prisoners yielded scant results and sometimes led to disastrous effects.

Before the great wave of arrests began, and therefore before we had first-hand experience of prison ourselves, our opinions on the subject were very literary, as were our ideas about the criminal underworld. If you wanted to bring to mind a credible Mafia boss you inevitably ended up recalling the character played by Marlon Brando in *The Godfather*. Finding yourself amongst drug pushers and kidnappers made you change your mind completely about many things you had simply accepted unquestioningly.

Prison always reflects the changes taking place in society. Thus there was no point in looking for Arsenio Lupin or the latest descendant of Robin Hood in the wings of San Vittore. With the virtual disappearance of the big bands of bank robbers the Mafia clans predominated, and in the course of their internal wars which continued even within the prison walls, there were attacks, knifings and executions on the stairs or in courtyards during the fresh air periods. Ultimately, even if no one had the courage or the honesty to admit it, the segregation of prisoners was a preferable situation to that of general promiscuity with the others. At least we could keep out of the way of the Mafia feuds. But this did not prevent us from joining in protests with the ordinary prisoners to improve living conditions, for better health care and for the abolition of article 90 which imposed severe restrictions in the maximum security prisons. The largest of these was the hunger strike in the summer of 1983 for the abolition of the old law on preventive detention, which at different times involved 10,000 prisoners all over Italy. We began it at San Vittore, and some months later a better law was approved.

Continuity and surrender

In Italian prisons the political prisoners have rarely if ever been a united, compact body. The divisions and affiliations of each group continued to survive inside, even if outside the original group had been completely dissolved. It's an old tradition of the left (and not only in Italy) to quarrel with your closest neighbours. This happened first between anarchists and socialists, then between socialists and communists, and it also happened between PL, the BR and the other organizations during the years of my imprisonment. Even so, as far as the rest of the prison population was concerned, the political prisoners were a single unit: you were 'the terrorist', and there was almost no point in explaining the difference between yourself and another militant.

But as the years passed and guerrilla warfare wore itself out, the dominant spirit of any group was the adhesion to a particular line of thinking, determined by the revaluation of each person's individual experiences. Only in a few instances did the original organizational link continue to hold things together. The defeat, temporary or otherwise, of the armed struggle was evident. That something in our plans and more particularly in our practice had gone wrong was certainly not something that required further demonstration. We had the only concrete proof that was needed – that we were where we were.

From this starting point, common to most of the political prisoners, there began a series of different paths, in many cases obviously conditioned by the concern to shorten the term of imprisonment. There can be no other explanation for the sudden conversion to the rules of the democratic game or even to catholicism after years spent with a revolver stuck in the belt. There's no doubt, the roads to Damascus are infinite in number.

But this is not true of everyone; there are those who continue to maintain or defend the ideas and actions of the past, and those who by study and reflection hope to reinvent a different idea of revolution more in keeping with the complexities of the present day. There is no one school of thought, and for every political position adopted there is a different attitude and a corresponding difference of treatment in prison. Certain prisons or some sections within them are reserved for those who display varying degrees of conciliation. At Bergamo, Alessandria and Rebibbia things are better, in fact as good as they can be in prison; at San Vittore worse, whereas Novara and Badu' e Carros (Nuoro) are sheer hell. In journalese all this is lumped under the terms 'dissociazione' and 'irriducibilità', but in reality the nuances are endless. The criticisms of one's own past do not always lead to dissociation — for many it merely goes as far as judicial silence and stops there.

The general election of 1983 was an occasion when these differences were made public. Parliament began to air the possibility of a law on dissociation which would reward those who distanced themselves unequivocally from the armed struggle. It was also a time when strange delegations of Socialist and Christian Democrat prelates began to wend their way towards the prisons. Even Archbishop Martini of Milan came. I remember some of my companions kneeling down and kissing his ring; even today I still wonder if it was the Jewish bit of me that made me turn my eyes away.

Scenes of daily life

I spent my prison years at San Vittore, or 'No 2', as they call it in popular Milanese ballads. No 2 Piazza Filangieri wasn't Rebibbia, as I said before, but nor was it one of the hell holes of the Italian prison system either. Things were so-so. If I think of many of my friends and many of my companions, I really cannot honestly complain. At least I always received a parcel with clean laundry, books and food — very rare for those in the special prisons. And once a week, by leaning over the 70 x 80 cm desk of the reception room where a proper embrace was impossible, I could at least squeeze and kiss the face of my woman or my sister, something which was impossible for those who looked and talked at each other through panes of glass.

I lived in a compact, all-male community, which in this respect was not dissimilar to a Franciscan friary or to a dormitory in a boarding school or barracks. As happens in any community of this type, squabbles and misunderstandings arose which were resolved in silences heavy with bitterness, in quarrels or in fights which after years of imprisonment had taken on the rituals and the jargon of prison life.

The truth is that men living alone are a bit comical, but they are also very different from the way people imagine them outside. For one thing, homosexuality is not nearly as common as is believed; when it does occur it is nearly always by mutual consent and is rarely violent. What can be violent, however, are the scenes of jealousy which take place, but these happen even with respectable people. A lot of pornography was consumed, both the written word and films, as well as geographical and travel magazines. As an old cell mate of mine used to say, we cherished all different aspects of the great natural world which God created for the benefit of man and of which we were being deprived. But at the same time there was also an attempt to remain men, men alone, with our dignity and our vanity.

I have never in my life seen such a quantity of cosmetics as I saw in No 1 wing of San Vittore, even if I include those belonging to all the women I've been with. Not growing old also involved acquiring creams, oils and special soaps or practising complicated and painful gymnastics during the fresh air periods. At first all this upset me quite a lot, but later on I happened to reflect on a girlfriend of mine also implicated in the Milan *Prima Linea* trial. She used to descend the steps of the courtroom cage moving and bestowing smiles around her like a Broadway star. That kind of behaviour irritated me a bit in that particular place — she was about 22 years old and already had been in prison for three. I must admit it took me quite some time to realize that only the most censorious of moralists could have criticized her or deprived her of that tiny joy, of that infantile exhibition of vanity.

But it wasn't simply a question of vanity, even if the Bible does say that everything is vantiy. There was also courage, affection, solidarity and friendship, and that indefinable feeling of belonging to a clan, family or group which, no matter what, will never conform to the rules of 'their' game. And there was no shortage of opportunities to show this.

But I like to remember the congenial, family aspect, the meals taken together with a clean table cloth often improvized from old sheets, and cutlery neatly arranged next to the plates. Prisons in Italy do not have communal refectories. Everything takes place in your cell. Usually the meals provided are foul, so people cook for themselves at their own expense. You would let the people in the cell next door taste what your mother had put in your food parcel, and for those who had no money, companions who worked would manage to pass on a part of their pay.

This is what I prefer to remember. I know it's got nothing to do with gastronomy but is something much more profound — it's the ability to remain men even in hell, even when the memory of what you once were seems to be fading into the distance like a dream. It means that if nothing else, we weren't the monsters they made us out to be.

ORGANIZATIONAL TENDENCIES IN ITALIAN REVOLUTIONARY GROUPS
by Mario Massardi

The diagrams overleaf do not represent a genealogical tree because too many branches and offshoots are missing; nor are they a skeleton outline of a vertical structure, but rather a pattern of organizational tendencies in a continual state of forming and dissolving. The ideal organic picture would be more a horizontal than a vertical one, and some names traverse almost the whole nebulous entity of Italian guerrilla warfare in the most diverse places and groups. Fluidity of movement was also a feature within the organizations themselves, as was the frequent passage of militants or entire sections from one organization to another. The only ones with a more or less vertical line of progression are the Red Brigades; for the others the path through the armed struggle was often determined by the original group to which they belonged in the factory, the district or the school, or else by some common cultural matrix — ideological guide lines determined at the start, such as Marxism/Leninism, anarchism, labourism etc, which brought them together even under different denominations.

It is rather like Le Carré's spies who would have studied at Oxford or Cambridge in the years prior to the Second World War, during the period when volunteers went to fight in the Spanish Civil War, of widespread Marxism even within academic circles in Britain and America. Thus someone who was twenty years old then will turn up without realizing it as a mole in an English spy story. It's a bit like what happened to many of our lads who found themselves accused of acts of terrorism simply because they were born in one district rather than another, or went to one school instead of another.

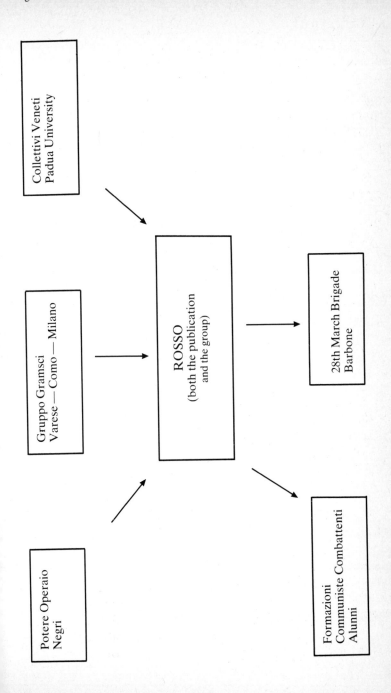

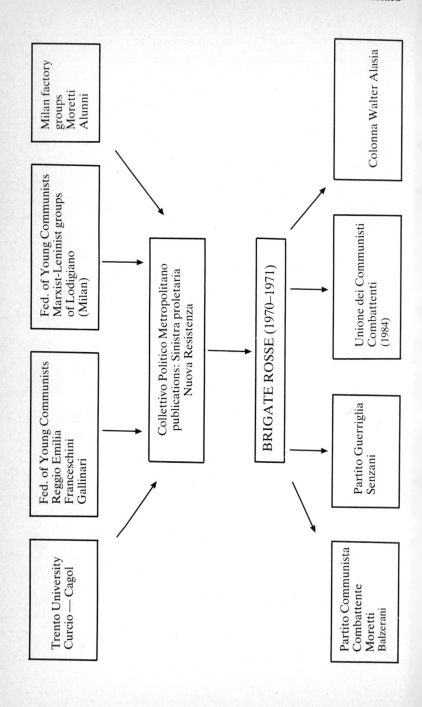

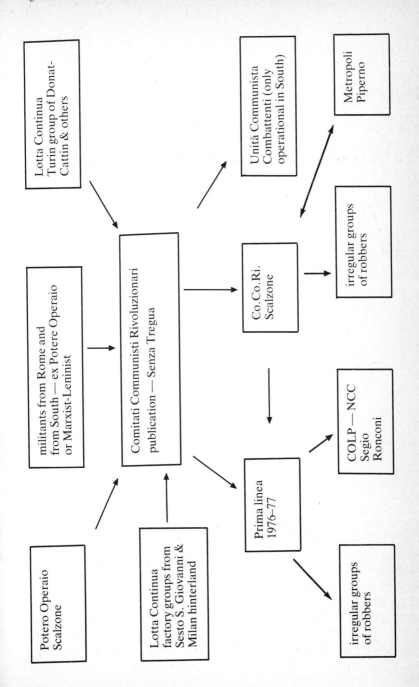

INTERVIEW WITH ADRIANA FARANDA

**Paliano Prison,
26th February 1987**

Biographical note

Adriana Faranda was born in Sicily in 1950. She became actively involved in politics in 1968 whilst a student at Rome university. She militated in Potere Operaio *and* Formazioni Armate Comuniste *before joining the Red Brigades in 1976. She was arrested in 1979 and given a 30 year prison sentence. She became dissociated from terrorism during 1983/84.*

———————————

With regard to your initial political commitment, I think you once described this as the result of a coming together of various elements — the '68 movement, your own development as a person, the experience of being in Rome at that particular time — that it was almost necessary to be involved in some way.

Things are never quite as clear as that. Countless others lived in Rome at the same time as me: kids of my age who weren't as involved as me, either in the political struggles or in the choices of the successive years. I suppose really it was the way I experienced the events of that time, my own personal stand-point on the problems, the crises, the hopes and the expectations that we had as well as what was happening outside which determined that particular path. It certainly would have been difficult to stand outside it all, especially for those who started university in 1968 with so much going on. And then we began to confront the problems of the working classes; there were all the extra-parliamentary groups. In one sense it would have been difficult to pull out, but many did. Nothing was automatic, nothing can ever be automatic.

It's a big step from political commitment of, let's say a normal kind, to the commitment that you had. I don't imagine it happened overnight, but was a gradual thing.

Yes, there were lots of little steps which led to where I ended up.

I suppose September/October 1976 was a decisive time for you, [ie when she entered the Red Brigades] *by which time you'd evaluated the other possibilities and had rejected them. Would you say that was a point of no return?*

Yes, I suppose so. But even then it wasn't a major leap in the true sense of the word. It was just another stage. But still, as you say, it was a point of no return. But more than a point of no return, it was a choice: choosing to enter the Red Brigades — to become clandestine and therefore to break off relations with your family, with the world in which you'd lived until the day before — is a choice so total that it involves your entire life, your daily existence. It means choosing to occupy yourself from morning till night with problems of politics, of organization, and fighting; and no longer with normal life — culture, cinema, babies, the education of your children, with all the things that fill other people's lives. These things get put to one side, ignored, because they simply do not exist any more. And when you remove yourself from society, even from the most ordinary things, ordinary ways of relaxing, you no longer share even the most basic emotions with other people. You become abstracted, removed. In the long run you actually begin to feel different. Why? Because you are different. You become closed off, become sad, because a whole area of life is missing, because you are aware that life is more than politics and political work.

I've often wondered how it was possible to live like that, separated from the mass of normal people, the people whom you aimed to represent. How did you reconcile those difficulties — by means of the irregular members who had contacts in the factories etc?

Yes, exactly, this was of critical importance. In practice we lived through the thoughts of normal people — or what we thought were the thoughts of normal people who worked in the factories and lived in the working-class districts — by means of those who actually did live in these situations. In a sense we were not once but twice removed. We had to trust in our impressions which in fact were only the subjective impressions of others. And living like that undoubtedly creates a series of ambiguities and misunderstandings. But at the same time, at what you could call a popular level, there is always a kind of hatred of power, of the ruling classes; there's always a feeling of frustration and discontent that the man in the street has. So that in those days, and even at the time of the Moro kidnap, there was a reaction of 'at last someone's doing something, it's about time, they had it coming to them. Now let them pay for it.' And this means absolutely nothing. It isn't consensus with a particular line of politics or of combat, it doesn't mean consensus with anything. All it signifies is a non-committal expression of discontent. And these same people today would stand back quite calmly if, say, an '*irriducibile*' were executed, if for example the armed struggle became more desperate and the death penalty existed. I think there's a kind of shallowness which means that blame must always be attributed. Today, for example, it might be the fault of the Christian Democratic party; tomorrow of the terrorists and the next day of someone else.

Yes, I remember hearing that some people were pleased on the day Moro was kidnapped.

Well obviously, you can see how with great ingenuousness and scarcely any understanding of mass psychology we interpreted this as support for the Red Brigades — which it wasn't in the slightest.

That reminds me of the interview a journalist did at the Fiat factory gates after the Casalegno attack. Even though the workers didn't particularly approve of the action they were indifferent to Casalegno's fate.

That's exactly what I mean. And just imagine what happens when, instead of an attack on a journalist with whom they have no contact, a department head or a manager is wounded. Then it's even easier to off-load your aggression, just at a verbal level alone.

By having discussions and arguments with the irregular members, we who were clandestine and who had no contact with anything, believed for a while that we understood what the situation was; what people outside thought. Though that went on for some time, it wasn't all that long. There were a number of things which made Valerio and me stop and think. For example, when all the rest of the extra-parliamentary movement spoke out — and it's not as if they stayed silent when the BR were in action. As far as the Moro kidnap was concerned, they held meetings, they made their own assessments, and even asked the BR quite explicitly to release Moro alive. And these things clashed with the way the Red Brigades wanted to see things, with their wish to think everyone was in agreement. I mean, imagine anyone saying 'no' to the kidnap of a Christian Democratic politician after 30 years of wrong-doing and misrule.

But in fact it wasn't like that; in fact there were many people who were in disagreement, who said: 'No. Stop. Wait: that's not the right road.' It was impossible to ignore a whole area of militants whose political origins you shared. It was absurd, suddenly there was a feeling almost of enmity

between you. We became so far apart that they were seen as
counter-revolutionaries. And you weren't just separated
from a part of yourself, from a part of your own history, but
separated from a whole area of people who like you were
outside the system, outside the games played by the
politicians. You had the feeling of squeezing yourself into an
ever-tighter corner.

An ever decreasing minority . . .

The minority of a minority of a minority! It got to the point
where you saw 99.99% of the population, of extant beings, as
real enemies. Obviously we didn't see things in such clear
terms then. But it did become clearer all the time, to the point
at which we left the Red Brigades because of this increasing
separation, the squeezing in of our environment. By that time
the Red Brigades could no longer speak any language except
their own.

*I'd like to ask you about violence. I know that you personally
have never killed anyone, but you must have taken part in all
the discussions, must have thought about it a lot. For those of
us who have never been involved, I think the most difficult
thing to understand is how people can kill, even though the
victim may be considered a hated symbol and not a human
being. How do you overcome this — I mean to kill another
person is not a natural human tendency, unless it be in
self-defence or in anger?*

Yes, I know. I think a person's relationship with violence is,
as you say, the most incomprehensible thing. It takes the
coming together of so many different elements for one person
to go out and kill another. First of all, there is a very high level
of abstraction, which serves to project a series of feelings over
a whole category of people and over the symbols that
represent this category. And in carrying out this mental
process of abstraction, you can attribute a series of
responsibilities or blame for things on to the category: things
which are also concrete facts — the real unhappiness of
people, deaths at the workplace, homeless earthquake

victims, kids who die of heroin because someone allows it to happen; and also our own friends, comrades killed during demonstrations by the police. Within this attribution of blame and responsibility there is also a burden of passion with which one person goes to attack another. But it isn't easy to explain because in part it's a rational mechanism and in part not.

You once said that when you shoot or kill, the violence is in some way reciprocal. In other words, that you yourself experience violence at the same time as you administer it. I'm not exactly sure what you mean by that.

In my opinion there are very strong contradictions within the ideal which you have in your mind, the model of society you want to construct, within the idea you have of the right kind of relationships between people — of mutual love, reciprocal tolerance, help and so on. You convince yourself that to reach this utopia of idealized relationships it is necessary to pass through the destruction of the society which prevents your ideas from being realized. Violence is a necessary component of this destruction. The concept of the purifying bloodbath is axiomatic to the model of the socialist revolution. There were a whole series of cultural models which indicated that any major change in history had always passed through conflicts of the most violent type, between those defending the old social order and those wanting to impose the new. If you accept the premise of the inevitability of violence, you accept that it is a necessary price to pay, even though it has absolutely nothing to do with what will come afterwards. Still, you do experience a contradiction, despite the emotive push of anger, despite the ideals you have, despite the people you are trying to save from the ruin of tomorrow. You do feel it as extraneous, something which you are obliged to use but which displeases you, which you don't like. And at the moment when you go to attack another person there is a part of you which you have to silence and mutilate, a part of you which rebels and says 'no!'

Some things we only understood afterwards: That violence

can actually make you unclean too: that violence only leads to violence — it's not true that violence can purify anything; that hatred gives birth to hatred; that every time you use violence you diminish yourself. At the time you are partly aware of this internal contradiction but feel it as something inevitable, something which you don't like, but which you perforce must do, the price to pay, to your own detriment in human terms.

You must have often faced up to the possibility of dying yourself, as something that could happen at any time. How much did you think about that? Obviously, on the day of a particular action you must have, but I mean on a day-to-day level.

It is something you feel all the time at a day-to-day level. You live with it constantly because as I said before, when you live clandestinely, you project a lot of anger on to the category of, for example, policemen and carabinieri. And you read their instruction manuals, about their training exercises. You make them become almost like machines. Not machines just because they are technically specialized and therefore dangerous for you, but because subjectively they are ruthless. You begin to imagine a whole category of the forces of law and order lined up against you. You convince yourself that if they come across you in the street then the most natural thing in the world to do is to shoot you. And when you say 'you are my enemy' then the relationship is one of mutual hatred and destruction. From that moment on, you start to play a political game and you have the feeling that you may die all the time.

Though I suppose necessarily there is some element of habit in it too, probably some kind of defence mechanism. Otherwise it could become an obsession, you could get paranoiac, only fit for a mental home. You would spend all your time looking round about you, wondering if you were being followed, if people were watching you. Yes, you do get used to living with this feeling of watchful fear, it's always there and understood. But then you feel, well, I have to die sometime. It won't be nice when it happens, but it's not something to despair about. Personally I've always been fatalistic about it. I always said, if one night they come knocking at my door, well there they are, they've arrived. If they want to kill me, they'll kill me. If they don't need to kill me, well that's wonderful. In the meantime, I'll sleep!

I'd like to ask you about the participation of women. There has been quite a high proportion of women in the Red Brigades. Do you think the motives for which a woman takes up the armed struggle are the same as for a man?

That's a question of I don't know how many million dollars! I find it difficult to answer because ever since I left behind a particular way of dividing up the world I have always refused to make that sort of distinction. It's difficult to say how the motivation of a man fits into a category definable as male, and that of a woman into a female one. I don't know if it's possible to draw up demarcation lines. Probably each human being has his or her individual reasons which belong to them alone and in which a man/woman difference cannot be defined. In general I think for the men it was a more rational problem, for the women it was an involvement more at the level of tangible emotion, more maternal, if you like, as if they felt things more directly; disasters and injustices which happened on the other side of the world. The involvement of women was tilted slightly more in this direction: in one way more rational, but on the other more visceral, more immediate. But perhaps there is another substantial difference amongst the women who have confronted problems of combat and violence. Women remain enemies of any type of power whatsoever; they have a feeling of real hostility towards it. Even when talking about the seizure of power, there is always a trace of recalcitrance, almost an identification of the evils of humanity with the very existence of a power exercized over others. It's something they always feel, continually. It's a rebellion, though more than rebellion, it's a conviction that the power of one individual over another is a source of disaster and injustice.

Emotionally and mentally, how did you live through the days of Moro's kidnap? Did you feel fear, anguish, triumph?

Well, it's extremely difficult . . .

Obviously with hindsight you see everything differently.

It's not just a question of hindsight, it's that there is never one dominant emotion, so many feelings come together. At the beginning there certainly was a sensation of intoxication because we had succeeded in doing something which had seemed impossible. But then there were doubts, worries that Valerio and I had expressed even before the kidnap. But what was happening was such an enormous thing, there is never just one possible emotion. There was the sensation that we, the bunch of us kids, had brought off this incredible thing; very aware of course of being completely responsible for it, but at the same time there's the feeling you have when you've done something which is larger than yourself. You say, 'my God, what do I do now!' Apart from other worries there was also incredible fear about how to handle the situation, the requests for an exchange of prisoners etc. I mean, we had to decide how to act with regard to a whole series of other questions affecting all the aspects of Italian political life. But we only realized afterwards just how much the Moro kidnap could have critically affected a whole series of national and international balances.

But it was your intention to create and stir up contradictions, it was just what you wanted!

Yes, but I don't think we realized just how deep these would go, how dangerous the destabilization could have been. Yes, obviously we wanted to open up contradictions as far as possible. But at that moment, remember, we were just a little group of people with a programme of political work ahead of us: the expansion of the armed struggle, the gathering together of a number of other groups to create a situation of organized struggle and of organized revolution. This was work which was to take years. And only much later did we realize, God, absolutely anything could have happened.

Are you thinking of an intervention by the CIA for example?

I think anything at all could have happened. It absolutely terrifies me now!

Do you think there could have been a dramatic reaction from the far right?

Yes, certainly, that could have happened! I have no way of evaluating the specific possibilities, all I know is that in a moment of destabilization like that, anything at all could have happened and luckily it didn't. But the Red Brigades didn't think of that. They said, 'Great, let's open up rifts in the institutions: Moro is an extremely important man, so with him in our hands we probably have about an 80% chance of winning this battle, of having the existence of guerrilla warfare recognized in Italy, and an exchange of prisoners in his place is always possible.' They hadn't even begun to envisage the delicacies of political equilibrium or the potential international repercussions.

Some have suggested that the security services 'let you be' at certain moments when they could have intervened; that, for example, they knew where Moro's prison was but did not act to save him. Either during or afterwards, did you wonder about this yourself, that someone might have given you some space, that someone might have had an interest in leaving you be?

No, I really don't think so at all, absolutely not. There have been so many falsehoods written about all that, and things with very serious implications — for example [*she refers here to the film, Il Caso Moro*] a very serious manipulation of dates regarding Via Montalcini. It's not true that the police went there during Moro's imprisonment. They arrived a month later.

There has been so much speculation about Via Fani too, overestimations of your military expertise, suggestions that the Mafia or the CIA collaborated.

Absurd things, absolutely ridiculous. I and all the others had a reaction of great annoyance to all that. Not because we have a past that has to be defended, not because we've done wonderful things and we want to take the glory for them, but it's a problem of identity. I have very grave responsibilities for certain crimes, for the suffering of victims and of families, for the upheaval of people's lives and tranquillity. Nonetheless I did these things for specific reasons, for principles. If I had ever suspected that in the midst of all this there could have been any contact whatsoever between the security services and even one member of the Red Brigades, the influence of any tiny part of the power structure that we were fighting, I simply couldn't have done anything at all, I couldn't have gone on. I would have had an immediate reaction, like getting out completely or denouncing them all. It would have lost all significance, and I know for the others it would have been the same.

Nor is there objectively any proof for this sort of thing. All it is is the wild speculation of people who refuse to accept the banality of the whole Red Brigades phenomenon, who want to find proof that occult forces or international groups were conspiring against the particular political group to which they belong. So the PCI 'historian' sees a conspiracy against the historic compromise, etc. You can put anyone at all into it and it means absolutely nothing. Nowadays people are beginning to accept it, but until two years ago it was unthinkable that in Via Fani there were nine people, all of them Italian. Nowadays people are even beginning to revaluate the military dimension of things like that. Even a few days ago, with the terrible killing of those two boys (*the two police escorts murdered in a BR attack on a post office van in Rome on 14th February 1987*) you could see just how little it takes to assassinate people when you take them by surprise. You don't need people who have been instructed in Palestinian training camps, or anywhere else for that matter. When you do that kind of action for the first time it might seem really dangerous. You imagine the guarding squads as monsters and that if you don't fire one bullet after another they'll have you in pieces just by looking at you. But nowadays people realize that all it takes is four determined people to start shooting. . . .

You were reported recently as saying in court that one of the reasons for kidnapping Moro was to try and find out more about the Piazza Fontana bomb attack.

Newspapers are never quite accurate. What I actually said was that one of the reasons the Red Brigades seized Moro was that they were interested in finding out from him the mechanics of political power and the process of decision-making: decisions which affected the entire class system, the productive forces, institutions. Having said that, it's true there was also an area of interest, although much less significant, in learning about the 30 years of DC government, attempted *coups d'état*, 'state' massacres, etc.

In fact Moro did talk about these things during his interrogation.

Yes, but this was just one of the things which interested the Red Brigades. It's not as if he was kidnapped for that.

And if he had given anything away . . ?

Obviously if he had, let's say, satisfied the expectations that the Red Brigades had, I don't think he would have been killed. The Red Brigades would still have stuck to all the preliminary stages, would still have made the same request for an exchange of prisoners. But in the end, I think, if he had satisfied our expectations, from his own point of view it would have been a public suicide. And if he had done that there would probably have been no sense at all in killing him.

Did you take the Socialist initiative seriously, the possibility that the government might have released Besuschio or Buonoconto? Was this regarded as a real possibility?

No one really believed they would release Besuschio. We did think that Buonoconto might have been released from prison, but this was considered an act of outright provocation: he was ill and needed to be at home. The government might have tried to pass it off as an act of clemency, but it was seen as an attempt to put a noose around our necks and a trap for public opinion too. It would have had no political value whatsoever and would have put the Red Brigades into an even worse light if, despite Buonoconto's release, they had gone ahead and killed Moro.

So it was by no means certain that Buonoconto's release would have led to Moro's liberation?

Not at all. There were many ways in which they could have reacted. In one way they were anxious for the whole thing to finish. And it would have certainly put them in a rather difficult position, but at the same time, since it didn't correspond to what the Red Brigades were expecting, there was no guarantee they wouldn't have killed him anyway.

Did the appeals made by the Pope and Kurt Waldheim have any significant effect on you?

In one way, yes. But in a sense there was also mild disappointment. The Red Brigades were very interested indeed in all that was moving in the background. Pope Paul's appeal had quite an effect because in one way or another he could have some influence over the DC and over the possibility of their opening up a dialogue. After all, the appeal was from the spiritual head of the Catholic Church. But there was disappointment too, because it was a purely humanitarian appeal which asked the Red Brigades to release Moro without any conditions, without getting anything in return.

Which you took to mean as being on the side of the DC?

Well, it was really an appeal from a purely Christian point of view. It was an appeal to humanity. But it did have political significance in the sense that there was a recognition of the Red Brigades.

He appealed to 'the men of the Red Brigades'; said he loved you.

Exactly. There was a recognition of the Red Brigades as people, as social beings, not as criminals or assassins. It brought out a positive aspect which we ourselves had been trying to press for. In other ways we were disappointed. We thought the Pope might also have explicitly exhorted the DC to go some way towards meeting our requests. It was a very utopian way of looking at things!

And Waldheim's appeal?

With Waldheim it was more or less the same thing. It was an extremely important appeal: certainly more important than that of Pope Paul VI. But at that time the Red Brigades were beginning to get restless. That appeal came after the communication requesting the release of the 13 prisoners. I don't know, perhaps if it had come sooner it might have had a different weight. There had been a hardening on the part of the Red Brigades in relation to the silence of the DC. After a specific '*aut aut*' request like that it would have been difficult to go back.

Did the so-called 'historic leadership' which at that time was in Turin have any particular influence on you? I mean, Curcio was talking to Guiso who was talking to Craxi. It's said that Curcio was in favour of Moro's release. Did what they said have any effect on you?

Yes, but not all that much. For example, at their trial they read out a document which discussed conditions in the special prisons. This could have looked like an invitation to propose some initiative there, or at least for us it looked like that. But others didn't interpret it that way. As far as that document is concerned, I don't think it had the weight of a political directive for those outside. But I don't know if at that time there were contacts between those inside and those outside. I don't think those in prison had as much pull as has sometimes been suggested, though.

You didn't see Moro after his kidnap, but you must still have been in a position to pick up things, to know what went on. Would you say the political image you had of him corresponded to the real man?

No, I don't think so, no. I think the experience disorientated and unbalanced things for those who had the most direct contact with him, even if they refused to accept it. For instance, they were convinced that he must correspond to a certain image they had of him as carrying out certain functions, incarnating certain tendencies. And when these things were not corroborated by any proof, by admissions or by his reactions, instead of questioning the theoretical basis of their analysis they said, 'Well he's playing ignorant, won't admit anything, won't reply.' From the human point of view this had quite a devastating effect, although at a very removed level. But the very fact that it was never referred to afterwards shows there was real discomfort on the part of those who knew him and talked to him.

Are you referring to those who are neither 'pentiti' nor 'dissociati?'

Yes, yes. And then later we read Maria Fida's books, read descriptions of him as a father, husband etc, and then we realized that he was totally different. But that aspect was so secondary as to be almost non-existent, it was totally put aside.

Can you understand how Maria Fida's faith has helped her to forgive you?

I think I can understand it better on a human, personal level than on a religious one.

After Moro had been killed you said that you had a certain respect for decisions taken collectively, and that for that reason you didn't leave the Red Brigades immediately. You said you needed time to evaluate your own feelings with regard to the others. You mentioned a kind of internal survival for which you were fighting. Though obviously you would have hardly decided to leave the Red Brigades on May 10th, for security reasons alone.

Yes, but it's really what you said at first. When you get involved in a long term project which absorbs you totally, then you have to accept certain rules. You accept for example that when there are political disagreements you follow the majority line. You support the others. It's a kind of pact of obedience. Even when you don't agree you have to follow things through, bring them to completion. And also, when you live clandestinely you are continually surrounded by doubts. You live in an unreal situation. If someone confronts me and says the problems of the working-class districts are one thing and not another and that I'm cut off from things, I can't just go there myself and talk to the people, in that district. I might feel my ideas were only my own conviction and didn't correspond to reality. A terrible personal insecurity grows up, so you say, 'Let's wait a minute. Perhaps it's me that's wrong, let's wait a bit and have some other proof.' So before breaking off a relationship with people with whom you have shared literally everything, before reaching conclusions and making judgements about these people, you think very carefully. From the point of view of affection, it's a very difficult move to make.

What did you think you would do after leaving the Red Brigades?

We thought it was necessary to go on fighting, but fighting in a completely different way from that of the Red Brigades. Starting from the premise that there was no need to go and kill people. We wanted to establish what the real needs of people were and give pre-eminence to them.

What do you mean, go back to the origins of the Red Brigades, back to the factories?

We believed that the armed struggle should no longer be the determining factor, the be-all and end-all. We wanted to be internal to the development of something. We believed that a project for Communism should bring together all aspects of life: housing, health, culture, education, etc. We didn't want to isolate ourselves in one area alone. We were concerned about everyday life; the nuclear family, the problems of community living, how people relate to each other, and different types of experiment with this. At that time the most important thing for us was experimentation with new ways of living and working, of producing, looking after people, educating children. And we felt the armed struggle should only intervene when it was absolutely necessary to open up space for this wish to experiment. And the wish was there, it was real.

So you didn't intend to give up the armed struggle, just use it differently?

The armed struggle was to be internal to what people really wanted to do, rather than drag them along behind it. Of course, in the end people rejected the armed struggle. It didn't take us long to find that out! But in fact I'm sure if we had been around for another year we would have certainly given it up, too.

But in the months after leaving the Red Brigades you couldn't have done much. You must have had to remain in hiding.

No. We moved around much as we had done before, taking the usual precautions.

Can you explain how you felt at the moment of your arrest: a great fear, or perhaps even relief?

Relief, no. Although that came later, when I'd overcome the first stage, when I was able to rediscover things I'd lost, like contact with my daughter. But at that particular moment I felt in an agonizing sense that I had been captured in a photograph, as if I were a prisoner in that position, paralyzed. It was very much the way I had imagined dying. I felt as if my whole being, my emotions and hopes were all disappearing and that I was nothing but a fighter, a political militant fighter. I felt my life was over, that I could no longer express anything. And I thought of all the things I wished I had done and which were suddenly closed off to me, forbidden. You feel that a phase is over, and you don't know if you can begin to live again. And because you don't know what the next stage will be you don't know if you'll have the possibility of being yourself, because in prison you can't express anything.

Was the path to dissociation a long and difficult one?

That too was a process which matured very gradually. Although I am absolutely convinced that even if we had not been in prison we would have reached the same conclusions as we have today. Inside you get there just the same, but with more effort. On the one hand it's easier because inside you have no problems of survival — to be on the run and to have an arrest warrant out in your name means you can't just go out to work like other people. In that sense the armed struggle can be a justification for existence, you can't accept defeat. Outside, you have more opportunity to evaluate things, for understanding more quickly that the armed struggle is extraneous to what people want, to social evolution. Inside, you have no means of doing that, you have to make your judgements indirectly, at a distance from society.

But it's not a traumatic leap, it's more a matter of a thousand little stages. It encompasses everything though; reasoning, valuations, questions which involve not just one action, not one way of conducting the armed struggle, not one revolutionary project — everything. It involves the revolution itself; Marxism, violence, the logic of enmity, of conflict, one's relationship with authority, a way of working out problems, of confronting reality and of facing the future.

Now that you consider you did wrong, is it difficult for you to salvage the good from the bad of your past? This seems to me to be the most difficult problem.

Yes, it's hard, but I think I can. Perhaps because I haven't taken one huge traumatic leap. It's not as if I was one person one day and a different one the next. I think I've managed to retain my wholeness as a person, to maintain a thread of coherence. Even the fact that I experience horror, a real pain for what happened in Rome recently when those two policemen were killed so viciously and a third only survived by chance, is a sign of that. In this sense of emotional involvement and of injustice I recognize the same person I was 15 years ago, and that's what I consider is the good part to be saved. If you like, it's the capacity not to feel indifferent to other people's misfortunes.

Do you think those who killed on 14th February were motivated differently from you?

I'm still trying to understand what they had in mind. I'm not trying to minimize what we did or our responsibilities, but violence was much more widespread in those days. Of course, we falsified things too. But they think that their violence is in some way legitimized. We thought ours was and we were wrong. Still, in our day there hadn't been such a violent crisis within the armed struggle. There wasn't the social isolation from violence that there is today. There hadn't been the ferocious self-criticism by the very people who gave birth to these movements. These kids have far more opportunity to evaluate the criteria than we had; to stop for a minute and to think. And then I suppose many of them are on the run and are desperate, they probably see no way of integrating themselves into society, so they have developed a kind of personal anger, as if they were waging a private war against the state. But they still have the presumption to think that they embody the feelings of a whole mass of people. The international struggle is just a tangent. They cannot accept defeat, so instead they go on fighting, aiming higher and higher. It's almost as if there were a strange, almost unconscious mechanism defending the very reasons for fighting, an attempt to escape the negative judgement handed down to the armed struggle in Italy.

ALDO MORO'S LAST LETTER

Note

There are 39 known letters written by Aldo Moro from his Red Brigades prison, of which 24 were delivered during his imprisonment. The other 15 were discovered later. On the principle that there were gaps of coherence between letters, in particular in those to his family, it is believed he may have written many more, and that some at least would have been written to the families of the murdered bodyguards.

It is impossible to know how far the letters were a genuine expression of his feelings and how far his captors influenced their contents. Yet in the last letter to his wife, probably written around May 6, there is no more anger or pleading, merely resignation to the death he knew was close at hand. This letter is therefore the closest glimpse we are likely to have into Aldo Moro's state of mind in those last few days. For this reason it is reprinted in full. It was unfinished and unsigned. The punctuation has been left as in the original.

———————————

Let all be calm. The only accusations to be against the DC. No to Luca at the funeral.

My dearest Noretta,

After a moment of wild optimism, due perhaps to a misunderstanding on my part of what was said to me, I think the decisive moment has arrived. It doesn't seem relevant to discuss the thing in itself, or the incredible penalty which I am having to pay for my moderation and my tolerance. With the best of intentions I did of course make a mistake in steering my course through life. But it's too late to change now. All that remains to be said is to recognize that you were right. We can only say that we might have been punished in some other way, we and our little ones. I want it made clear that the DC with its absurd and incredible behaviour bears full responsibility. It lies here, this should be stated with the same firmness that any honours eventually offered should be refused. Then of course there are many, many friends (though I don't know their names) who did not act as they should have done, either believing mistakenly that they would do me harm by speaking out, or too worried about their own positions. A mere one hundred signatures would have made negotiations unavoidable. But that's all past history. As for the future, I am possessed of the most intimate tenderness for you just now, the memories of each and every one, a great big love full of apparently insignificant memories but which in reality are precious. You dwell united in my memory. It will seem as if I am with you. I beg you all to live in the same house, Emma too if possible, and when you need help turn to good and dear friends to whom you'll be so thankful. Hug and kiss all of them for me, face by face, eye by eye, hair by hair. Let my immense tenderness towards each one be passed on through your hands. Be strong, my dearest, in this absurd and incomprehensible trial. These are the ways of the Lord. Remember me to all our relations and friends with great affection and to you and all of them a deep embrace, the pledge of my eternal love. I would like to know with my little mortal eyes how it will look afterwards. If there is light it would be lovely. My dearest, feel me close to you always and hold me tight. Hug and kiss Fida, Demi, Luca (especially Luca) Anna, Mario the little one yet to be born, Agnese Giovanni. I'm so grateful for what they did. Everything is useless when others will not open the door.

The pope didn't do much: perhaps he'll regret it.

THE ITALIAN PARLIAMENT,
THE POLICE AND THE JUDICIARY

The Italian Parliament

Italy has two parliamentary chambers, the Chamber of
Deputies and the Senate. The functions of each are virtually
identical, and both must approve all legislation passed,
although the Chamber of Deputies initiates and is the centre
of greatest parliamentary activity. Apart from a small
proportion of honorary Senators, (former Prime Ministers, a
cross-section of distinguished figures from public life) both
chambers are elected democratically. The head of state is the
President of the Republic, who is elected for a seven-year
term by the Senators and the Deputies, plus representatives
from the 20 regions. The President is responsible for
dissolving Parliament and the calling of a general election
and, once elections have taken place, for inviting a potential
Prime Minister to form a government. The invitation may not
necessarily go to the leader of the largest parliamentary party,
but to the person most likely, in the President's judgement, to
be able to reconcile differing political parties and factions into
a workable governing majority. The maximum life of a
legislative period is five years, although in practice no one
Prime Minister has ever held office for this length of time.

Parliament can and frequently does sanction changes in the governing coalition. The parties responsible for drafting the Constitution of 1946, which include those listed below with the exception of the MSI, Greens, Radicals and Proletarian Democracy, comprise the so-called 'constitutional arc.'

The Italian system of proportional representation produces a broad political span unrepeatable under the UK and US voting systems. The main parties, in descending order of parliamentary representation in the Chamber of Deputies (as from the general election of June 1987) are as follows:

Christian Democratic Party (*Democrazia Cristiana*, DC): 34.3%; 234 seats.
Secretary: Ciriaco De Mita
A populist centre-right party, it derives its support from all classes and geographical areas, although is strongest in southern and north-western Italy. Economic policies rely on continuance of a strong political presence in the extensive public and semi-public sectors.

Italian Communist Party (*Partito Comunista Italiano,* PCI): 26.6%; 177 seats.
Secretary: Achille Occhetto
Its intellectual basis of Marxism/Leninism gradually replaced by more moderate stance of Togliatti, Longo and Berlinguer. Since 1944 declared objective has been change through peaceful means rather than violent revolution — 'the Italian way to Socialism'. Strongest support comes from the cities of the centre-north and the central Italian band comprising the regions of Reggio Emilia, Tuscany and Umbria.

Italian Socialist Party (*Partito Socialista Italiano*, PSI): 14.3%; 94 seats.
Secretary: Bettino Craxi
A party torn by internal conflict throughout the 1950's and '60s, the PSI is now firmly established in a centre-left position. In the course of Craxi's secretaryship the party has shown itself to be pro-West, pro-NATO and anxious to play a

prominent role in industrial modernization and innovation. However, its left-wing faction and pressure from the grass roots on issues such as nuclear energy, ecology and defence could still cause shifts in party policy.

Italian Social Movement Party/National Right (*Movimento Sociale Italiano/Destra Nazionale*, MSI/DN): 5.9%; 35 seats.
Secretary: Gianfranco Fini
Strongly right-wing, reactionary and authoritarian. Historic and idealogical links with Fascism. Fiercely anti-communist.

Italian Republican Party (*Partito Repubblicano Italiano*, PRI): 3.7%; 21 seats.
Secretary: Giorgio La Malfa.
Most respected of smaller 'lay' or non-catholic inspired parties. Policies directed primarily to maintenance of strong economy. Rejection of undue state intervention. Promotors of technological innovation in industry; in favour of close links with US and Western Europe.

Italian Social Democratic Party (*Partito Socialista Democratico Italiano*, PSDI): 3.0%; 17 seats.
Secretary: Antonio Cariglia
Close in spirit to the PSI, from which it broke away in 1947, the party tries to find an intermediate path between the PSI and the DC. Takes an anti-nuclear stance; major preoccupations are with employment and housing, reform of the legal system.

Radical Party (*Partito Radicale*): 2.6%; 13 seats
No 'secretary,' as it considers itself a European group, rather than an Italian political party.
Public image of colourful, 'showbiz' party. Champions specific causes, especially with reference to minority groups, civil rights. Policies concern reforms in legal and political structures, non-violence, unilateral nuclear disarmament.

The Greens (*Verdi*): 2.5%; 13 seats
Like the Radicals, they reject the label of political party, but
most frequent spokesman is Professor Gianni Matioli.
Policies are in line with those of other European Greens,
namely concerned with protection of the environment,
pollution, animal protection, abolition of nuclear power
stations, unilateral nuclear disarmament and the search for
alternative renewable energy sources.

Italian Liberal Party (*Partito Liberale Italiano*, PLI): 2.1%;
11 seats
Secretary: Renato Altissimo
Contrary to its name, the PLI is the most conservative of the
lay parties. Defends interests of big business, landowners.
Considerable support from private sector employers' association, Confindustria. In favour of free market economy,
reduced state interference.

Proletarian Democracy (*Democrazia proletaria*, Dp): 1.7%;
8 seats
Secretary: Giovanni Russo Spena
Led from 1978 (its first parliamentary representation) until
July 1987 by Mario Capanna, former student leader of '68,
Dp appeals most to the young, those dissatisfied with
traditional, stuffy image of PCI. Emphasis on workers' issues:
unemployment, black market exploitation; also drugs,
housing, environment.

The Police

The Italian police force has three main divisions:

1. *Carabinieri*: largest and most important group. Admi-
nistratively part of the army, the carabinieri are ultimately

responsible to the Minister of Defence. Many of their functions are identical to those of the

2. *Polizia di Sicurezza* (PS): like the carabinieri, the PS operates nationwide, but is under the direction of the Minister of the Interior. Responsibility delegated through regional Prefects — the regional representatives of central government — and Questors — provincial chiefs.

3. *Guardia di Finanza*: responsible for guarding Italy's borders and for enforcing customs and fiscal regulations.

The judiciary and the criminal process

The Italian judiciary is an autonomous, self-regulating body controlled by the Superior Judicial Council (*Consiglio Superiore della Magistratura*, CSM). One third of the CSM is nominated by Parliament, the other two thirds by the magistrates themselves.

The state prosecution is represented by the offices of the *Pretura* and the *Procura*. The latter handles all serious crime, such as acts of terrorism. When a serious crime is committed the *Procuratore Generale* or a *Sostituto Procuratore* (Deputy Procurator) initiates investigations in conjunction with the police and carabinieri, and is responsible for issuing arrest warrants. When a suspect is arrested and charges have been brought, the accused is brought before a *giudice istruttore* (instructing judge) whose role is to evaluate the charges brought and to decide whether or not they justify sending the suspect for trial. During the *istruttoria* the suspect is assisted by a lawyer, either of his own choosing or someone appointed by the state to defend him. If the *giudice istruttore* decides the charges are not valid the suspect is released. Otherwise he goes forward to the *Court of Assizes*, or '1st grade trial.'

The prosecution case in court is continued by the *procuratore generale* or his deputy. Trials are conducted under the inquisitorial system, whereby the accused must prove his innocence, rather than under the accusatorial system as used in Britain, whereby a suspect is innocent until proved guilty. Trial is by jury, formed of both *giudici populari* (popular judges) who are ordinary citizens, and of *giudici togati* (robed judges) who are professional lawyers. A *giudice a latere* (lateral judge) ensures that correct legal procedures are observed. The *Presidente della Corte* (Court President) passes the final sentence.

After sentence has been passed in the Court of Assizes, either defence or prosecution can appeal against the verdict, and in this case the whole trial is re-run through the Appeal Court, and a '2nd grade' trial takes place. After this, or if no appeal is made, the case goes forward to the Court of Cassation. This court is not generally responsible for the evaluation of evidence but for the technical observance of the law, to provide an assurance that all the correct procedures have been implemented. If not, the judgement of the previous trial can be overturned and a new trial be called. Unlike the Courts of Assizes and Appeal which are administered locally, the Cassation Court operates only in Rome. Once a verdict has been approved by the Cassation Court the sentence becomes definitive and the accused cannot be retried for the same offence.

In theory the lengthy procedures outlined above should provide the maximum guarantees for justice to be done; in practice many problems arise from the time which is needed to pass from the arrest of a suspect to his final or definitive sentence. Terrorism trials have on occasion taken up to ten years to reach a definitive verdict. Recent legislation has reduced the delays to some degree. A complete reform of the penal code is due to take effect from September 1989 which will replace the inquisitorial with an accusatorial system, eliminate the figure of the instructing judge and bring all evidence for judgement into open court hearing.

LIST OF PRINCIPAL ORGANIZATIONS
OF THE REVOLUTIONARY LEFT IN ITALY

Autonomia Operaia, AUTOP, (Workers' Autonomy)
Grew out of dissolved *Potere Operaio* in 1973. Centres of greatest support — Veneto region (esp. Padua) and Rome. Aim of spontaneous insurrection by the masses. Stress on individual liberty — from work, from centres of power and from politics. Promoted 'sabotage', 'rejection of work' and 'proletarian expropriation'. Leaders (Negri, Scalzone and others) remained in the open and expressed their views publicly. Strongest 1976–77, decimated by arrests April 1979.

Avanguardia Operaia (Workers' Vanguard)
Born Milan 1968, with roots in factories through *Comitati unitari di base* (Cub) (Unified base committees). Low level of violence. Disappeared 1976–77.

Brigate Rosse, BR, (Red Brigades)
Emerged Milan 1970. In period of maximum strength (1978–80) membership estimated at around 500, of which probably only 50 full-time and clandestine, distributed through 7 'columns' in Milan, Rome, Turin, Veneto region, Naples, Sardinia (very briefly) and Genoa. Between 1970–80 carried out over 439 terrorist attacks, including 55 murders and 68 woundings. To date the BR have carried out total of 18 kidnaps, of which 15 for political reasons, 2 for ransom and 1 to provide urgent medical assistance for one of their members.

Gruppi di Azione Partigiani, GAP, (Partisan Action Groups)
Emerged Milan area 1969. Largely financed by Giangiacomo Feltrinelli. Many members were former partisans. Main aim: to provide armed response to any attempt by neo-fascist right to stage coup d'état.

Lotta Continua , LC, (Continuous Struggle)
Formed Turin end 1969 by group of intellectuals with links to factories. Leader Adriano Sofri. Nationwide organization,

concerned with problems of workers in large metropolitan areas. Actions consisted of occupation of houses; demonstrations; political propaganda through eponymous newspaper, expropriation. Concern with prison conditions. Level of violence relatively low.

Nuclei Armati Proletari, NAP, (Armed Proletarian Cells)
Emerged Naples 1972–74, with bases in Florence, Milan and Rome. Lasted until '76–'77 when virtually merged with BR. Main area of concern — prison conditions and politicization of prisoners. Committed 4 murders, 6 woundings, 3 kidnaps (1 political, 2 for ransom).

Potere Operaio, Potop, (Workers' Power)
Emerged Pisa 1968. Centred on factories but quickly spread nationwide. Principal ideologue — Toni Negri. Appealed for mass agitation, propaganda and violence on mass scale. Very anti the reformism of PCI and trade unions. Dissolved in 1973 when many entered *Autonomia Operaia.*

Prima Linea, PL, (Front Line)
Based Milan and Turin where emerged in 1976 from assorted groups. Defined self as 'point of aggregation of groups of guerrillas for the organization of armed proletarian power'. Unlike BR, considered itself a service structure, a link between armed party and workers. 1976–80 carried out 16 murders, 23 woundings.

Senza Tregua, (Without Truce)
Formed in 1975 in Milan to oppose reformist movement from within factories. Largely working class, served as recruitment ground for other militant groups.

NB of the above groups, only the *Brigate Rosse, NAP* and *Prima Linea* can really be considered terrorist organizations, ie who considered murder and wounding as integral to political strategy.

LIST OF THE PRINCIPAL ACTS
OF THE RED BRIGADES
1970–1988

3/3/72	Milan. Kidnap of Idalgo Macchiarini, Personnel manager, Sit Siemens. Released same day.
10/12/73	Turin. Kidnap of Ettore Amerio, Personnel manager, FIAT. Released after 8 days.
18/4/74	Genoa. Kidnap of public prosecutor Mario Sossi. Released after 35 days.
17/6/74	Padua. Raid on MSI offices. 2 party workers killed.
14/10/74	Robbiano di Mediglia (Milan). Murder of carabinieri marshal Maritano.
6/6/75	Asti. Kidnap of Vallarino Gancia (for ransom). Freed next day in police raid, during which Mara Cagol shot dead.
8/6/76	Genoa. Murder of public prosecutor Francesco Coco and 2 bodyguards.
12/1/77	Genoa. Kidnap of Pietro Costa, shipowner. Released after 81 days on payment of 1.5 billion lire.
28/4/77	Turin. Murder of Fulvio Croce, President of Turin lawyers' association.
16/11/77	Turin. Shooting of Carlo Casalegno, deputy editor of *La Stampa*, who died 13 days later.
14/2/78	Rome. Murder of Riccardo Palma, Cassation court judge with responsibility for prison reforms.
10/3/78	Turin. Murder of carabinieri official Rosario Berardi.

16/3/78	Rome. Kidnap of DC President Aldo Moro and murder of his 5 bodyguards. Moro was murdered 55 days later.
11/4/78	Turin. Murder of prison guard Lorenzo Cotugno.
20/4/78	Milan. Murder of prison guard supervisor Francesco De Cataldo.
21/6/78	Genoa. Murder of Police Commissioner Antonio Esposito.
10/10/78	Rome. Murder of Geralamo Tartaglione, Cassation court judge.
24/1/79	Genoa. Murder of Guido Rossa, PCI member and trade unionist.
29/3/79	Rome. Murder of Italo Schettini, DC regional councillor.
3/5/79	Rome. Raid on DC local HQ, Piazza Nicosia. Murder of 2 police, 1 carabinieri officer.
13/7/79	Rome. Murder of Col. Antonio Varisco, responsible for courtroom security.
8/1/80	Milan. Murder of 2 carabinieri and one police officer.
25/1/80	Genoa. Murder of carabinieri colonel and driver.
12/2/80	Rome. Murder of Vittorio Bachelet, Vice President of Superior Judicial Court.
16/3/80	Salerno. Murder of public prosecutor Nicola Giacumbi.
18/3/80	Rome. Murder of Girolamo Minervini, Cassation court judge.
19/5/80	Naples. Murder of Pino Amato, DC regional councillor.

12/11/80	Milan. Murder of Renato Briano, Executive of Magneti Marelli.
28/11/80	Milan. Murder of Manfredo Mazzanti, Executive of Falck.
12/12/80	Rome. Kidnap of judge Giovanni D'Urso, responsible for allocation of prisoners to special or top security prisons. Released after 34 days.
31/12/80	Rome. Murder of General Enrico Galvaligi, responsible for security in special prisons.
27/4/81	Torre del Greco (Naples). Kidnap of DC regional councillor Ciro Cirillo and murder of his 2 bodyguards. Released after 88 days.
20/5/81	Porto Marghera (Venice). Kidnap of Giuseppe Taliercio, Esecutive of Montedison. Murdered 46 days later.
3/6/81	Milan. Kidnap of Renzo Sandrucci, Executive of Alfa Romeo. Released after 51 days.
11/6/81	Kidnap of Roberto Peci, brother of 'pentito' Patrizio. Murdered 54 days later near Rome.
17/12/81	Verona. Kidnap of General James Lee Dozier, NATO commander. Freed by police special unit 42 days later.
13/7/82	Naples. Murder of deputy police commissioner Antonio Ammaturo and driver.
22/1/83	Rome. Murder of prison wardress Germana Stefanini.
3/5/83	Rome. Wounding of Gino Giugni, adviser to government on labour legislation.
15/2/84	Rome. Murder of Leamon Hunt, US director of UN peacekeeping force in Sinai.

25/3/85	Rome. Murder of Ezio Tarantelli, trade union consultant and government adviser.
10/2/86	Florence. Murder of former Republican party mayor, Lando Conti.
21/2/86	Rome. Wounding of Antonio Da Empoli, economic adviser to PM Craxi.
14/2/87	Rome. Murder of 2 police officers escorting cash carrying P.O. van, and seizure of 1.15 billion lire.
20/3/87	Rome. Murder of Licio Giorgieri, responsible for weapons procurement for Italian Air Force.
16/4/88	Forlì. Murder of DC Senator Roberto Ruffilli, adviser to Prime Minister De Mita on institutional reform.

INDEX